Gilded Flesh

Coffins and afterlife in Ancient Egypt

Rogério Sousa

Oxford & Philadelphia

In loving memory of my godmother, Odete
who shines beautifully among the Imperishable Stars

Published in the United Kingdom in 2019 by
OXBOW BOOKS
The Old Music Hall, 106–108 Cowley Road, Oxford OX4 1JE

and in the United States by
OXBOW BOOKS
1950 Lawrence Road, Havertown, PA 19083

© Oxbow Books and the author 2019

Hardback Edition: ISBN 978-1-78925-262-0
Digital Edition: ISBN 978-1-78925-263-7 (ePub)

A CIP record for this book is available from the British Library

Library of Congress Control Number: 2019948187

All rights reserved. No part of this book may be reproduced or transmitted in any form or by any means, electronic or mechanical including photocopying, recording or by any information storage and retrieval system, without permission from the publisher in writing.

Printed in the United Kingdom by Short Run Press

Typeset in India for Casemate Publishing Services. www.casematepublishingservices.com

For a complete list of Oxbow titles, please contact:

UNITED KINGDOM	UNITED STATES OF AMERICA
Oxbow Books	Oxbow Books
Telephone (01865) 241249	Telephone (610) 853-9131, Fax (610) 853-9146
Email: oxbow@oxbowbooks.com	Email: queries@casemateacademic.com
www.oxbowbooks.com	www.casemateacademic.com/oxbow

Oxbow Books is part of the Casemate Group

Front cover: Inner coffin of Kha. Museo Egizio in Turin (S.8429).
Back cover: Top: Painted box from the Tomb of Kha. Museo Egizio in Turin (S 8617-18).
    Bottom: Painted box from the Tomb of Kha. Museo Egizio in Turin (S 8613).

Contents

List of figures iv
Preface xi

1. A dwelling by the Nile: The Predynastic grave of "Gebelein Man A" 1
2. On the path to Sokar: Solar splendours in the Mastaba of Ti 9
3. Facing the sun: The shaft tomb of Senebtisi 24
4. Flying back home: The grave of the "Gurnah Queen" 42
5. A house on the edge of the world: The Tomb of Kha and Merit (TT 8) 54
6. The Garden of Heaven: The family tomb of Sennedjem (TT 1) 93
7. The healing light: The burial assemblage of the priestess Tabasety 128
8. The divine brotherhood: The Tomb of the Priests of Amun 147
9. Conclusion 172

Bibliography 189

List of figures

Except when otherwise stated in the captions, the drawings published in the volume are by the author. All the photos from the Tomb of Kha were kindly provided by the Museo Egizio in Turin.

Maps
Map 1. Egypt: The sites mentioned in the text.
Map 2. Gebelein. Map of the site.
Map 3. Saqqara. Map of the site.
Map 4. Deir el-Medina. Map of the site.

Chapter 1
Fig. 1. Gebelein. View of the Eastern Hill.
Fig. 2. Ernest Wallis Budge.
Fig. 3. Gebelein Man A with a reconstructed assemblage of burial goods. British Museum (EA 32751). © The Trustees of the British Museum.
Fig. 4. A typical grave from Nagada II (above). Tattoos found on the Gebelein Man A (below left) and on the Gebelein Woman (below right).
Fig. 5. Jar decorated with a Nilotic landscape. Nagada II.

Chapter 2
Fig. 6. The Saqqara plateau with the funerary complex of Djoser Netjererkhet (aerial view).
Fig. 7. Auguste Mariette.
Fig. 8. The Tomb of Ti (19th century).
Fig. 9. The entrance of the mastaba.
Fig. 10. Reconstruction of the mastaba.
Fig. 11. The courtyard.
Fig. 12. The serdab of the offering chamber.
Fig. 13. Plan of the tomb.
Fig. 14. The false door in the offering chamber.
Fig. 15. Decoration of the offering chamber (detail).
Fig. 16. Decoration of the offering chamber, eastern wall. Drawings from Wild 1966. Composition by the author.

List of figures

Fig. 17. Decoration of the longitudinal gallery (detail).
Fig. 18. Decoration of the offering chamber (detail).
Fig. 19. The statue of Ti. Egyptian Museum in Cairo.
Fig. 20. The burial chamber.
Fig. 21. The stone sarcophagus of Nebka (?) from the unfinished Northern Pyramid of Zawyet El Aryan. Services des Antiquité d'Égypte, 1904.

Chapter 3

Fig. 22. The Pyramid of Amenemhat I in Lischt.
Fig. 23. The Expedition of the Metropolitan Museum of Art in Thebes, 1925. Archives of the Egyptian Expedition, Department of Egyptian Art.
Fig. 24. Plan of the Mastaba of the Vizier Senuseret with the position of the shaft-tomb of Senebtisi. In Arnold 2018, Pl. 149.
Fig. 25. Double offering table. Metropolitan Museum of Art (12.181.197).
Fig. 26. Plan of the tomb of Senebtisi with the reconstructed burial assemblage. Drawing after Mace, Winlock 1916, Fig. 1.
Fig. 27. Burial assemblage of Senebtisi, comprising an outer rectangular coffin (reconstructed), an inner rectangular coffin (Metropolitan Museum of Art, 08.200.45a-b), one anthropoid coffin (reconstructed) and a canopic box (reconstructed), with human-headed vases. Drawings by the author after Mace, Winlock 1916.
Fig. 28. Bow. Metropolitan Museum of Art.
Fig. 29. Beadwork apron of Senebtisi. Metropolitan Museum of Art (08.200.29a).
Fig. 30. Circlet and golden rosettes of Senebtisi. Metropolitan Museum of Art (07.227.7).
Fig. 31. Necklace with sa-amulets (07.227.11), necklace with shell pendants (07.227.8). Metropolitan Museum of Art.
Fig. 32. Necklace with shen-ring. Metropolitan Museum of Art (07.227.9).
Fig. 33. Large collar with falcon headed terminals. Metropolitan Museum of Art (08.200.30)
Fig. 34. Bracelets and anklets. Metropolitan Museum of Art (08.200.25–.28).
Fig. 35. Clasp. Metropolitan Museum of Art (07.227.10).
Fig. 36. Girdle with a falcon. Metropolitan Museum of Art (08.200.42a).
Fig. 37. Acacia bead girdle. Metropolitan Museum of Art (07.227.13)
Fig. 38. Nekhakha sceptre. Metropolitan Museum of Art (07.227.15).
Fig. 39. Arrangement of the body adornments found in Senebtisi's mummy as if worn by a living person.
Fig. 40. Anthropoid coffin of Hapiankhtifi of Mir. Metropolitan Museum of Art (12.183.11c-2).
Fig. 41. Anthropoid coffin of Sobekhat after photographic documentation in Yoshimura et alli 2018.

Chapter 4

Fig. 42. White Chapel of Senuseret I at Karnak.
Fig. 43. The hills of Dra Abu el-Naga in Thebes, aerial view.
Fig. 44. William Flinders Petrie, 1886.
Fig. 45. The grave of the "Gurnah Queen" as it was found in 1908. Photographic records of Petrie Museum of Egyptian Archaeology.
Fig. 46. Composition of the burial.
Fig. 47. The rishi coffin of the "Gurnah Queen" (front view). National Museums of Scotland (A.1909.527).
Fig. 48. The rishi coffin of the "Gurnah Queen" (side view). National Museums of Scotland (A.1909.527).
Fig. 49. The "Gurnah Queen". Drawing by the author after the facial reconstruction by Manley at al. 2002.
Fig. 50. Rishi mask. World Museum in Liverpool (M11020).

Chapter 5

Fig. 51. The Theban Mountain (El-Gurn) and the village of Deir el-Medina with its necropolis.
Fig. 52. The Tomb of Kha in the northern sector of Deir el-Medina's necropolis.
Fig. 53. Ernesto Schiaparelli.
Fig. 54. The shaft to the Tomb of Kha at the time of its discovery. Schiaparelli excavations, 1906. Museo Egizio Archive.
Fig. 55. Cobbled wall, sealing the entrance to the Tomb of Kha. Schiaparelli excavations, 1906. Museo Egizio Archive.
Fig. 56. Plan and section of Kha's tomb drawn by Francisco Ballerini. Museo Egizio Archive. Copyright of the Museo Egizio in Turin.
Fig. 57. The corridor preceding the funerary chamber of Kha at the time of its discovery. Schiaparelli excavations, 1906. Museo Egizio Archive.
Fig. 58. The funerary chamber of Kha at the time of its discovery. Schiaparelli excavations, 1906. Museo Egizio Archive.
Fig. 59. The clearance of the tomb with the objects being transported to the Valley of the Queens. Schiaparelli excavations, 1906. Museo Egizio Archive.
Fig. 60. The funerary complex of Kha.
Fig. 61. Pictorial decoration of the funerary chapel and the funerary stela of Kha kept in the Museo Egizio in Turin (C. 1618). Drawings from Vandier d'Abbadie, Jourdain 1939, Pl. III, IV and VIII.
Fig. 62. A typical house in Deir el-Medina.
Fig. 63. Cup with loaves (S. 8234).
Fig. 64. Sealed jar (S. 8516).
Fig. 65. Wine jar with festive decoration and stand (S. 8224).
Fig. 66. Festive jars (S. 8619, 8620, 8621, 8622).

List of figures

Fig. 67. Funerary chair of Kha (S. 8333).
Fig. 68. The Ka statuette of Kha (S. 8335).
Fig. 69. Stand with a lustration bowl (S. 8222.2).
Fig. 70. Papyrus shaped lamp (S. 8628).
Fig. 71. Basket (S. 8417).
Fig. 72. The bed of Kha (S. 8327) and stool (S. 8614).
Fig. 73. The bed of Merit (S. 8629) with headrest (S. 8631) and stools (S. 8510, 8512).
Fig. 74. Cosmetic box of Merit (S. 8479) and broidered rug (S. 8528).
Fig. 75. Alabaster ointment vessels (S. 8322, S. 8445).
Fig. 76. Scissor, blades and grind stone.
Fig. 77. Folding cubit (S. 8391).
Fig. 78. Writing tools (S. 8387).
Fig. 79. Implements and tools (S. 8386, 8395–96).
Fig. 80. Decorated box with cloths (S. 8212).
Fig. 81. Decorated box (S. 8617–18).
Fig. 82. Tunics and underwear of Kha (S. 8530). Decorated box with cloths (S. 8613).
Fig. 83. Gifts offered to Kha: scribe's tablet (S. 8388), senet game board previously belonging to Banermeret (S. 8451.1), cup with the cartouches of Amenhotep III (S. 8355), situla with the name of Userhat (S. 8231), royal cubit given to Kha by the Pharaoh Amenhotep II (S. 8647).
Fig. 84. Shabti of Kha (S. 8337).
Fig. 85. Models of tools and model coffin with shabti of Kha (S. 8338–8339).
Fig. 86. Coffin set of Kha: outer rectangular coffin (S. 8210), middle coffin (S. 8316) and inner coffin (S. 8429).
Fig. 87. Coffin set of Kha.
Fig. 88. Book of the Dead of Kha (S. 8316/3=8438): Adoration of Osiris by Kha and Merit.
Fig. 89. Book of the Dead of Kha (S. 8316/3=8438): The deceased in the form of Ba-bird.
Fig. 90. Middle coffin of Kha (S. 8316): detail of the headboard.
Fig. 91. The scene of Duamutef on the inner coffin of Kha (left) and on the inner coffin of Merit (right).
Fig. 92. Middle coffin of Kha (S. 8316): detail of the case.
Fig. 93. Coffin set of Merit: outer rectangular coffin (S. 8517) and anthropoid coffin (S. 8470).
Fig. 94. Coffin set of Merit.
Fig. 95. Mummy mask of Merit (S. 8473).
Fig. 96. The mummies of Kha (S. 8316) and Merit (S. 8471).
Fig. 97. X-Rays of the mummy of Kha: The head is adorned with a shebiu-necklace, large earrings and a snake-head amulet.
Fig. 98. X-Rays of the mummy of Kha: The thorax is protected by a finely carved heart scarab suspended on a wire.

Fig. 151. Eugène Grebaut, Mohamed Abdel Rassul and Georges Daressy standing between the burial sets unearthed from the tomb on the 5th of February. Archives of the Collège de France.
Fig. 152. Procession of bearers carrying the coffins towards the steamer. Illustration by Émille Bayard published on the nº 2510 of L´Illustration on the 4th of April of 1891 (with thanks to Dik van Bommel).
Fig. 153. Perspective of the tomb.
Fig. 154. The stairway connecting with the transverse gallery.
Fig. 155. The coffin set of Hori and the possible relation with the statues of Nephthys and Isis.
Fig. 156. A typical burial assemblage from the late 21st Dynasty: outer and inner anthropoid coffins, mummy-cover, shabti-box with shabtis, Osiris statue with Book of the Dead, stela.
Fig. 157. The Basic scheme. Lid of Tabasety. Museum of Ancient Art in Aarhus.
Fig. 158. Left: the lid as a sacred gate (Basic Scheme). Right: Gate in the Tomb of Nefertari.
Fig. 159. The Classical scheme. Lid of Djedmutiuesankh. Geographical Society of Lisbon.
Fig. 160. Left: the lid as a royal tomb (Classical Scheme). Right: Ostracon with the plan of a royal tomb.
Fig. 161. The Complex Scheme. Outer lid of Butherkhonsu. Kunsthistorishes Museum in Vienna.
Fig. 162. The Complex Scheme. Inner lid of Djedmutiuesankh. Egyptian Museum in Florence.
Fig. 163. Left: the lid as a sacred ceiling (Complex Scheme). Right: Funerary cover of Asetemkhebit, from the Royal Cache.
Fig. 164. The mummy and the "semiotic wrapping" provided by coffin decoration.
Fig. 165. Examination of a Mummy of the Priests of Ammon (1891). Oil on canvas, by Paul Dominique Philippoteaux. Photo credit: Peter Nahum at The Leicester Gallery, London.
Fig. 166. Showcase with a sample of unwrapped mummies from Bab el-Gasus at the Giza Museum (Room 85/86)
Fig. 167. Plan of the tomb with the original position of the burial sets. Drawing after Niwiński, 21st Dynasty Coffins from Thebes, table 1. The drawing includes the original burial chamber located in the shaft and the reviewed position of the burials, according to the notes published by Daressy (1900: 147–148).

Preface

The study of funerary material culture in Ancient Egypt is often an overwhelming task given the exceptional richness of the archaeological sites. For methodological reasons, when approaching the study of funerary archaeology, scholars tend to deal with complexity by limiting the focus of their analysis to a certain category of objects. I did it myself on several occasions, namely on the study of pictorial decoration of the "yellow" coffins, crafted in Thebes during the 21st Dynasty. This analytical approach is certainly necessary, particularly in terms of the organisation of each object and its relation with the whole corpus. Since the "yellow" corpus of coffins is particularly rich both in terms of the quantity and quality of the objects, from the beginning I found it useful to study them as an ensemble. Before a particular object, I use the seriation method in order to understand its relation with the rest of the corpus.

This "holistic" approach to a specific category of objects led me to the current work, where I examine coffins in their original archaeological context. Over the years, several authors have pointed out the importance of integrating funerary contexts in our understanding of individual objects. Regarding the funerary materials of the Third Intermediate Period, David Aston is the author of a very important work that attempts to reconstruct the original composition of the burials dating from this period, which is normally a difficult task given the lack of accurate records.

Recently, more attention is being given to the organisation of the burial assemblage as a whole with funerary sites being increasingly studied as holistic unities. Coffins, in particular, have been studied together with other categories of funerary objects, attempting to explore how the same idea often manifests itself in a variety of media. These approaches have inspired me to write this book, attempting to understand the layout and use of the "yellow" coffins at the light of the global trends that moulded and shaped funerary material culture since the Neolithic to the end of the 21st Dynasty.

Either formulated as a simple grave or an elaborated architectonic complex, each tomb is designed as a sacred space carefully arranged according to implicit theological conceptions and funerary beliefs which are consistent with political and socio-economic factors of its time. This multidimensional phenomenon is often difficult to perceive given the implicit nature of Egyptian magical procedures. However, if we take funerary items as discrete units of meaning, integrating a broader semiotic unit, then we may try to reconstruct the meaning of each category of objects in a given burial. This "semiotic" approach also allows us to understand how different media were used to express the same idea, and how changes in religious conceptions interfered in the construction of meaning in the funerary space. A funerary object often works as a "hypertext", literally linking a particular tomb with religious texts of a magical nature, such as Coffin Texts or the Book of the Dead. The intertextuality between funerary texts and funerary items deeply shaped the layout and evolution of the objects themselves.

In sum, when seen from a semiotic perspective, each burial is representative of the Egyptian model of the universe, and it is this model that I would like to reconstruct in each of the tombs I selected for this book. I use these eight tombs as case studies to understand how high elite burials were arranged in different moments in time. The selection focuses, as much as possible, on undisturbed high elite burials, simply because the wealth of semiotic unities provides a better understanding of the organisation of the tomb as a whole. In each burial, we examine the tomb together with the burial assemblage so as to understand its overall organisation.

Secondly, we examine the role coffins performed as units of meaning in the overall burial assemblage, including the tomb itself. This holistic ensemble is understood as the "text" revealing the world view underlying each tomb.

This approach allows us to understand a phenomenon specific to Egyptian funerary archaeology, consisting of the interrelation between visual culture and materiality. In the Egyptian mindset, representations and texts are often used as substitutes of the objects themselves. We will therefore, look at tomb decoration and burial equipment as integrating the same phenomenon.

Regarding Egyptian coffins, in particular, it is clear that they perform a much wider role than that of simply body containers. Coffin decoration played an important role in the continuous semiotic reshaping of these objects. Originally, coffins and sarcophagi remained undecorated, as well as the burial chambers themselves. Coffin decoration only took shape from the late 5th Dynasty onwards, with the growth of Osirian beliefs. From then on royal funerary chambers started to be decorated with the Pyramid Texts, providing a safe journey into the afterlife. Private coffins, too, received texts and images aiming at securing an eternal supply of food.

The decoration of coffins is thus deeply rooted in the Osirification of funerary practices, which would be maximally expressed in the creation of the anthropoid coffins in the mid-12th Dynasty. However, from the late Middle Kingdom onwards, funerary solar beliefs started to play an increasing role in this process, leading to the creation of a wide variety of anthropoid models, reaching its apex at the end of the Ramesside Period with "yellow" coffins, literally being used as a "canvas" to illustrate the nightly journey of the sun god.

A long process separates the plainly undecorated body containers, to the heavily decorated yellow coffins. Such development was only possible with the skills of craftsmen and a thorough organisation of workshops, mastering the management of material goods and, most importantly, the organisation of labour involving carpentry, sculpture, inscriptions and pictorial work. The examination of the selected tombs also allows us to infer how the knowledge associated with coffin production was transmitted through generations and how changes associated with coffin decoration interfered in the organisation of labour.

This book would have not been possible without the support of several Museums and the cooperation of their curators. I am deeply indebted to the support provided by the Museo Egizio in Turin, who generously provided me with the photographic records of the objects published in this book. I would like to thank the Director of the Museum, Christian Greco, and his staff, namely Federica Facchetti, for their generous support and endless patience.

I would like to acknowledge the Metropolitan Museum of Art, in allowing me to use their photographic resources, as well as providing the valuable support of its curator, Janice Kamrin, who kindly assisted me in my requests.

A sincere appreciation is due to the Antikmuseet in Aarhus and to its Director, Vinnie Nørskov, for letting me study the burial assemblage of Tabasety, which turned out to be such an exciting experience. I also thank the Museum for allowing me to publish the photos of the Tabasety burial assemblage, which were kindly provided by Mikkel Randlev Møller. This appreciation is extended to all the museums who allowed me to publish photos of the objects kept in their collections, such as the Egyptian Museum in Cairo, the National Museums of Scotland, and the British Museum, who kindly accepted my publication requests.

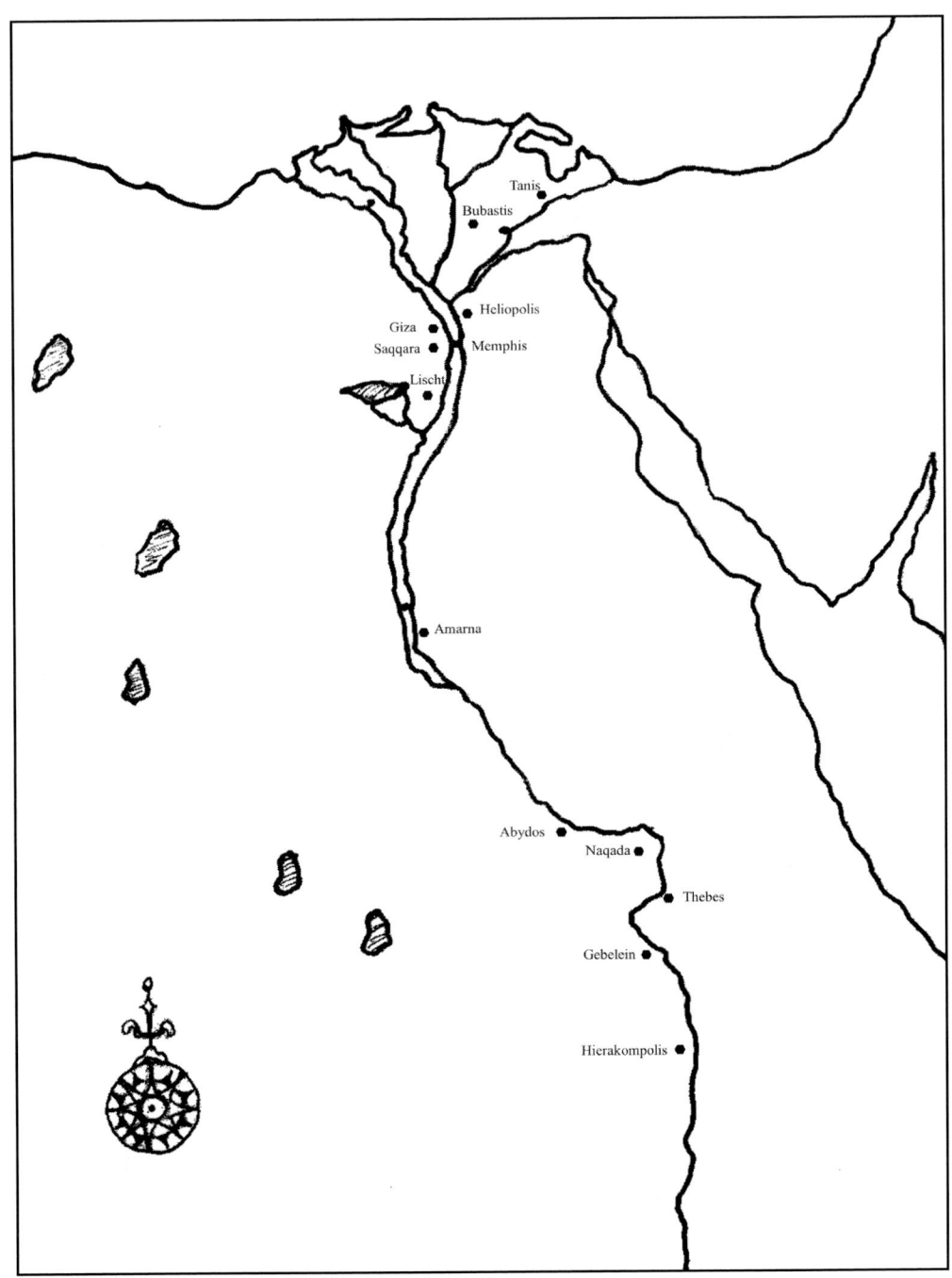

Map 1. Egypt: The sites mentioned in the text.

Chapter 1

A dwelling by the Nile: The predynastic grave of "Gebelein Man A"

Thirty kilometres south of Luxor on the western bank of the Nile, two desert hills stand out from the wide, lushly green floodplain (Fig. 1). The site has been known by the Arabic name of Gebelein, meaning "two rocks". These long narrow hills lay parallel to the course of the Nile, creating a wide valley which was periodically flooded, creating a lake that would give the townspeople direct access to the Nile. Such a location may have been seen as extremely favourable by ancient settlers.

In pharaonic times the place was already known as the "Two rocks of Anubis", Inerty Anupu.[1] As Anubis was the guardian deity of the necropoleis, such invocation suggests an association with a burial site. Evidence of this is abundantly found in the western hill with tombs dating back to the Neolithic Age when the Nile floodplain was not yet a unified territory. During this period, known as Predynastic, the Valley and the Delta were inhabited by different cultures, with those in the south presenting an increasing specialisation of labour and hierarchical organisation, a phenomenon particularly well documented in funerary sites. Together with the settlements in Hierakompolis, Abydos, and Nagada, Gebelein shows a concurrent development of funerary material culture in elite burials.[2]

Discovery

In the 1890s, while looking for Predynastic mummies to add to the British Museum's collection, Ernest Wallis Budge (Fig. 2), the keeper of Egyptian and Assyrian Antiquities in the British Museum, was guided by a local inhabitant to a spot where a group of six Predynastic graves was found by the villagers. According to the patterns of occupation of the necropolis, it is currently believed that this spot was located at the south-east side of the westernmost of Gebelein's hills, where Predynastic rock carvings had also been found.[3]

Fig. 1. Gebelein. View of the Eastern Hill.

Budge provided a brief account of these findings in his notes:

> One of the largest of the graves had been dug partly under a small projecting spur of the hill, and it was nearly covered by two or three large lumps of stone which seemed to have been placed there after the burial of the body. These were tightly jammed together, and to this fact the body in the grave owed its preservation in a complete state.[4]

In fact, the grave held a male adult, now known as Gebelein Man A (British Museum, EA 32751), found in a perfect state of preservation. The body was buried in a contracted position, laying on the left side, with the face hidden by the hands. Short, curly tufts of ginger-coloured hair were preserved on the scalp. Around the body pots and flint tools were disposed.

Fig. 2. Ernest Wallis Budge.

1. A dwelling by the Nile: The predynastic grave of "Gebelein Man A"

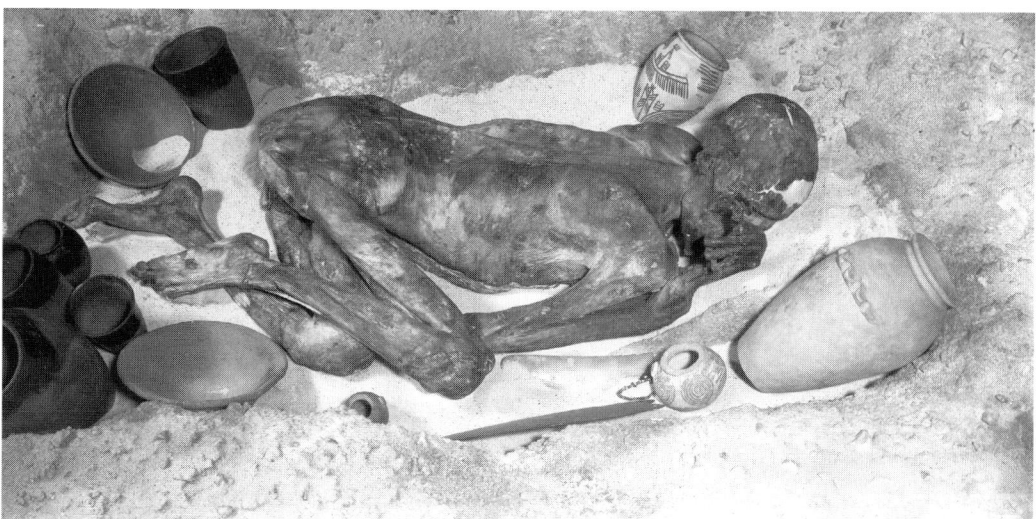

Fig. 3. Gebelein Man A with a reconstructed assemblage of burial goods. British Museum (EA 32751). © The Trustees of the British Museum.

The grave was covered with lumps of stone to protect the body from the predatory action of scavengers, and to sign the burial to the living members of the community, who could use this "superstructure" to perform funerary rituals.

In his records, Budge adds a few notes on the adjacent graves:

> We then turned our attention to the other graves, and took out three men with their flints and pots, and one woman. One man was wrapped in a skin, a second in a mat of palm fibre, and the third was rolled up in a reed mat. The woman was without covering, and the only pot in her grave contained what seemed to be a sort of dried porridge.5

The mummies found in Gebelein were shipped to the British Museum in 1900, where they still remain. Gebelein Man A, popularly known as "Ginger", has been on display in the permanent galleries of the Museum, together with a reconstructed sample of objects which had not been originally found in his grave (Fig. 3).

The features of the burial and the modern analysis of the human remains indicate that Gebelein Man A lived during the middle Predynastic Period, around 3500 BC, a phase known in Egyptian archaeology as Nagada II.[6] Contemporary imaging techniques made it possible to have a closer look at the circumstances surrounding his death. The 3D visualisation of the CT carried out on his body had shown that he died violently at a very young age (eighteen to twenty-one years), as the result of a single penetrating wound to the back. The scans show that he was stabbed by a blade at least 12 cm long. Since no other wound was found, it is unlikely that he was killed in a battle. Instead, he seems to have been caught by surprise and stabbed in the back.

Daniel Antoine, the curator of physical anthropology at the British Museum, identified dark smudges on the upper right arm that have been revealed as tattoos of a bull and sheep. On the female mummy, known as Gebelein Woman, found in the same cluster of tombs, researchers also found tattoos in the form of four small S-shaped motifs (Fig. 4). Together, these burials provide the oldest known examples of this practice. It is interesting to note the use of similar S-shaped motifs in the decoration of contemporary ceramic pots, as well as other Nilotic motifs (Fig. 5).

Mummification and burial

It has been believed that the arid environment, as well as direct contact with the hot sand, had been sufficient to assure the natural mummification seen in Predynastic corpses. Recent analysis, however, carried out in the Predynastic mummy S. 293 kept in the Museo Egizio in Turin, suggests that this result might actually have been facilitated by the use of unguents. Dating slightly earlier from the same period than those found in Gebelein (3600 BC), the mummy S.93 was originally buried lying on his left side, curled in a foetal position, possibly clothed in a full-body shroud, and lain beneath a thin covering of earth.[7] Detailed analysis of chemical residues present on the corpse itself, and its funerary coverings, revealed that the mummy had not been left to the tender drying mercies of the wind and sand. Instead, both the body and the textiles which wrapped it had been carefully coated in a special "balm" – a mixture of preserving agents that comprised plant oil, conifer resin, an aromatic plant extract or balsam, and a sugar derived from plant gum.

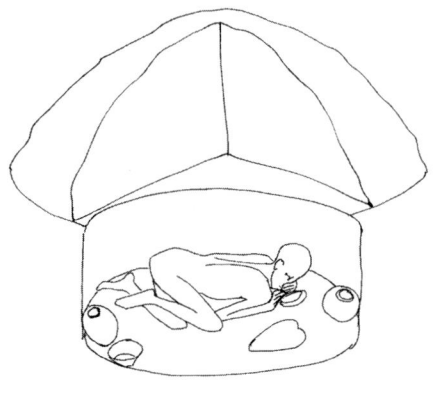

Fig. 4. A typical grave from Nagada II (above). Tattoos found on the Gebelein Man A (below left) and on the Gebelein Woman (below right).

The mixture represented a sophisticated combination of ingredients designed not only to preserve but also to prevent spoilage. In particular, some of the ingredients comprising the balsam, and the conifer resin, had strong antibacterial qualities. The resin came from a species not native to Egypt, and thus it had to be imported. These ingredients were typical in combination and proportion of "those employed by the Egyptian embalmers when their skill was at its peak, some 2500 years later." Mummy S.93, and by implication other preserved bodies dating from the same period, "represent here the literal embodiment of the antecedents of classic mummification, which would become a central tenet of ancient Egyptian culture."[8]

1. A dwelling by the Nile: The predynastic grave of "Gebelein Man A"

We do not know if the body of Gebelein Man A underwent a similar process, but the excellent state of preservation in which he was found reveals that it was correctly prepared to resist natural decay.

Moreover, it is clear that his body was buried observing ritual conventions. The bodies from Gebelein's Predynastic tombs were carefully positioned in the graves, with the head pointing south and the face turned towards the west. The dead were laid on their left side, in the foetal position, with arms and legs flexed. This position might have been adopted to convey the idea of rebirth, expressed as the return to the womb of a cosmic mother goddess, perhaps associated with the cycles of the Nile flood and the sun.

It is noteworthy that the hands in most of the Gebelein burials are positioned in front of the face, perhaps originally holding a cup containing food or drink.

The bodies from the six graves uncovered by Budge were naked, sometimes wearing belts or wrapped in linen. Later excavations at the site unearthed other graves of the Late Predynastic and Early Dynastic periods. Some of the bodies are wrapped within mats, of a type traditionally used for sleeping on.[9] This practice suggests the grave's identification with the deceased's dwelling, one that encloses the body within, as coffins eventually would do.

Today it is impossible to know with certainty the original composition of the grave goods buried with Gebelein Man A, as they were not recorded by Budge and his team. However, the dating of the burial allows us to have at least a rough idea of its content. Flint tools and pots were relatively common in this period. Besides the undecorated black topped pots in use since the early stages of the Nagada culture, new types of funerary artefacts were introduced in the Nagada II pottery, displaying for the first time painted figurative decoration. They depict the Nilotic environment, such as low hills, ripples of water and flocks of ostriches. The boats commonly depicted on the Nagada II pottery emphasise the importance of the Nile as the main means of communication.[10] These motifs were depicted in a variety of media, including pottery and cloths, perhaps alluding to the beginning of the flood (Fig. 5).[11]

Fig. 5. Jar decorated with a Nilotic landscape. Nagada II.

Concluding remarks

The mummies acquired by Budge clearly belonged to members of Gebelein's local elite. The size and structure of the grave of Gebelein Man A suggest that, despite his young age, he held an important status in his community. It is likely that his premature death may have resulted from his status.

The Predynastic graves in Gebelein show that a sophisticated vision of the afterlife was already taking shape in Predynastic settlements, in which the preservation of the body played a central role. The use of funerary balsams reveals that knowledgeable and highly skilled personnel was supported by the local ruling elite with the purpose of providing "magical" media that could enable them to achieve immortality.

The use of mats in the grave suggests the association of the tomb with a household, alluding to death as an eternal sleep.

An interesting aspect detected in Predynastic graves is the paramount role played by visual culture. The motifs painted on pots, cloths, and even on tomb walls show that pictorial decoration already plays an important part in recreating a magical realm where life in the Nilotic cosmos is celebrated (Fig. 5). However, the role of images was not strictly funerary, as they were used also in tattoos, obviously carried out during the lifetime of the individuals, certainly with relevant social and religious significance. The meaning of visual culture, with its Nilotic associations, was surely embedded in the wide system of beliefs and practices of these communities.

The importance of visual culture would remain a distinctive feature of Egyptian funerary culture. Nilotic references thus pervade the imaginary of life and the afterlife. This process is closely intertwined with the development of the hieroglyphic writing system itself, and for this reason, it was certainly associated with status and power. Visual culture and status will always remain closely associated with Egyptian elite burials.

Finally, the burials suggest that cosmic elements such as the Nile's flood, the sun, and perhaps a great mother goddess already played a part in the imaginary associated with the deceased's rebirth. It is possible that, later on, this funerary mother goddess would be known as Hathor, the goddess of joy, love, and rebirth. In fact, on Gebelein's eastern hill, opposite the Predynastic necropolis, the Temple of Hathor was built at the beginning of the Old Kingdom (*ca.* 2600 BC) and was still active in the Ptolemaic Dynasty (332–30 BC). The importance of this cult in Gebelein was such that in Greek times, the city was known as Aphroditopolis, and also Pathyris, from Old Egyptian Per-Hathor ("Domain of Hathor"). It is, therefore, possible that a local cult was already carried out to an early form of the cosmic mother goddess.

1. A dwelling by the Nile: The predynastic grave of "Gebelein Man A"

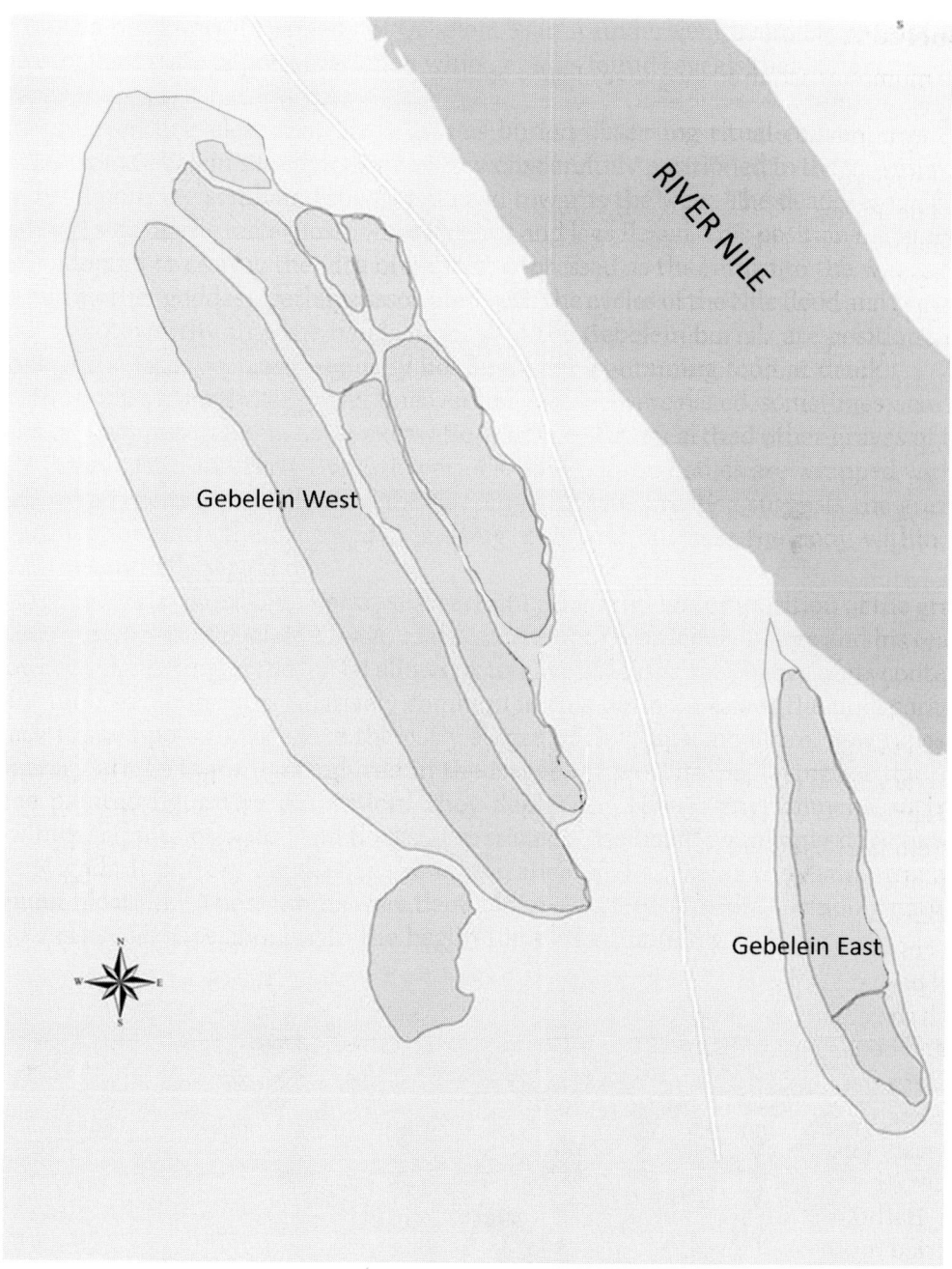

Map 2. Gebelein. Map of the site.

Notes

1 Fiore Marochetti, 2013.
2 Ugliano 2015, 44.
3 Taylor, Antoine and Vandenbeusch 2014, 31.
4 Taylor, Antoine and Vandenbeusch 2014, 31.
5 Taylor, Antoine and Vandenbeusch 2014, 31.
6 Taylor, Antoine and Vandenbeusch 2014, 36.
7 Ugliano 2015, 41.
8 Jones *et al.*, 2018.
9 Taylor, Antoine and Vandenbeusch 2014, 36.
10 Taylor, Antoine and Vandenbeusch 2014, 36.
11 Ugliano 2015, 44.

Chapter 2

On the path to Sokar: Solar splendours in the Mastaba of Ti

According to Manetho, the Egyptian priest who wrote the *History of Egypt* commissioned by the Hellenistic ruler Ptolemy II, Memphis was founded by Menes, the first king of Egypt, to celebrate the unification of Upper and Lower Egypt under his sole rule. The capital of this unified kingdom was built where the Nile leaves the valley, squeezed by the desert mountains and opens its arms towards the Mediterranean forming the flat, marshy land of the delta. In antiquity, this city was known as Ieneb Hedje, the "White Wall" (*i.e.* the "Shining City"). And indeed, the white city must have looked like an island of light engulfed amidst the luxuriously green fields.

In the nearby western cliffs of the desert, a wide plateau, today known as Saqqara, was chosen to build the necropolis of the capital city, becoming a place sacred to Sokar, the underworld god of light.

Built around 2600 BC for Djoser Netjererkhet, the huge funerary complex towered by the Stepped Pyramid overlooked this contrasting landscape as no other building had done before (Fig. 6). Under the supervision of Imhotep, royal architect and priest of Heliopolis, the use of stone in large scale was for the first time essayed, giving rise to the Old Kingdom (2686–2160 BC) which would give Egypt nearly 500 years of peace, the longest in human history ever recorded. During this Age of the Pyramids, kings and their high officials would transform the deserted area into one of the most thriving places in the ancient world.

Royal necropoleis and pyramid complexes were heavily shaped by royal ideology developed under the influence of solar theology. The pyramid provided the king with much more than a tomb, standing as a cosmic manifestation of the pharaoh and showing his ascent to heaven and unification with the gods.

During the Old Kingdom, these royal complexes formed a true "pyramid field" along the western edge of the desert. Most of the kings from the 4th Dynasty built their monuments in the plateau of Giza, overlooking the sacred city of Heliopolis,

Fig. 6. The Saqqara plateau with the funerary complex of Djoser Netjererkhet (aerial view).

while the kings from the 5th Dynasty elected the smooth plateau of Abusir to build their funerary complexes. Both royal necropoleis, the burials of the king's family and of his high officials were literally built as the shadow of the king's pyramid. Elite individuals adopted the use of a mastaba-tomb, a bench-shaped structure (hence the Arabic name) provided with a chapel, which the living could enter, with rooms for performing the cult of the dead.[1] During this period, Saqqara seems to have been overlooked, but by the end of the 5th Dynasty, pyramid complexes eventually returned to the sacred plateau of Sokar. A man, simply called Ti, the "rich", may have played an important role in this process, building an impressive mastaba in Saqqara, away from the kings he served which were buried in Abusir pyramid field.

Discovery

Auguste Mariette was guided into Saqqara in 1850 by a local Bedouin tribe (Fig. 7). At that time he could hardly see any of the splendour of this ancient necropolis. Centuries of neglect covered the plateau with gravel and only the Stepped Pyramid stood out from this sea of sand. However, accidentally, he noticed a sphinx with its head above the sands, which eventually led him to find, one year later, the celebrated Serapeum, the tomb of the sacred Apis bulls. This was only the beginning of one of the most fascinating adventures in the history of Egyptian archaeology. Despite his many activities all over Egypt, Saqqara would always remain a source of new discoveries for Mariette.

Only ten years later, not far from the Serapeum, Mariette made another exceptional find, when he uncovered the Mastaba of Ti (Fig. 8). This once imposing building still lies partially buried in sand, which makes the right perception of its original context and layout difficult for the modern visitor. However, in antiquity, the building would have stood out from the landscape around and become the focus of tomb robbers. Despite the magnificence of the tomb, nothing seems to have been found by Mariette in the burial chamber, and not even fragments of Ti's mummy had been recorded. However, an over life-size stone statue of Ti was found by Mariette in its original setting (Figs 17–18). It is now on display in the Egyptian Museum in Cairo and stands out as one of the most impressive private statues from the Old Kingdom.

When Mariette cleared the tomb, the texts inscribed on the walls provided an impressive biographical record of Ti who had served under several kings of the 5th Dynasty. The long list of titles includes high responsibilities in the royal administration, such as "overseer of all cattle", "overseer of marshlands", "overseer of scribes of the king's documents", "overseer of all works of the king". Other titles show he was engaged with the royal funerary cults performed in the pyramid field of Abusir ("overseer of the *ba* pyramid of Neferikare", "Overseer of the pyramid of Niusere", "Overseer of the sun temple of Reneferef", "Overseer of the sun temple of Sahure", "Overseer of the sun temple of Neferikare"). Given his important position, Ti was one of the few individuals who had access to the king. He was "Sole companion", "King's acquaintance", "much loved" and for this reason he took personal care of the king's most private needs: "Director of hairdressers", "Overseer of king's meals", "Overseer of the king's regalia", and "Director of the palace".

The magnificent mastaba built by Ti on the edge of the sacred plateau of Saqqara thus crowned an outstanding career.

Fig. 7. Auguste Mariette.

Fig. 8. The Tomb of Ti (19th century).

The structure of the tomb

Originally, the core of the mastaba-tombs was solid, composed of rubble or blocks of stone, and a mudbrick chapel was built towards the east side, in order to provide the interface between the living and the dead. Approaches to the undecorated burial chambers were via shafts sunk through the superstructure.[2] However, under the influence of royal complexes, during the 5th Dynasty, the former massive structure of the mastaba was transformed into a cult complex provided with pillared chambers, galleries, and serdabs (hidden chambers where the statues of the deceased were kept).[3]

Ti raised his splendid mastaba with all the innovations introduced in his time. Today it remains engulfed by the sand and it is reached through a descending causeway leading to a pillared portico (Fig. 9). However, in antiquity, this monumental portico would proudly rise from the desert plateau, welcoming the living with an "Appeal to the living" addressed by Ti on the walls flanking the portico.

Fig. 9. The entrance of the mastaba.

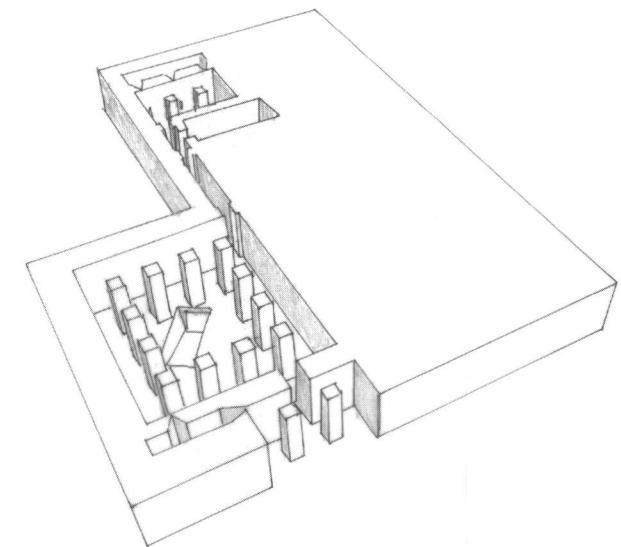

Fig. 10. Reconstruction of the mastaba.

It is likely that Ti may have expanded his mastaba during his long life. The typical rectangular plan of it was slightly changed and a columned courtyard was attached to the rectangular building, forming an L-shaped structure (Fig. 10).

A courtyard is a rare feature in private tombs and it was surely designed after the plan of royal funerary complexes, which included a monumental courtyard in the temple of the pyramid. Ti's imposing courtyard was provided with a portico with twelve monolithic square pillars inscribed with the name and titles of the owner (Fig. 11).

2. On the path to Sokar: Solar splendours in the Mastaba of Ti

In the Mastaba of Ti, the courtyard is associated with several other exceptional features. One of them is a secondary serdab, hidden on the façade of the building, where the statues of Ti and his family would be able to see the sunlight (Fig. 12). Another exceptional feature found in this location is the access to the underground passage leading towards the burial chamber. This structure was certainly equipped with an altar where the offerings were ritually purified before being presented in the funerary cult.[4]

Fig. 11. The courtyard.

Despite these exceptional features, the remaining structure of the tomb is fairly conservative, displaying a relatively simple plan, which included a longitudinal gallery, two transversal chambers, one serdab and secondary burial chambers for Ti's wife and sons (Fig. 13).

The most important room of the mastaba was the main offering chamber with a double false door on the west wall (Fig. 14). This is by far the most important ritual device included in the tomb, whose origins are to be found in royal complexes built from the beginning of the 5th Dynasty onwards.[5] The false door was designed as a magical gate connecting the world of the living with the realm of the dead king. Flanking these magical gates, a wealth of decoration was provided showing offerings being brought to the king who was seated before an offering table.

Fig. 12. The serdab of the offering chamber.

Unlike the motifs associated with the divinisation of the king, which remained exclusively used by the monarch, the themes associated with food offerings were allowed to be used by his subjects. With its many rooms and galleries lavishly decorated, the Mastaba of Ti clearly shows how important these themes became for private individuals to display the boldness of their status.

Despite the diversity of subjects featured on the Old Kingdom mastabas, all of them derived from the false door motif. This was the unsuspected beginning of the visual splendours seen in the Mastaba of Ti.

Pictorial decoration

With the exception of the funerary chambers, which remained undecorated, the walls of the mastaba were profusely decorated with painted reliefs. The repertoire of scenes is divided into three main subjects and these are not randomly distributed in the tomb.

Scenes regarding the provision of the tomb are closely associated with the cult of the Ka performed before the four false doors set up in the tomb, all of them oriented to the west side. The courtyard is provided with a false door for Ti's son. The false door of Ti's wife, Neferhotep, is found in the first section of the longitudinal gallery and the room is entirely decorated with offerings associated with her funerary cult. The second section of this gallery is provided with a transversally arranged room entirely decorated with food provisions and offerings, and for this reason, it has been described as a "storeroom". The offering chamber of Ti is the most impressive of the tomb, showing a double false door on the west wall and a vast array of food offerings (Fig. 14). Long lines of offering bearers replicate the scenes featured in royal complexes alluding to the kingly domains.[6]

Much space is devoted to the depiction of agricultural pursuits, fishing and fowling, bread and beer production, butchery and meat processing, workshops and crafts, including metal workers, boat-building and stonemasons (Fig. 15).[7] This extensive repertoire of "daily life" scenes aims at providing Ti with the funerary goods he needs, while at the same time, celebrates the success and career of the deceased. The high status of the deceased is enhanced by widening the variety of activities which he manages to oversee. The scenes showing Ti and his family adopt the royal canon introduced during the 5th Dynasty: the wife is no longer depicted at the same scale, reduced to less than half the size of her husband (Fig. 16, 17). The deceased thus figures in his tomb as a landowner overseeing his own domain.

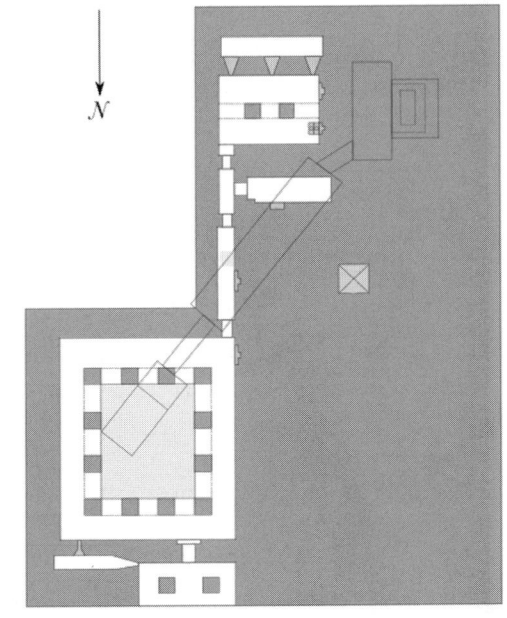

Fig. 13. Plan of the tomb.

Fig. 14. The false door in the offering chamber.

2. On the path to Sokar: Solar splendours in the Mastaba of Ti

Fig. 15. Decoration of the offering chamber (detail).

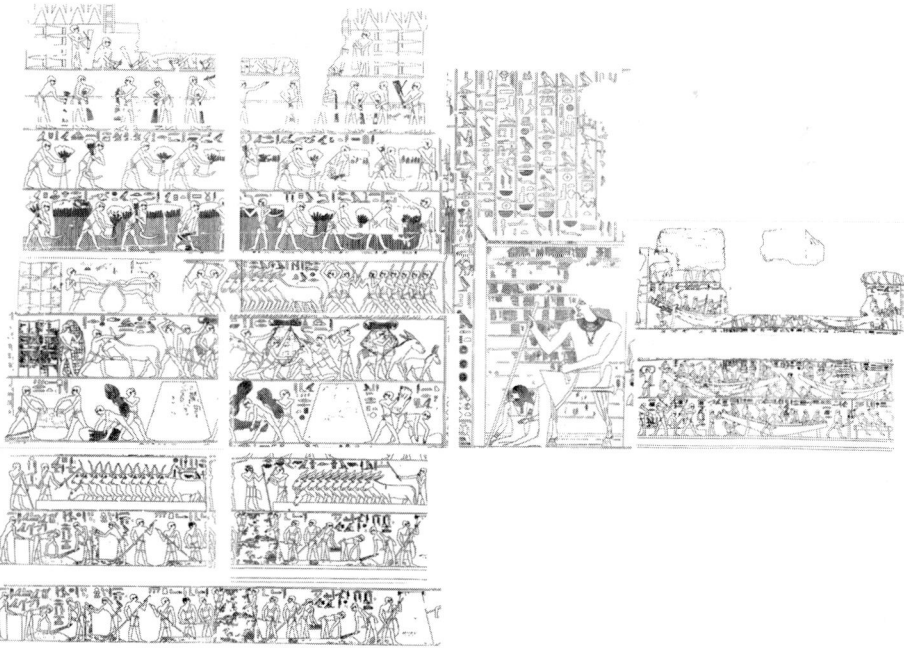

Fig. 16. Decoration of the offering chamber, eastern wall. Drawings from Wild 1966. Composition by the author.

Fig. 17. Decoration of the longitudinal gallery (detail).

Other scenes play a symbolic role, subtly alluding to the journey of the deceased to the underworld. The hunting scene in a papyrus marsh recalls royal models depicted in the pyramid complexes (Fig. 18).[8] The harpooning of the hippopotamus, in particular, has a ritual significance as it serves the purpose of depicting the deceased opposing the enemies of Re.[9] In the Mastaba of Ti, the scene achieved an outstanding level in terms of composition. The serene majesty of Ti's silhouette stands out from the geometrical background of tall and vertical papyrus stalks, while his brave men defeat the group of dangerous hippopotami. The perils of this hunt are further emphasised by showing the fearful beasts fighting against each other.[10] The hunting scene thus shows the struggle against chaos and the triumph of *maat*. The hidden dangers are mastered by the deceased, the beasts are beaten, and he triumphs over chaos.[11]

Other nautical scenes featured in the tomb play a different role and convey another reading of the papyrus marsh. Next to the false door of Ti's wife, a peaceful journey is depicted, showing Ti pleasantly wandering with his wife and sons on a papyrus barque, suggests an association with regeneration (Fig. 17).

Finally, scenes depicting the deceased carried by his men on a litter, full of dignity, allude to his journey to the "Beautiful West", *i.e.* to the funerary cortege that carries his mummy to the necropolis.

Fig. 18. Decoration of the offering chamber (detail).

There is a hint of the influence of the cult of Re in the subject matter of the reliefs.[12] The scenes are lively depicted and often labelled with inscriptions recording a conversation between the different characters. Such picturing of human, animal, and plant life might well have originated as an expression of man's dependence upon the vital force of the sun in the Temple of Re in Heliopolis, later adopted in the decoration of royal funerary complexes.[13]

In a way or another, all these decorative elements can be seen as an extension of the "false door", which is the central symbol of the funerary cult. Always located on the west wall, this magical door "opens" to the underworld and, more specifically, to the burial chamber. In the tomb of Ti, the orientation of the false doors of Ti and Hotepnefer with their respective burials chambers is clear. Through this door, the Ka of the deceased was able to leave the underworld in order to take the offerings dedicated to him by the living.[14] This "door" opened a magical passage through which the living and the dead could meet.

The serdab

Next to the double false door, hidden in its serdab, stood the statue of Ti's Ka (Fig. 12). Unlike the general trend observed during the 5th Dynasty, when the statues in stone become smaller and the use of wood was often preferred, the stone statue of Ti is life-sized, featuring a rather classical style. The importance given to this statue is also seen in the tomb's reliefs, some of them illustrating the transportation of the statues of the Ka to the necropolis. Small slits open on the wall allowed the statue to see the offerings and scent the incense,[15] while keeping it hidden.[16]

This timeless image, depicts the deceased literally as a three-dimensional hieroglyph (S 42 from the list of Gardiner) meaning "statue", *i.e.* the "living image" of Ti, which was expected to perform the same role assured by his body, which was holding intact his Ka, his power of life. This image was necessarily invested with extreme dignity and power, embodying the idea of a superior human being, who excelled himself in his service of the king.[17]

In the reliefs, the depiction of Ti gives an impression of strength and severe maturity. He is shown with a prominent nose, large lips, short beard, and long wig (Fig. 18). The treatment of his body is anatomically correct, carefully defining muscles and bones as to suggest the body of an accomplished athlete. The statue, on the other hand, shows a smoother treatment of the anatomical features. Despite its monumentality, it suggests a younger portrait, beardless,

Fig. 19. The statue of Ti. Egyptian Museum in Cairo.

and with a shorter wig (Fig. 19). Despite these hints of idealisation, the nose, and the lips are consistent with Ti's two-dimensional depictions.

The burial chamber

The burial chamber of Ti was excavated directly below his double false-door. Contrasting with the profusion of decoration carved on the walls of the superstructure, the burial chamber remained undecorated and only the massive stone sarcophagus was found there (Fig. 20).

Fig. 20. The burial chamber.

The stone sarcophagus of Ti is rectangular, with arched lid and raised end-pieces. This design typically suggests the layout of a "house".[18] A U-shaped boring at each end of the lid enabled the use of ropes to lower it into place.[19] These were intended to be broken off after the funeral, but as in many other tombs, they were left in place. As additional support, walls were constructed between the sarcophagus and the bedrock surface to hold up the lid until after the funeral, when it was slid into place.

In the most elite internments, the sarcophagus, called Neb Ankh ("Lord of Life") played the most important role. For religious reasons, great importance was given to the orientation of the sarcophagus, which was positioned in the burial chamber with the head pointing northwards and the long left side towards the east. This position was adopted after the royal model used in the pyramid complexes, where the north played an important role, as the Imperishable Stars pointed the way to immortality for the king.

Carvings on the inner walls of Ti's stone sarcophagus makes it likely that a wooden coffin had been used. However, if such a coffin existed, nothing was found in situ. Private coffins from this period are rectangular, with flat lids.[20] They evolved from the short wooden boxes introduced during the Early Dynastic Period (1st–2nd dynasties), where the body was still buried in a contracted position following a long tradition.[21] Some of these body containers were designed as huts after the domestic concepts associated with Predynastic graves. Besides wooden boxes, a wide range of domestic objects are often used as body containers, such as mats, baskets, vases and pots, and animal skins.[22] With the development of mummification practices in royal circles, the extended position of the corpse was eventually adopted by the elite, originating in rectangular shaped wooden coffins. In the necropoleis of Giza and Saqqara, coffins are plain and the decoration is restricted to a single incised line of an offering-text running round the upper part of the box.[23] In the most elite burials, where a large stone sarcophagus was included, the main purpose of the coffin was to provide a light body container to transport the mummy to the tomb, preserving the deceased from any form of "contamination". The opaqueness of these undecorated coffins prevented undesired interactions between the living and the dead.[24] It is, therefore, plausible to assume that the mummy of Ti was carried to the necropolis and buried in such a wooden coffin.

Inside the coffin, the mummy was placed on its left side, facing the East, *i.e.*, the false door, the land of the living, and the rising sun.[25] During the 5th Dynasty, the mummy did not show the typical layout of a "cocoon" as it would be the rule from the Middle Kingdom onwards. After being prepared with balsams and eviscerated, the body was wrapped in linen and the autonomy of the limbs was maintained. This was carried out in such a way that the mummy could be dressed with garments and decorated with jewels.[26] Sketches featuring anatomical details, such as the eyes, nose, mouth or nipples were outlined on the mummy wrappings to complete the decoration.[27] This was meant to create an underworldly "statue" for the Ka, one that would remain hidden inside the sarcophagus. The desire to establish an identity between the mummy and the statue of the Ka often led to bizarre results: in some cases, the mummy was covered up with a layer of plaster which was moulded and sculpted in order to better reproduce the style of a statue.[28] The corpse was thus literally transformed into a "living image" ("statue") of the deceased.

Concluding remarks

The Tomb of Ti is an outstanding achievement in terms of visual culture. At first glance, those images seem to feature episodes from daily life. However, this would be incorrect, as they show the afterlife as it was understood in the Old Kingdom, as an ideal reflection of the earthly life. Unlike the king, who ascended to heaven and united with the gods, elite individuals aspired to live in the underworld together with their ancestors. Their tombs functioned as the entrance to the underworld where the Ka of the deceased would be maintained. Besides the funerary goods, most of the scenes are designed to assure their ongoing production.

It would be misleading to understand these scenes as historical documents in *stricto senso*. Despite the fact that some scenes allude to the supervision of goldsmiths, it would be unwise to take this information as historical, as most of the scenes are included as part of a "classical" repertoire featuring the *mise en scéne* of cosmic order in Egypt.

Borrowed from royal complexes and solar temples, the visual culture featured on mastabas conveys a cosmic programme rather than a biographical account. For instance, the scenes showing the deceased undertaking the journey to the dangerous forests of papyri where he faces the beasts that threaten the cosmic order: these images do not exactly replicate an earthly journey, but rather the iconographic repertoire developed under the inspiration of the solar cult. In the solar imaginary, the forest of papyri is understood as a primordial territory of rebirth and regeneration. In fact, the magical role of the forest of papyri is transferred to the tomb itself, with its chambers and rooms seen as the interior of these forests, where regeneration takes place.²⁹

The prominence of the sun cult is clearly implicit in the cycles represented, presenting an ideal world with everyone living in *maat*.³⁰

Royal imagery deeply pervades the layout of the tomb. The imposing double false door, the overwhelming asymmetry between Ti and his servants, the long lines of offering bearers, the monumentality of his statue and the solar courtyard are some of the boldest statements of Ti's status. Ti featured himself as an Akh, an "efficient spirit", who as the king, was able to keep *maat* in his own dominion so that life on the banks of the Nile could keep its own cycles in motion.³¹

Fig. 21. *The stone sarcophagus of Nebka (?) from the unfinished Northern Pyramid of Zawyet El Aryan. Services des Antiquité d'Égypte, 1904.*

However, in the Mastaba of Ti, solarisation plays an even bolder role, as it changed the tomb's plan. The open courtyard connected the light of the sun with the underworld, where Ti's mummy rested inside its sarcophagus.

Despite its simplicity, the undecorated monumental sarcophagus is the most sacred piece of his tomb. It was the embodiment of the sacred "ground", perhaps seen as a womb, that held the deceased and prepared him for a new rebirth. This imagery is clearly detected in royal burials. Despite the considerable leap forward between the royal sarcophagus of the Old Kingdom and the simple Predynastic oval graves, a genealogical continuum can be traced in between. Instructive in providing this link is the royal sarcophagus of Nebka, a rectangular block of stone integrated into the pavement of the burial chamber with an elliptical interior and an elliptical lid (Fig. 21). The structure is reminiscent of the Predynastic oval burial pits, with the difference that the interior of this "sarcophagus" functioned to hold an elongated body.³²

This sophisticated imagery, firmly embedded on royal tombs, is revealing of Ti's personal expectations regarding the afterlife. However, despite his close relationship with the king and royal ideology, it is surprising to see that he chose not to build his "mansion of eternity" next to the royal complexes in Abusir and turned his attention to the ancestral necropolis of Saqqara instead.

Ti constructed his "house of eternity" in Saqqara, apparently without any association with a royal complex. It is important to point out that when he decided

Chapter 3

Facing the sun: The shaft tomb of Senebtisi

The Faiyum is the largest oasis of Egypt. It extends over a wide desert depression to the west of the Nile, 80 km south of Cairo. The oasis grows around the Lake Qarun, watered by a channel of the Nile, the Bahr Yussef, *i.e.* Joseph's Canal. This biblical allusion to the Pharaoh's dream announcing seven years of famine after seven years of wealth is perhaps more than accidental. When the Theban king Amenemhat I ascended to the throne, founding the 12th Dynasty, he inherited a country which not long ago had known famine and social unrest. With the Two Lands again unified under his rule, he chose the Fayum oasis to build his new capital city.

In antiquity, the lake was much wider than today and on its banks, wildlife flourished in ways that today we can only dream of. The lake nurtured all kinds of fish and the marshes swarmed with thousands of birds. Over the years, the successors of Amenemhat I would transform the Fayum oasis into the granary of Egypt and the role of the king as the nourisher of the people was indeed greatly valued, exactly as we learn from the biblical tale of Joseph.

Unfortunately, nothing remains of Ity-Taui ("The Seizer of the Two Lands"), the new capital city of Amenemhat I, not even its location, and only the faint remains of the royal necropolis built around the Fayum give us a glimpse of its former splendour. Amenemhat I built his pyramid in Lisht, in a splendid location, between the Nile floodplain and the Fayum. Unlike the pyramid fields of Giza or Saqqara, which towered over the landscape around, the monument of Amenemhat I was built on a low platform of the desert, thus closely connected with the green fields flooded by the Nile (Fig. 22). Despite the beauty of the site, Amenemhat's choice would not turn out to be the wisest in terms of preservation. The easy access to the site dictated its fate, and for centuries it has served as a quarry.[1] Originally over 55 m high, today the pyramid is depleted to around 20 m.

3. Facing the sun: The shaft tomb of Senebtisi

Fig. 22. The Pyramid of Amenemhat I in Lischt.

Additionally, the ground waters submerged the burial chamber of the king in modern times, preventing its archaeological exploration. Like the pyramid, most of the tombs of the necropolis of Lisht were badly affected by humidity and were found in a poor state of preservation.

This was the situation of the Tomb of Senebtisi, an elite woman that lived under the 12th Dynasty. Her shaft tomb was excavated in the mastaba complex southwest of the pyramid of Amenemhat I, belonging to the vizier Senuseret, who served under the kings Senuseret I and Amenemhat II.

Discovery

Senebtisi's shaft tomb (Tomb 758) was unearthed by the Metropolitan Museum of Art Expedition in its first season in Egypt. In January 1907 Albert Lythgoe began work in the cemeteries at Lisht, assisted by Arthur Mace and Herbert Winlock who was just starting his archaeological career (Fig. 23).

The precinct included nearly 15 subsidiary shallow pit tombs (Fig. 24). Unlike the remaining tombs of the funerary complex, the axis of the burial pit of Senebtisi was not N-S, but E-W, which probably resulted from the lack of available space in the precinct. This is relevant because the orientation of the tomb determined the position of the mummy in the burial chamber, which should be laid with the head to the north, facing east. However, the site where the pit was excavated did not provide enough space along this axis, and the burial pit had to be excavated along the E-W axis. The situation was corrected by excavating the burial chamber in transversal position.

Fig. 23. The Expedition of the Metropolitan Museum of Art in Thebes, 1925: (back row, left to right) Herbert E. Winlock, Walter Hauser, Albert M. Lythgoe, Harry Burton, Charles K. Wilkinson, Norman de Garis Davies; (centre row, left to right) Helen Winlock, Nina de Garis Davies, Lucy Lythgoe, Minnie Burton, Miss Willis; (front row, left to right) Walter Cline, Barbara Winlock, Frances Winlock, G.M. Peek. Archives of the Egyptian Expedition, Department of Egyptian Art.

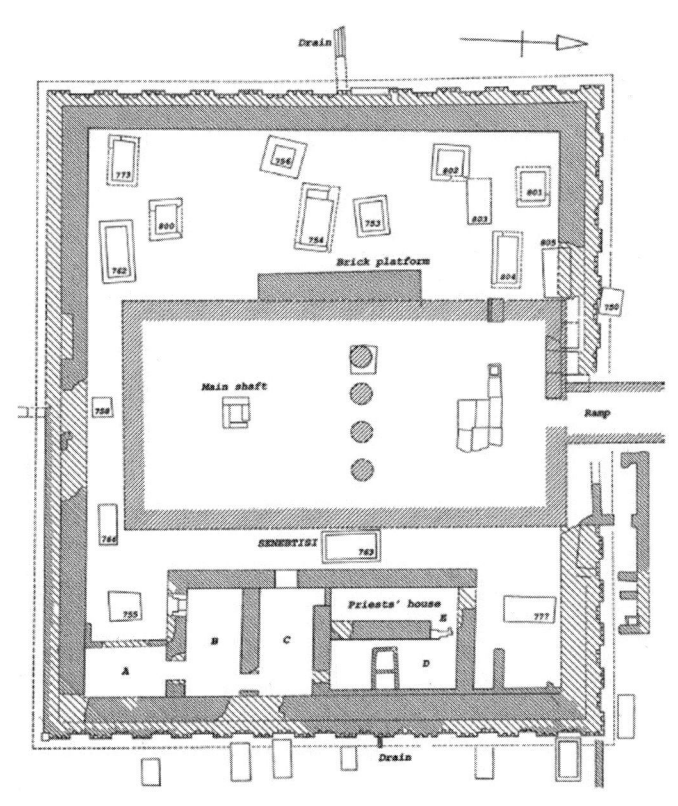

Fig. 24. Plan of the Mastaba of the Vizier Senuseret with the position of the shaft-tomb of Senebtisi. In Arnold 2018, Pl. 149.

3. Facing the sun: The shaft tomb of Senebtisi

The pit, filled to the top with heavy rubble, was 6.85 metres deep. The upper part of the shaft was lined with bricks and covered with a heavy coating of plaster. The floor of the pit was roughly cut.

The offering chamber opened out of the pit from its west end, carved slightly on a lower level. It was concealed by a brick blocking found intact; roughly square, irregularly cut. The ground was strewn with food and drink offerings contained in a multitude of pottery jars, dishes, and saucers (Fig. 25). When Mace and Winlock entered the offering chamber, they found a wig box, thrown out by plunderers, probably when they were caught.[2] This event occurred before the definitive sealing of the burial pit with rubble.

The burial chamber was carved transversally leading north (Fig. 26). Despite the visit of the ancient tomb robbers, it was found relatively intact. However, humidity produced severe damage to the organic materials. The nested coffin set was positioned according to the ritual conventions, with the headboard leaning on the north wall. It comprised two rectangular wooden coffins and a magnificent anthropoid coffin, entirely gilded.[3]

On the floor, placed alongside the coffin set, lay a long wooden chest probably holding staves and two small shrine-shaped boxes which may have contained wooden *shabti*-figures, i.e. small sized wooden replicas of the mummy, a new type of funerary artefact introduced in this period.[4]

A niche carved on the east wall of the burial chamber held the canopic box of Senebtisi.

Despite the poor state of preservation of the organic materials, the painstaking documentation work carried out by Mace and Winlock allowed the full reconstruction

Fig. 25. Double offering table. Metropolitan Museum of Art (12.181.197).

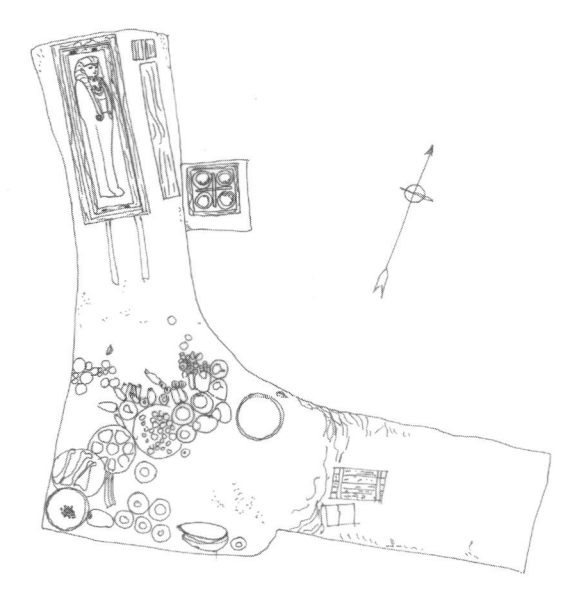

Fig. 26. Plan of the tomb of Senebtisi with the reconstructed burial assemblage. Drawing after Mace, Winlock 1916, Fig. 1.

of the original layout of most of the lost objects of the burial assemblage, which had been thoroughly published in a remarkable monograph published by the Metropolitan Museum of Art.[5]

Rectangular coffins

The outer coffin, probably made of sycamore-fig, had succumbed to the humidity of the tomb.[6] It was about 211 cm long, 72 cm wide, 116 cm high, elegantly decorated with stripes of gold against red paint imitating cedar (Fig. 27).

The inscriptions had been badly preserved but the few vestiges that remain show that they were designed after the patterns developed in the mid-12th Dynasty. At this time, it was customary to decorate the long sides of the coffin with a horizontal band of hieroglyphs at the top, and below this, four text columns. On the short ends, there were two columns,[7] and on the left long side, an eye-panel was featured.[8]

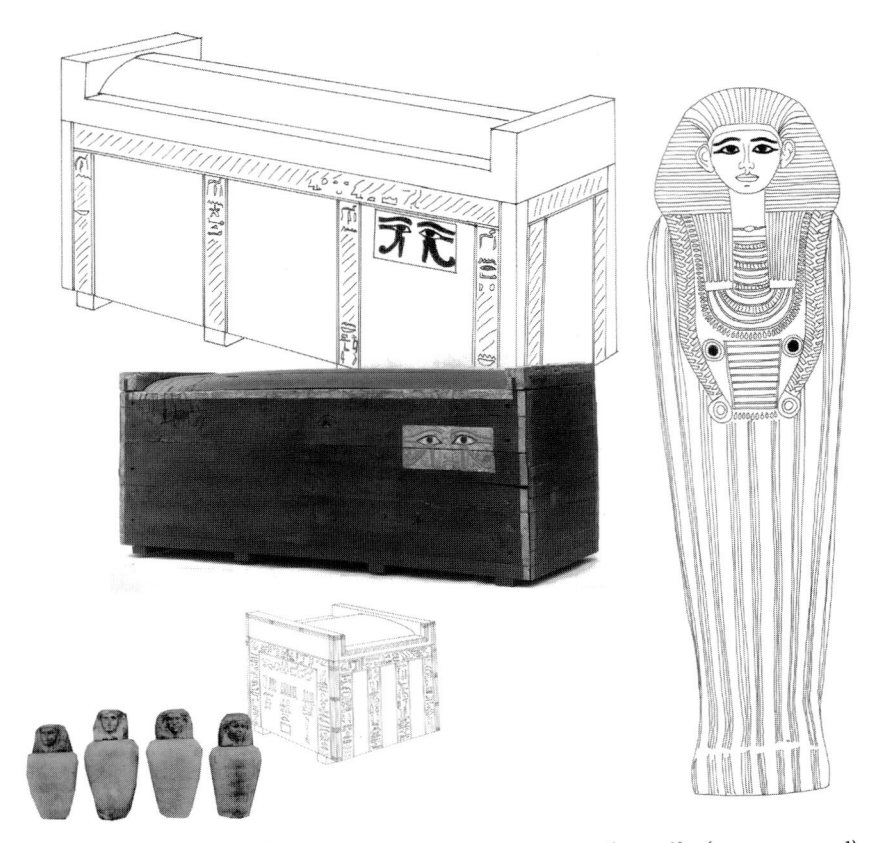

Fig. 27. Burial assemblage of Senebtisi, comprising an outer rectangular coffin (reconstructed), an inner rectangular coffin (Metropolitan Museum of Art, 08.200.45a-b), one anthropoid coffin (reconstructed) and a canopic box (reconstructed), with human-headed vases. Drawings by the author after Mace, Winlock 1916.

The coffins were ritualistically positioned in the burial chamber so that the head of the mummy would be oriented to the north. This alignment defined the coffin cosmologically, like a miniature representation of the world.[9] The lid was equated with the sky, and so it was customary to be inscribed with a longitudinal inscription alluding to the rebirth provided by the heavenly mother goddess Nut.

The right side faced west and related to topics concerning the west, sunset, and entering the underworld. The bottom was linked to the night and the underworld.

The left side was turned to the east side, providing access to the world of the living. Here, the dominant themes were the offering ritual and sunrise, with the eye panel featured near the head end of the wall allowing the deceased to see the sunrise and enjoy the funerary offerings.[10]

The outer coffin of Senebtisi seems to observe this scheme, with the lid inscribed with a spell conferring the protection of the sky goddess Nut. References to Duamutef (west side) and Nephthys (north side) subsist, showing that they allude to the protection conferred to the deceased's limbs by the four Sons of Horus during the embalming ritual.[11]

Other inscriptions would provide the deceased with the deification of his body parts through the identification with the Great Ennead, the primordial beings begotten by the sun god.[12] In all, this elaborate set of references defined the rectangular coffin as a *qereset*, i.e. a proper "burial place".

This wealth of inscriptions and iconography provides a vivid contrast with the undecorated character of the Old Kingdom coffins, which were defined by their opaqueness.[13] The absence of decoration stressed the impenetrability of the container, isolating the deceased and creating a protective barrier.[14] The addition of depicted elements re-connects the deceased with the funerary rituals and make them permanent.[15]

The eye-panel, on the left long side, breaks the impermeability of the coffin, providing a passage between the interior and the exterior.[16] Made of inlaid stone, they show the eyes of the deceased on the exterior of the coffin, a phenomenon that triggered the full "anthropomorphisation" of the body container, as we may see in the coffin set of Sebnetisi.

The inside of the outer box of Senebtisi was entirely coated in black pitch.[17] Inside the box, was found a well-preserved, rectangular coffin of cedar, mounted with a gold foil and having a low, vaulted lid with transverse end boards.[18] Owing to the excellent cedar wood of which it was made, this second coffin had suffered comparatively little.[19] It was 194 cm long, 55 cm in width, 75 cm in height (Fig. 27).

The chief emphasis of the decoration was in the colour and texture of the cedar wood, which had been rubbed down to a smooth surface. The dark texture contrasts elegantly with the gilded bands, finely decorated with incised lines. The eye panel stands out from the dark background. It is formed of plaster overlaid with gold foil, and the eyes are of alabaster and obsidian. The only inscription of the coffin is on a gold band 6.6 cm wide down the centre of the lid. The signs were inscribed in plaster and gold leaf was rubbed in.[20] This text is an utterance taken from the Pyramid Texts and is addressed to the sky goddess Nut:

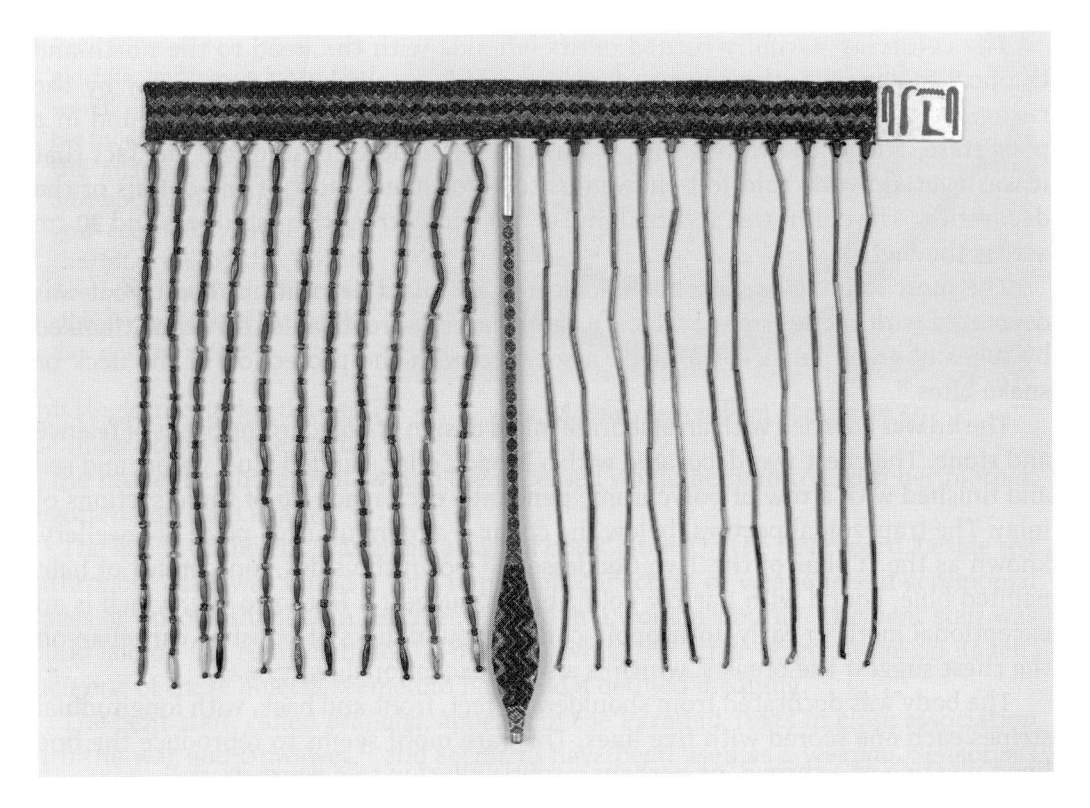

Fig. 29. Beadwork apron of Senebtisi. Metropolitan Museum of Art (08.200.29a).

The distribution of the emblems on the right and left sides of the apron presupposes the fact that the deceased who wears it would face the east, with the right side turned to the south and the left to the north.[38] This apron is a kingly attire with Osirian significance.[39]

The space between the mummy and the coffin lid was filled out by twelve fringed shawls.[40] The mummy of Senebtisi was wrapped in alternating layers of sheets and bandages. They were covered over the front with a coating of resin, poured in a liquid form after it had been laid in position, inside the coffin. The pitch had run down to the left side of the body and must, therefore, have been poured when the mummy was laid on its left side.[41]

The outer wrappings of the mummy were adorned with jewellery embedded in the layer of resin. The head was adorned with a headdress of gold wire (Fig. 30). This delicate and charming parure consisted of a circlet of fine twisted gold wire. Ninety-eight little rosettes of beaten gold adorned the area where the divine wig would have been located. This was a divine attire of Osiris, also found in coffin decoration.

Three necklaces were disposed on the neck. One of them was composed of three strands of tiny ball beads of carnelian, green feldspar, and blue frit divided into sections by sets of gold beads. On the exterior strand were attached 25 pendants of beaten gold in the form of small bivalve shells (Fig. 31 below).

Another necklace featured two strings of little green feldspar beads enclosing 21 *Sa*-amulets of electrum, carnelian, silver, green feldspar, and ivory (Fig. 31 above). These are shaped after the hieroglyph *sa* (V 17), meaning "protection". They represent a rolled-up reed mat carried by marsh dwellers as a lifejacket.[42]

The third necklace also makes use of hieroglyphic signs. It is composed of beads shaped as small offering *hes*-vases of carnelian, green feldspar, blue frit, and gilded paste, with a pendant in the form of a gold *shen*-ring inlaid with carnelian and blue paste (Fig. 32).[43] Meaning "encircle", the *shen*-ring (V 9) represents everything the sun encircled during the course of the 24 hours but it also alludes to the protection conferred to what remains within it.[44]

Around the waist girdles of small acacia beads were found.

Inside the wrappings was the bulk of the funerary jewels. The throat was adorned with three *wesekh*-collars.[45] Two of them are made of multicoloured beads. In both cases, the terminals are gilded: one of them presents rounded undecorated terminals, while the other shows falcon-headed terminals

Fig. 30. Circlet and golden rosettes of Senebtisi. Metropolitan Museum of Art (07.227.7).

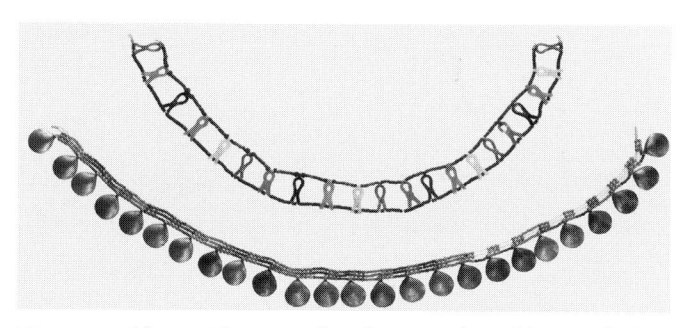

Fig. 31. Necklace with sa-amulets (07.227.11), necklace with shell pendants (07.227.8). Metropolitan Museum of Art.

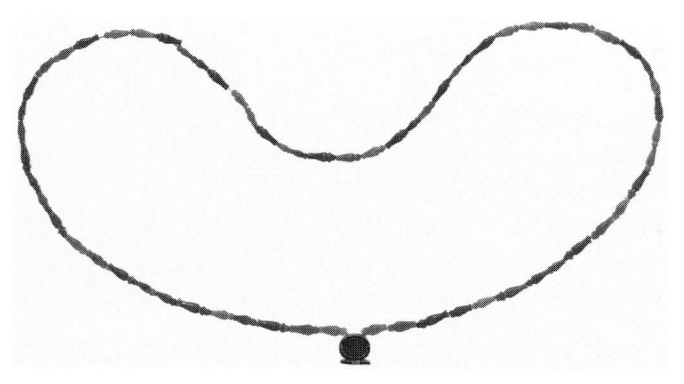

Fig. 32. Necklace with shen-ring. Metropolitan Museum of Art (07.227.9).

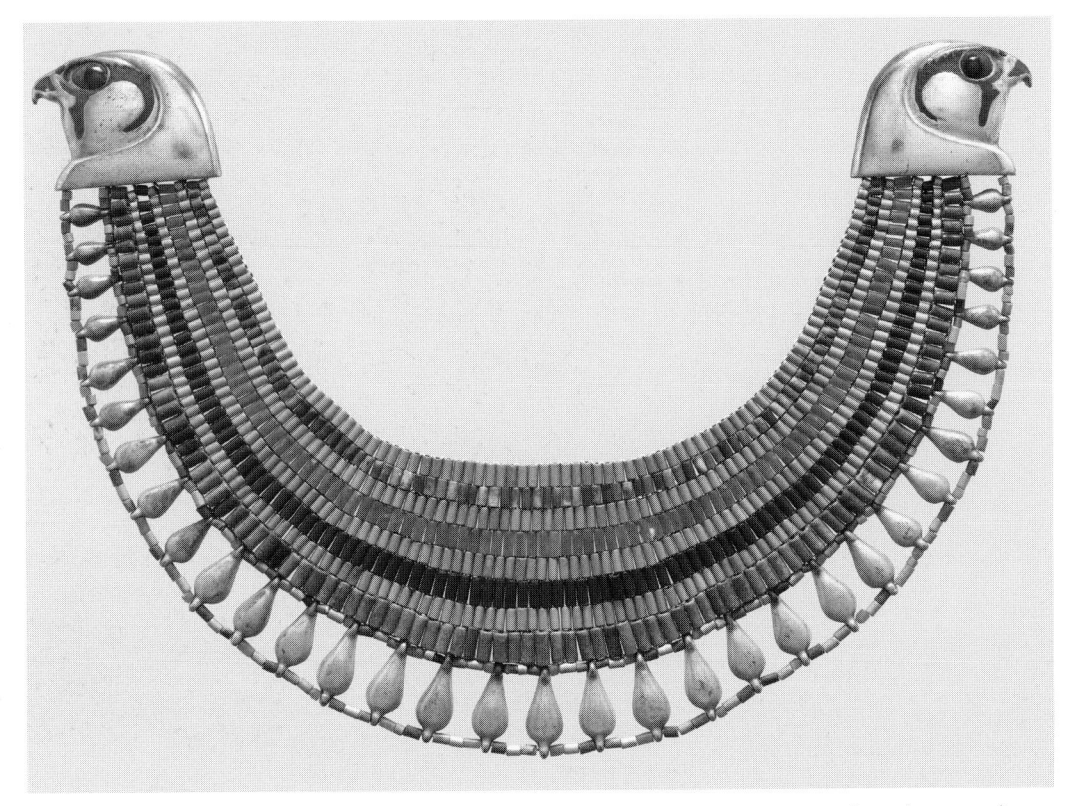

Fig. 33. Large collar with falcon headed terminals. Metropolitan Museum of Art (08.200.30)

with inlays of obsidian and lapis-lazuli (Fig. 33).[46] The third collar is the "collar of Gold", made of a piece of sheet copper cut to shape and overlaid on both sides with gold foil. On the front, the outlines of the gold beads, pendants, and terminals are engraved in the surface of the foil.[47]

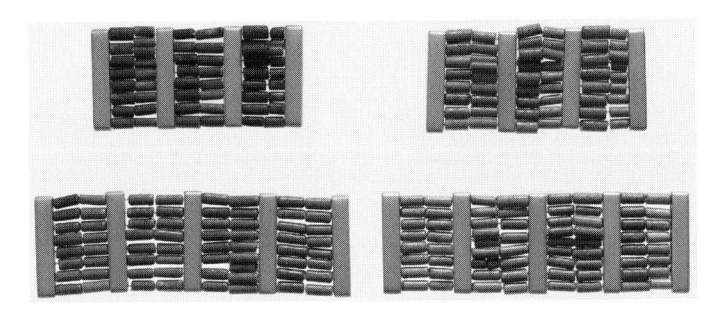

Fig. 34. Bracelets and anklets. Metropolitan Museum of Art (08.200.25–.28).

On the wrists and ankles wide bracelets and anklets of tubular beads were disposed (Fig. 34).[48] These too are ritual objects with Osirian significance. A bracelet of faience tubular beads is fitted with a gold clasp in the form of a corded square knot,[49] probably an early design of the *tjet*-amulet, the so-called "Isis knot",[50] alluding to the life-giving protection conferred by Isis (Fig. 35).

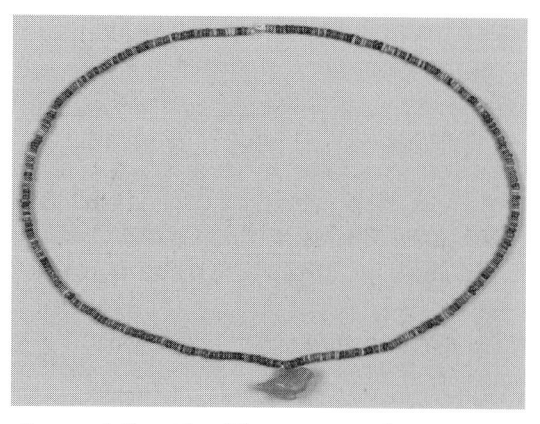

Fig. 36. Girdle with a falcon. Metropolitan Museum of Art (08.200.42a).

Fig. 35. Clasp. Metropolitan Museum of Art (07.227.10).

Also noteworthy is a girdle of faience disk beads supporting a small carnelian amulet in the form of Horus depicted as a crouching falcon (Fig. 36). It was worn about the hips and abdomen of the mummy of Senebtisi in such a way that the falcon lays over the embalmer's incision on the left side of the body.[51] The function of this object was to the seal the incision, a role later on performed by the "Eye of Horus", the *wedjat*-plaque.

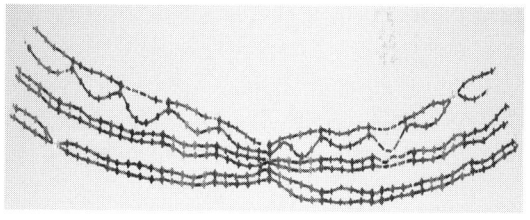

Fig. 37. Acacia bead girdle. Metropolitan Museum of Art (07.227.13)

Another girdle was made up of six strands of small ovoid beads in the shape of acacia seeds, separated by groups of minute disks of gold, carnelian, green feldspar, and lapis lazuli, in addition to a yellowish composition imitating ivory, also used for acacia beads (Fig. 37).[52]

The royal sceptre *nekhakha* completed the funerary equipment of Senebtisi (Fig. 38). It is composed of three long, tapered streamers suspended from the end of a short handle. It probably derived from an implement used to collect *ladanum* from the leaves of the cistus plant (or other gum bearing plants) which could then be used in the preparation of incense.[53] As a royal sceptre, it was seen as a symbol of authority and as a magical object probably associated with the divine powers of the king.

The body, that of a small woman, about fifty years old, and with the teeth in almost perfect condition, lay extended with the hands together over the lower abdomen. The state of preservation of the mummy was poor and it was mostly reduced to the skeleton. The method used in the mummification was surprisingly conservative:

the arms and legs were individually wrapped, and the brain remained within the cranium.[54]

The viscera had been extracted through an incision over the left groin and the body cavity packed with sawdust and wads of linen soaked in resin. The heart, wrapped in linen, had been replaced in the body, but the liver, intestines, and two other organs had been permanently removed and placed in the four canopic jars.

Canopic equipment

The canopic box was found in the niche carved in the east wall of the burial chamber (Fig. 26). It was made of fine cedar wood, but nevertheless it was in a poor state of preservation, within a cubical box (55 cm square and 62 cm high) with a vaulted lid. It was made to match the outer coffin, as it was painted red. Gold stripes on the edges and inscriptions completed the decoration.[55] The inscriptions refer

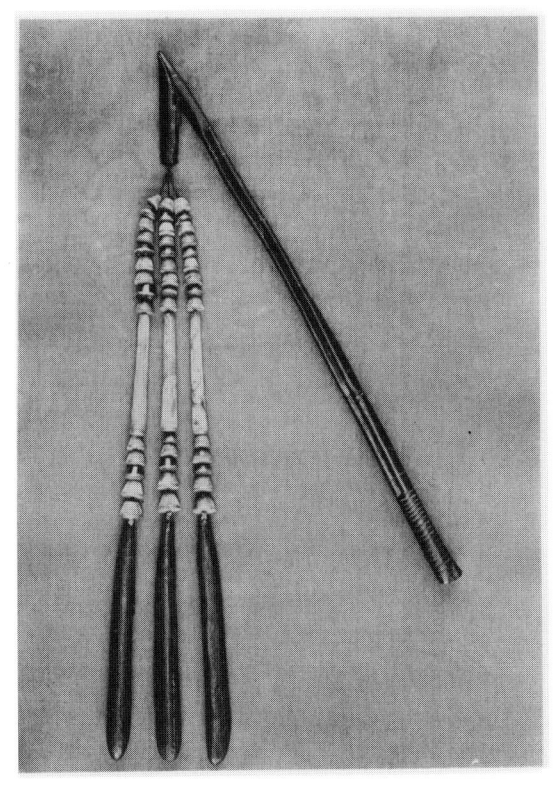

Fig. 38. Nekhakha sceptre. Metropolitan Museum of Art (07.227.15).

to funerary offerings and to the protection conferred by the four cosmic goddesses (Neith, Serket, Isis and Nephthys) to the four Sons of Horus (Qebehsenuef, Duamutef, Hapi and Imseti), and the four viscera of the deceased (intestines, stomach, lungs, and liver).

Inside, four vases of alabaster were found. The human-headed wooden stoppers of Senebtisi's canopic jars are beardless.[56] Since the anthropoid coffin was found poorly preserved, we cannot compare them with the gilded face of Senebtisi featured on the headboard of this object. However, these heads differ so much form one another that they seem to have been assembled from different sets. The jars themselves are of alabaster, handsomely grained and finely polished. They present different sizes and formats.[57] Two of the human organs in these jars have been identified as the liver and the intestines.[58]

Concluding remarks

The cemeteries surrounding the pyramids of the 12th Dynasty contained the tombs of the royal families and of the courtiers in the immediate retinue of the king. Built in the vicinity of Amenemhat's I pyramid, the mastaba tomb of the vizier Senuseret was a splendid monument. When the expedition from the Metropolitan Museum of Art uncovered the site, only faint remains of the original decoration of the mastaba were found. However, the few vestiges left suggest that it was beautifully ornamented with colourful reliefs, after the traditional layout used in mastaba tombs during the 5th and the 6th Dynasty. By the end of the 12th Dynasty, this funerary precinct started to be used to hold intrusive burials, and it is in this context that Senebtisi's shaft tomb was excavated.[59]

Judging by the quality of her funerary equipment, Senebtisi was a high elite resident of the capital city and undoubtedly a member of the royal court. Although making use of poorer materials, her burial followed in its general style, and in many of the individual objects included in her tomb, the features of the contemporary royal burials. Her outer rectangular coffin, painted red to imitate granite,[60] is clearly a wooden version of the stone sarcophagi found in the royal tombs in Dashur. The use of two nested rectangular coffins thus emulates the archetypical composition of the burial chamber which should be equipped with a stone sarcophagus and a rectangular wooden coffin.

The inner rectangular coffin of Senebtisi, in particular, is a fine object, belonging to the "court" type. It displays a simpler and yet sophisticated decoration. The earliest examples of this type belong to four princesses buried in the pyramid enclosure of Amenemhat II, at Dashur.[61] These coffins differ significantly in form and decoration from the brightly painted coffins used elsewhere. Here there is a severe but rich simplicity, relying for its effect on the natural color and tone of fine dark wood, relieved and accented by narrow bands of gold. This exquisite object carries with it a distinctive expression of status, only affordable to the highest elite of those times.

The gilded anthropoid coffin of Senebtisi is no less remarkable, showing an archaising layout, and exquisite inlaid decoration, including Hathoric motifs, which are exceptional at this early date. It is also interesting to point out the interaction between the black pitch covering of the interior walls of the rectangular coffins and the gilded foil covering the anthropoid coffin, as if the immortal flesh of the sun god (gold) rested within the darkness of the underworld. Perhaps not accidentaly, the only inscription included in the decoration of the inner rectangular coffin is an address to the sky goddess Nut taken from the Pyramid Texts, which during the late Old Kingdom had been exclusively inscribed in the royal burial chambers. This recitation invokes the cosmic mother goddess so that she gives birth to the deceased, as a new-born Osirian god, a privilege once exclusive to the king.

As we have seen, the symbolism of the anthropoid coffin is deeply rooted in the magical significance of the funerary mask, which was designed as a tangible manifestation of the Osirian resurrection. Once restricted to the king, this divine identification of the deceased with Osiris triggered what can be described as an "Osirification" of the Egyptian burial equipment. Anthropoid coffins, human-headed canopic vases, and *shabtis* are all examples of this phenomenon that took place at the beginning of the Middle Kingdom.

Described in Chapter 151 of the Book of the Dead ("Spell for the head of mystery"), the magical purpose of the funerary mask comprised several goals. In the first place it allowed the deceased to see.

The drive to see established a magical continuum between the different body containers, with the anthropoid coffin resting on its left side so that the headboard could gaze at the eye-panels from the inner and outer rectangular coffins.

The magical link uniting the different body containers is of course extended to the mummy itself. Another role attributed to the funerary mask (and so the anthropoid coffin) in Chapter 151 of the Book of the Dead is the power to drive away the deceased's enemies. For this reason, Senebtisi was equipped with weapons, since as an Osirian god she would be invested with the power to repel "his" adversaries (the Sethian agents of death).

Finally, the funerary mask provided the deceased with his divine manifestation as an Osirian god. Chapter 151 of the Book of the Dead makes clear that through mummification the deceased had become wholly divine, a transformation expressed through the equation of all parts of the head with deities.[62] Therefore, the anthropoid coffin depicts the deceased as a *sah*, *i.e.* an Osirian god.

The definition of the deceased in this manner is completed with the objects included in the mummy wrappings. In fact, most of the objects found in the mummy of Senebtisi are not personal jewels but funerary items expected to protect the mummy, such as the large collars, necklaces, bracelets, sceptres, and weapons. They all allude to the resurrection of Senebtisi as an Osirian god (Fig. 39).[63]

Some of the jewels placed in the mummy wrapping repeat those depicted on the anthropoid lid. This is the case of the large collars and the *seweret*-necklace. This shows a close interconnection between the magical equipment of the mummy and coffin decoration. In Senebtisi's coffin, nearly a hundred golden rosacea covered the head of the mummy, but in other burials, these motifs are depicted over the divine wig of the anthropoid coffin (Fig. 40).[64]

The royal girdle is also used in burial contexts as an attribute of Osiris, the king of the netherworld and, for this reason, it was eventually depicted on anthropoid coffins (Fig. 41).[65] The girdle shows the heraldic plants of

Fig. 39. Arrangement of the body adornments found in Senebtisi's mummy as if worn by a living person.

3. Facing the sun: The shaft tomb of Senebtisi

Fig. 40. Anthropoid coffin of Hapiankhtifi of Mir. Metropolitan Museum of Art (12.183.11c-2).

Upper and Lower Egypt in a way that the right side of the deceased is covered by the Upper Egyptian lilies, while her left side is covered by the Lower Egyptian papyri. This arrangement supposes the cosmic alignment of the deceased with the east. In this way, as the king of Egypt, the deceased would eventually rise from the underworld, facing the rising sun, with her left side turned towards Lower Egypt, and the right side to Upper Egypt, thus uniting the Two Lands in her own body and triggering a cosmic recreation.

The use of royal insignia in the funerary equipment is as symbolic as the use of weapons.[66] This fact has raised an interesting discussion regarding our prejudices and expectations for what we think as gender related objects. Military equipment is often seen as useful evidence to identify a male burial and royal insignia are obviously expected in royal tombs. However, during the Middle Kingdom high elite women are often buried with these artefacts. The regalia used in Senebtisi's burial are not exceptional and are surprisingly similar to those found in the tomb of the "king's daughter" Nubheteptihered at Dashur.[67] This shaft tomb was integrated with the pyramid complex of Amenemhat III and, according to Wolfgang Grajetzki, shows a typical example of the ritual items deposited in the burial during the late Middle Kingdom for a selected group at the royal court.[68] It is, therefore, logical to admit that Senebtisi integrated such an exclusive group which was able to use these important objects in a symbolic manner.

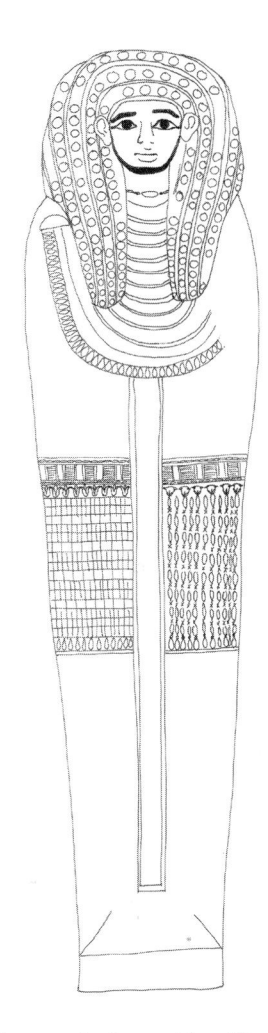

Fig. 41. Anthropoid coffin of Sobekhat after photographic documentation in Yoshimura et al. 2018.

Used in this context, royal objects, weapons, and staves played a symbolic and ritualistic role alluding to the "hour vigil", the last phase of mummification of Osiris, when these objects were given to him to acknowledge his kingship.[69]

These type of "court burials"[70] show a "silent" revolution taking shape. The burial chamber was no longer the undecorated place, where the mummy of the deceased was hidden to hold the vital powers of the Ka, as it happened during the Old Kingdom. Food supply still plays an important role in the burial equipment and, in fact, a number of vessels, vases and even an offering table (Fig. 25) were found in the offering chamber of Senebtisi's tomb. However, the burial chamber became a semiotic space, where each object worked as a sign encoding the re-enactment of a mysterious transformation, one that once was expected to occur with a king: the rebirth provided by the heavenly goddess Nut. The whole burial chamber was equipped like an embalming tent in such a way that the coffin and the burial goods formed a meaningful unit where the transformation into a godlike being was the main focus.[71] In other words, Senebtisi's burial chamber was prepared so that she could rise from the underworld and see the rising sun, eternally, in her cosmic manifestation of Osiris, the King of the Two Lands, *i.e.*, the King of All (Fig. 39).

Notes

1. Mace and Winlock 1916, 3.
2. Hayes 1953, 306.
3. Hayes 1953, 305.
4. Mace and Winlock 1916.
5. Mace and Winlock 1916, 3.
6. Hayes 1953, 305.
7. Willems 2018, 4.
8. Delvaux and Therasse 2015, 34, 44.
9. Nyord 2014.
10. Willems 2018, 6–7.
11. Grajetzki 2018, 240.
12. Nyord 2014, 42.
13. Nyord 2014, 38.
14. Nyord 2014, 38, 42.
15. Meyer-Dietrich 2006.
16. Nyord 2014, 39.
17. Van Walsem 2014.
18. Hayes 1953, 305.
19. Mace and Winlock 1916, 26.
20. Hayes 1953, 318.
21. Hayes 1953, 318.
22. Hayes 1953, 281.
23. Hayes 1953, 282.
24. Hayes 1953, 283.
25. Hayes 1953, 285.

26 Hayes 1953, 285.
27 Hayes 1953, 286.
28 Hayes 1953, 305.
29 Cooney 2007, 18.
30 Hayes 1953, 305.
31 Andrews 1994, 99.
32 Hayes 1953, 311.
33 Hayes 1953, 311.
34 Hayes 1953, 311.
35 Hayes 1953, 283.
36 Ikram and Dodson 1998, 145.
37 Hayes 1953, 306.
38 Hayes 1953, 309.
39 Hayes 1953, 309.
40 Ikram and Dodson 1998, 157.
41 Ikram and Dodson 1998, 116.
42 Andrews 1994, 43.
43 Hayes 1953, 231–232.
44 Andrews 1994, 77.
45 Hayes 1953, 307.
46 These collars allude to the protection conferred by Isis and Nephthys to the mummy of Osiris.
47 Hayes 1953, 308.
48 Hayes 1953, 307.
49 Hayes 1953, 231–232.
50 Andrews 1994, 45.
51 Hayes 1953, 308.
52 Hayes 1953, 231–232.
53 Hayes 1953, 286.
54 Ikram and Dodson 1998, 116.
55 Hayes 1953, 305.
56 Hayes 1953, 305.
57 Hayes 1953, 324.
58 Hayes 1953, 324.
59 Arnold 2008, Pl. 147.
60 Taylor 1989, 14.
61 Ikram and Dodson 1998, 198.
62 Taylor 1989, 25.
63 Miniaci 2014, 129.
64 Anthropoid coffin of Hapiankhtifi of Mir, 12th Dynasty. Hayes 1953, 312. See also the coffin of Sobekhat in Yoshimura *et al.* 2018.
65 Anthropoid coffin of Sobekhat. Yoshimura *et al.* 2018, 164. See also the sarcophagus of Merenptah in Grajetzki 2018, 236.
66 Yamazaki 2018.
67 Grajetzki 2018.
68 Grajetzki 2018.
69 Miniaci and Quirke 2009, 368; Grajetzki 2018, 235.
70 Mace and Winlock 1916, 114–116.
71 Grajetzki 2018, 240–242.

Chapter 4

Flying back home: The grave of the "Gurnah Queen"

During the Middle Kingdom, Thebes ("Uaset", the "Powerful One" in Egyptian) had already become a large city. Located on the east bank of the Nile, in the area today occupied by the village of Karnak, the settlement was at least 1 km long. Within its walls, Uaset was laid out in a regular plan, as in the case of most of the fortified cities built during the Middle Kingdom. An elite quarter was provided with large villas for the ruling elite, while the remaining city was composed of single room mudbrick houses aligned side-by-side along the narrow streets.[1] If seen from the sky, Uaset may have looked like an immense mudbrick honeycomb gravitating around its magnificent temple, the Apet Sut (the "Reckoner of Places"), built in white limestone and alabaster by the kings of the 12th Dynasty. This was the Temple of Amun, the centre of the world for the Theban cosmogony, delicately designed with rare grace and balance, with its elegant pillared porticoes facing the sunset (Fig. 42).

After the military successes of the 12th Dynasty, the occupation of the Delta territories by the Hyksos (Hekau-khasut, the "Kings of the Desert Mountains") led Egypt to a situation of political divide. During this period, Thebes again became the capital of an autonomous kingdom, with most of Upper Egypt under the influence of its kings, which formed the 17th Dynasty.

At this stage, the small hills of Dra Abu el-Naga, on the west bank of Thebes, were chosen to hold the royal burials. These hills faced the city of the living and the Temple of Amun on the opposite side of the river. The smooth slope of this hill was also the closest to the Nile and in the full sight to the rising sun. This strategic position provided the royal Theban elite with an unrivalled alignment that encompassed the social, political, and cosmic aspects of its rule (Fig. 43).

Not far from this hill, where the modern road turns to the Valley of the Kings, a disconcerting grave was found containing two intact burials of a high elite woman and child dating from the late 17th Dynasty.

4. Flying back home: The grave of the "Gurnah Queen"

Fig. 42. White Chapel of Senuseret I at Karnak.

Fig. 43. The hills of Dra Abu el-Naga in Thebes, aerial view.

Discovery

In 1908, the indefatigable archaeologist Flinders Petrie moved his attention to the Theban site known as El-Khor (Fig. 44), where two important discoveries had already been carried out, namely the coffins of king Kamose and queen Ahhotep, in 1857 and 1859 respectively.[2] On the 29th December, a new grave was uncovered dating from the same period (Fig. 45). A letter from Petrie dated 18 January 1909 to an unnamed correspondent gives an insight into the discovery of the burial:

> We have been about six weeks at Thebes. Our main purpose was to search the northern valleys, where it was reported that there might be tombs. We settled therefore at a small hill north of the road up to the Kings Tombs where some rock-tombs served for our workmen and my wife and myself, while some brick huts were built for dining rooms and bedrooms.

Fig. 44. William Flinders Petrie, 1886.

Fig. 45. The grave of the "Gurnah Queen" as it was found in 1908. Photographic records of Petrie Museum of Egyptian Archaeology.

4. Flying back home: The grave of the "Gurnah Queen"

Though we have cut innumerable trenches about the valleys, and on one spot kept 24 men and boys for over a month, yet only one tomb has been found in the desert valleys. That is a perfect burial of about the XVII dynasty. There was no valuable article in it, but the whole was an unusual and good group.

The grave had been covered over with boulders, which suggests that there was no intention for it to be re-entered, so the woman and child must have been buried in the same event.[3]

The woman was interred in a long anthropoid coffin, with gilded decoration, while the child was buried in a small white rectangular box (Fig. 46). Besides the coffins, the grave contained a wealth of artefacts. Around the main anthropoid coffin, several objects were disposed, all of them everyday life artefacts: a chair, two stools, a box containing linen soaked in unguent, and various ceramic vessels. There were also food offerings consisting of grapes, dates, dom-palm fruits, a pomegranate, and assorted loaves and cakes.

A second basket included a selection of goods that were probably seen as "precious", or "personal" objects, such as a beautiful stone bowl decorated in relief, and a ball of thread which might have been included in the burial to serve as a toy for the child.[4] A wide number of cosmetic objects was found, such as an oil-horn inlaid with ivory and ebony, a razor and hone, two flint flakes, two *kohl*-pots in obsidian and alabaster, a *kohl* stick, a bronze cutter, and a sharpening stone.

Particularly intriguing in this luxurious context is the humble carrying pole laid on the left side of the coffin, containing six pottery Kermaware beakers.[5]

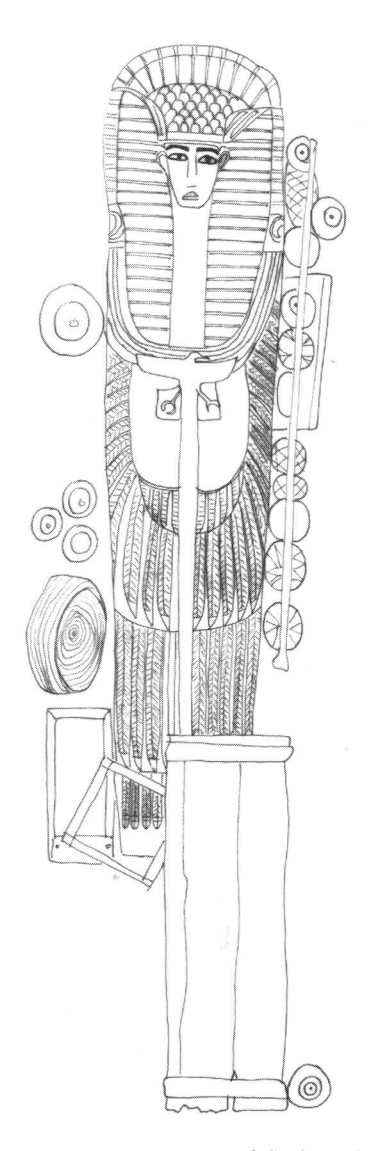

Fig. 46. Composition of the burial.

The coffin and the whole assemblage were offered by Flinders Petrie to the Royal Scottish Museum (now the National Museum of Scotland). The group was registered in the museum in September 1909 and immediately put on display.[6]

Long anthropoid coffin

The anthropoid coffin is a remarkable piece of funerary art belonging to the *rishi* type ("feathered" in Arabic), showing the deceased fully enveloped in feathers (Fig. 47). This

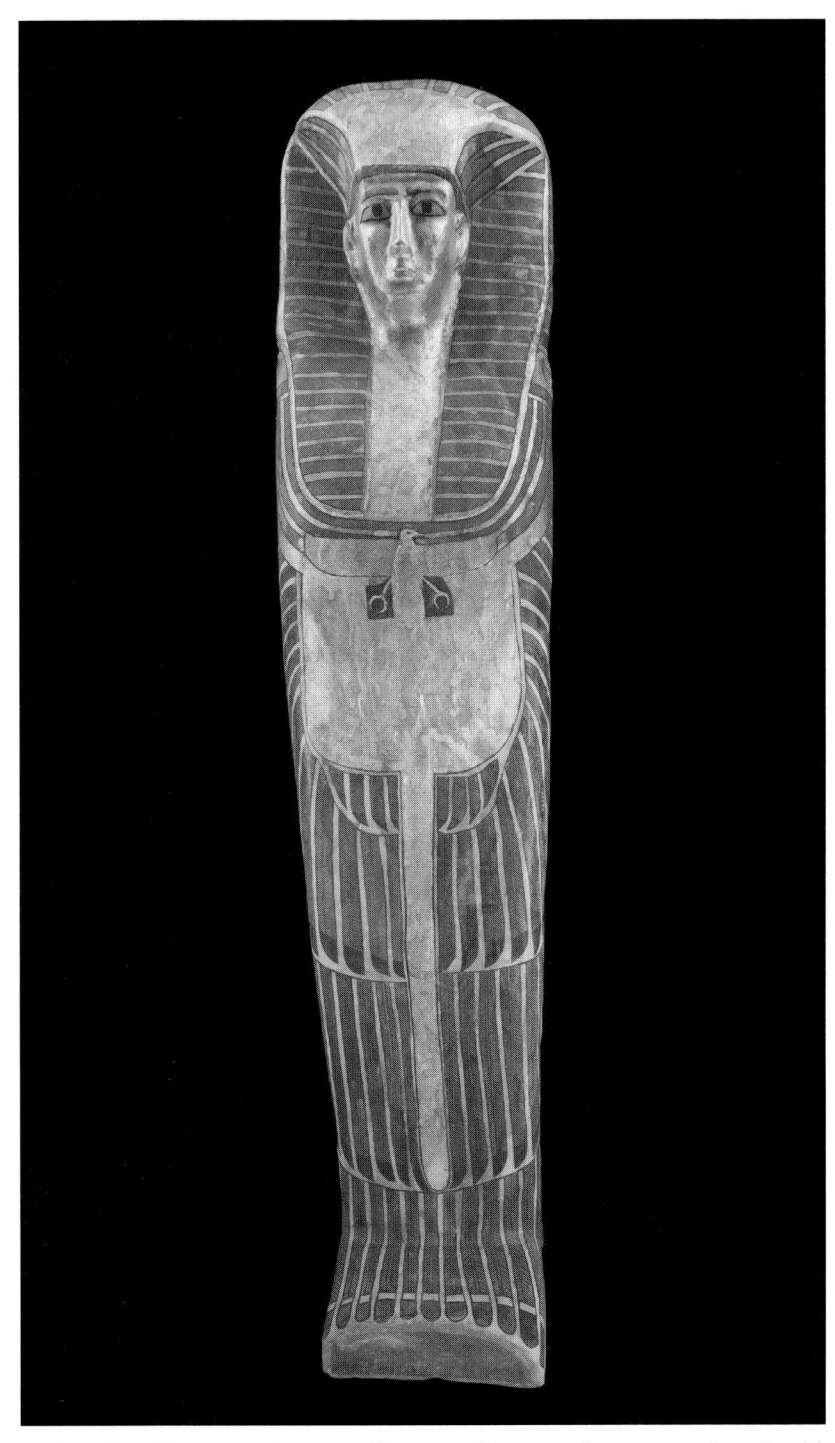

Fig. 47. The rishi coffin of the "Gurnah Queen" (front view). National Museums of Scotland (A.1909.527).

type of coffin appears in the archaeological record during the Second Intermediate Period associated with the Theban ruling elite. Unlike the previous form of anthropoid coffins, they are always used as a single piece without association with an outer rectangular coffin.[7] Following this practice, the anthropoid coffins were no longer laid on their left sides but placed on their bottoms.

The coffin is 2.08 m long. It was roughly hewn out of two different logs: tamarisk for the lid and sycamore for the box, both local Egyptian species of wood.

The whole has been plastered with fine gesso and painted, including gilded details.[8] The feathered patterning was painted in blue with black details on a yellow ground. Despite the splendid gilded decoration, the face is crudely carved showing the angular and wedge-shaped faces typically seen in the *rishi* corpus.[9] The eyes and eyebrows are naively painted and the ears are roughly modelled. The deceased uses the striped *nemes*-headdress worn by kings. The frontal section of the headdress is decorated with short feathers resembling drops.

Partly hidden under the lappets of the headdress, the *usekh*-collar is decorated with falcon-headed terminals.

On the chest is a sacred vulture, outstretching its wings towards both sides of the lid. From the feet of the avian goddess, a longitudinal band of inscriptions runs down the centre of the lid. The inscriptions were pressed or stamped into the plaster, then gilded. The column measures 1.08 m although the text is broken off after 72 cm, and reads:

> An offering which the king gives to Osiris, lord of Djedu, a voice offering of bread and beer, fowl and beef, for the spirit of ...[10]

The name and titles of the deceased should follow but they were lost. Attempts to find fragments of other hieroglyphs in the broken section using high-magnification digital photography was fruitless.[11]

The longitudinal band of inscriptions is flanked by two outstretched wings, displaying long pointed feathers.[12] The tail of the raptor is depicted on the footboard, showing long feathers with rounded tips.

The edge of the footboard is flattened, featuring concentric bands suggesting the shape of a mound. The underside shows two goddesses, perhaps Isis and Nephthys, raising their arms in joy.

The case is decorated as an independent box (Fig. 48). The sycamore-fig wood was gesso-covered and painted blue. This monochromatic decoration contrasts with the lavishly decorated lid. The interiors of both box and lid are undecorated.

Mummy

The coffin contained the mummified body of a slender woman, about 1.50 m tall, and several items, including an acacia headrest inlaid with ivory and ebony, and a basket containing a sceptre-head in the form of a flail.[13]

The mummy was unwrapped by the excavators at the time of discovery.[14] The deceased wore a magnificent collar of gold rings, a pair of gold earrings, two pairs

Fig. 48. The rishi coffin of the "Gurnah Queen" (side view). National Museums of Scotland (A.1909.527).

of gold bracelets, and a girdle of fine electrum rings (apparently worn in life) as well as a green scarab and an electrum button. The analysis of the gold of the woman's jewellery revealed that the collar and bracelets she was buried with are made from 90% pure gold, while her earrings are 95% pure.[15]

The examination of the human remains revealed that the woman was young when she died, probably between 18 and 25 years old. Bone examination suggests that she spent a great deal of time kneeling, which may have resulted from ritualistic activities. Petrie suggested that the woman's skull (Fig. 49) was not typically Egyptian, but recent examination of her skeleton, to determine whether she was ethically Nubian or Egyptian, has been inconclusive.[16] However, analysis of her diet, through the carbon and nitrogen isotopes in her bones, did point to a Nubian link.[17] It is, therefore, likely that she was born in Nubia and moved to Egypt as a child.

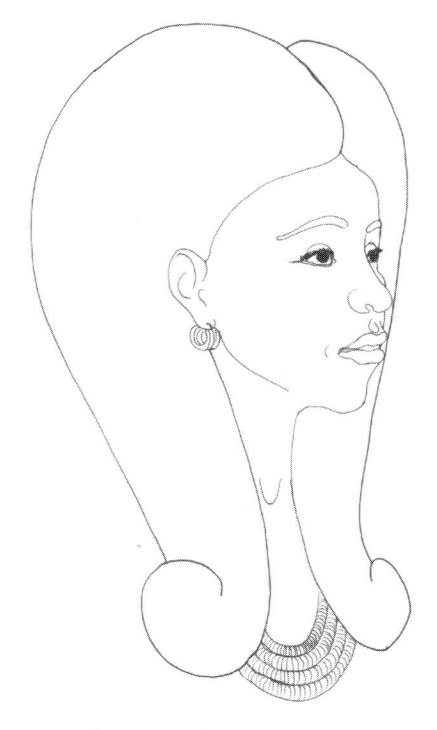

Fig. 49. The "Gurnah Queen". Drawing by the author after the facial reconstruction by Manley at al. 2002.

Short rectangular coffin

At the foot of the anthropoid coffin a white-painted rectangular coffin for a child was laid. The wood is sycamore-fig and cedar, covered in fine gypsum-plaster. One side and one end are composed of individual rectangular planks, while the other side and end are composed of two roughly rectangular planks. The lid and base are formed out of irregularly shaped planks.[18] The object is uninscribed.

Inside was found the mummy of a two to three-year-old child of indeterminate gender. The child wore a necklace of gold rings, a pair of gold earrings, a girdle and pair of anklets made from blue-glazed rings, and three ivory bangles, two on the left arm and one on the right.[19] The presence of this coffin, so closely associated with the female burial, suggests the child was a relative of the woman, most likely her child.

Concluding remarks

Taken as a whole, this exceptional group of objects belies the conventional wisdom about Thebes during the Second Intermediate Period as a relatively isolated provincial centre cut off from the trade and resources needed to acquire or manufacture luxury items of the type that characterise this burial.[20]

complete fusion of both individuals into one being. Osiris by means of identification with Re comes to life again as a new ruler/Re, ready for a new revivifying ritual for his father Osiris.[29]

The union of Osiris and Re thus results in a revolutionary vision of immortality associated with the rebirth of the sun god. The boldness of this insight again suggests its royal provenance. In this view, the manifestation of the deceased takes the form of the *Baw* of Osiris and Re.[30]

The change introduced with the *rishi* coffins suggests the adoption of royal solar beliefs by the Theban elite, a phenomenon that was only possible due to the political collapse of the 13th Dynasty. The way these visions were subsequently integrated into the shaping of *rishi* coffins was not exempt from experimentations and involved, on the part of Theban workshops, an active search to achieve a new design.[31] Comparison with contemporary *rishi* funerary masks provides an important parallel. It is common to find oddly unbalanced funerary masks with a very small head (Fig. 50). This distortion results from the attempt to depict a human-headed raptor and not the deceased himself. Together with the *rishi* coffins, these objects show the first documented attempts to depict the Ba-bird and attest a coherent process of osmosis, with the same image shaping different media.[32]

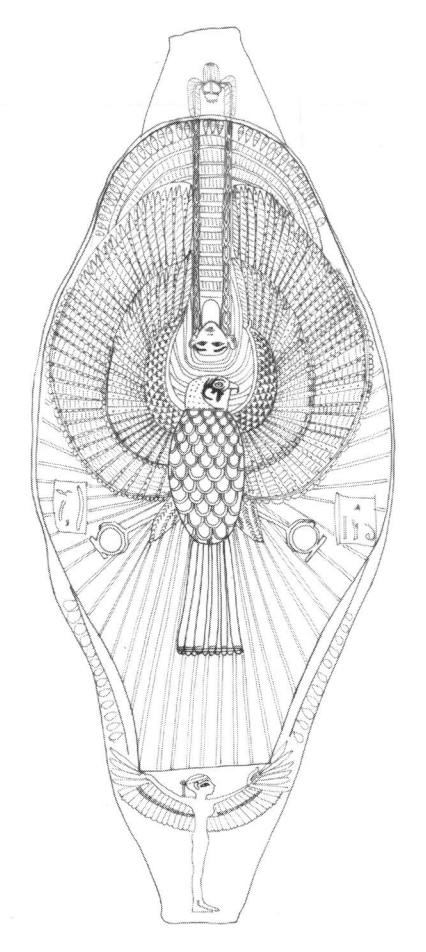

Fig. 50. Rishi mask. World Museum in Liverpool (M11020).

In all, the decoration of the lid is focused on the protection of rebirth,[33] showing the deceased as a newborn Ba-bird, rising from the primordial mound, *i.e.* the Osirian tomb, under the protection of her divine mother, the vulture goddess. Despite the beauty underlying to this imagery, other aspects underlying the *rishi* model may have contributed to an enthusiastic reception of the Nubian elite settled in Thebes. The use of feathers in the funerary equipment found in contemporary Nubian sites has been pointed out, and so the *rishi* coffins may have been seen as "closer" to Nubian funerary beliefs.[34]

In any case, depicted in an avian form, the Nubian princess is shown in her coffin rising from her tomb and flying away to join the journey of the sun. One can only speculate if she would fly back home in this form.

Notes

1. Kemp 1996, 205.
2. Petrie 1909; Manley and Dodson 2010, 23. Miniaci 2018, 259.
3. Manley and Dodson 2010, 26.
4. Manley and Dodson 2010, 23.
5. Veldmeijer and Bourriau 2009.
6. Manley and Dodson 2010, 23.
7. Miniaci 2018.
8. Manley and Dodson 2010, 23.
9. Hayes 1953, 29–30.
10. Manley and Dodson 2010, 24.
11. Manley and Dodson 2010, 23.
12. Ikram and Dodson 1998, 193.
13. Manley and Dodson 2010, 23.
14. Manley and Dodson 2010, 23.
15. Troalen *et al.* 2009.
16. Manley and Dodson 2010, 23.
17. Eremin *et al.* 2000; Manley and Dodson 2010, 26.
18. Manley and Dodson 2010, 26.
19. Manley and Dodson 2010, 26.
20. Manley and Dodson 2010, 23.
21. Manley and Dodson 2010, 23.
22. Manley and Dodson 2010, 23.
23. Miniaci 2018.
24. Manley and Dodson 2010, 26.
25. Miniaci 2018.
26. Miniaci 2018.
27. Miniaci 2018, 251.
28. Roehrig 1988, 131.
29. Miniaci 2010, 55–56.
30. Miniaci 2010, 55–56.
31. Miniaci 2018.
32. Miniaci 2018.
33. Miniaci 2018.
34. Bourriau 1997.

Chapter 5

A house on the edge of the world: The tomb of Kha and Merit (TT 8)

The Theban landscape is towered over by El-Gurn, the "Peak", the desert mountain that was sacred to the great mother goddess Hathor, who embodied regeneration and rebirth (Fig. 51). The significance of this mountain was such that pharaohs from the New Kingdom abandoned the royal practice of building pyramid complexes and chose to excavate their tombs under the shadow of this sacred mountain, in the *wadi* today known as Biban el Muluk (the "Valley of the Kings" in Arabic). In antiquity, the sacred *wadi* was named Set Aat, the "Great Place", an expression often associated with Isis.

Conceived as a mysterious Osirian crypt protected by the great goddess, the tomb holds the mummy of the king so that he could be united with the sun god during his nightly journey through the underworld. These mysterious tombs required a cultic area, associated with the floodplain, where the funerary cult of the king was carried out. Hatshepsut was the first sovereign to excavate a royal tomb in the Valley of the Kings associated with a "Temple of Millions of Years", built on the foothill of the Theban Mountain at Deir el-Bahari, the *Djeser Djeseru* ("The most sublime", in Arabic). Despite separated by the mountain, the tomb and funerary temple formed an inseparable unity with important cosmic and theological associations.

During the reign of Hatshepsut, the Theban landscape underwent extensive changes and it was entirely reshaped. On the east bank, a long processional causeway flanked by sphinxes was built between the Temple of Amun-Re in Karnak and the Temple of Opet in Luxor, allowing the sacred barque of Amun to participate in public festivals celebrating the cosmic renewal of kingship.

On the west bank, the queen designed an equivalent route from her magnificent funerary temple at Deir el-Bahari to Medinet Habu, where the Small Temple of Amun was built. These temples were united by a canal navigated by the sacred barque of Amun on the occasion of the Beautiful Feast of the Valley, the most important funerary festival in Thebes.[1]

5. A house on the edge of the world: The tomb of Kha and Merit (TT 8)

Fig. 51. The Theban Mountain (El-Gurn) and the village of Deir el-Medina with its necropolis. On the right the funerary temple of Hatshepsut in Deir el-Bahari is visible.

During the early part of the 18th Dynasty, the city and the Temple of Amun, in particular, were extensively renovated and enlarged. A number of quarters in Thebes had been demolished to allow the temple to be enlarged. The once entirely walled settlement was now extending itself along the new processional ways. A similar phenomenon occurred in the necropolis, with the private tombs and royal temples aligned along the canal that united Deir el-Bahari and Medinet Habu. These transformations reflected a new vision on the role played by the presence of god in history and society, as well as on the fate of each individual.

Hidden by the small hill of Gurnet Murai, the village of Deir el-Medina ("Monastery of the town" in Arabic) was founded in the early 18th Dynasty to house the artisans of the pharaoh, who worked in the construction of the royal tombs. Its ancient name was Set Maat, "The place of Order". This peculiar community which included sculptors, painters, draughtsman, architects, and scribes fermented with innovative approaches to the traditional repertoire of royal ideology.

Under Thutmose III, the village of Deir el-Medina underwent its first extension in order to accommodate the increasingly larger community of artisans working for the

Fig. 52. The Tomb of Kha in the northern sector of Deir el-Medina's necropolis.

pharaoh. Most of the houses were built side-by-side along a narrow road running the length of the village. This street may have been covered by reeds to filter the intense glare and heat of the sun, thus providing the villagers with maximal protection against the hostile environment of the desert. The houses, with an average floor space of 70 m^2, were made of mudbrick, with four to five rooms comprising an entrance hall, main room, two smaller rooms, kitchen with cellar and staircase leading to the roof.

Unlike most of the Egyptian settlements, Deir el-Medina was not located next to the Nile floodplain. For this reason, its necropolis was built on the neighbouring hills and not on the opposite side of the river as it was usually observed in Upper Egypt. In fact, the village is separated from its own necropolis by just a narrow street. The necropolis of the artisans was extended along the slope of the mountain, beautifully arranged in white terraces and platforms.

One of these chapels belonged to a couple, Kha and Merit, who lived in the mid-18th Dynasty (Fig. 52). We learn from the artefacts found in their tomb that Kha (his name equates him with the rising sun meaning "He who appears" or "He who shines") was an important foreman of Deir el-Medina. He held the post of *Hery Set-Aa* ("head of the Great Place", *i.e.* "foreman of the Valley of the Kings"), *Imy-ra kat em Set-Aa*

5. A house on the edge of the world: The tomb of Kha and Merit (TT 8)

("overseer of the works in the Great Place"), *Imy-ra kat Per-Aa* ("overseer of the works in the Palace") and *Sesh nisut* ("royal scribe").[2] His career spanned the reigns of at least three pharaohs: Amenhotep II (1428–1397 BC),[3] Tuthmosis IV (1397–1388 BC) and Amenhotep III (1388–1351 BC). With his wife Merit (her name means "The beloved one"), he had two sons (Amenemopet and Nakhteftaneb) and a daughter (Merit), with whom he was depicted in his funerary chapel. His burial chamber, found undisturbed and in pristine condition, thus provides a unique glimpse of the Theban society, in a period of exceptional wealth, teeming with new ideas that were gradually reshaping Egyptian religion and society.

Discovery

The funerary chapel of Kha had long been known by archaeologists. Despite being partially ruined, it was still extant with its beautifully preserved paintings. According to the usual structure of Theban tombs, it would have been expected to yield the underground chambers of Kha and Merit in a part of the courtyard in front of the chapel. However, this was not the case in this tomb and any trace of a shaft leading to the burial chamber of Kha was not found.

When the Italian archaeologist Ernesto Schiaparelli began his first season of excavations at Deir el-Medina in 1903, he decided to undertake a systematic work of clearance on the site, focusing on the northern part of the valley up to the cliff (Fig. 53).[4] This painful process is vividly described by Schiaparelli:

> The work was neither easy nor straightforward because the rubble was piled up incredibly high; it took four weeks' strenuous work with over 250 workmen divided into various teams working separately, but the results did not prove encouraging. As the work progressed and the sides of the mountain were gradually revealed, only a few tombs came to light. They were either shaft tombs or chamber tombs, but they had been plundered. The enormous piles of rubble we were removing, consisting of chips of limestone that had turned yellow or black due to weathering, mixed with human bones, fragments of vases, as fluid as water, bore unambiguous witness to extensive and recent violation.
>
> But, after a month of backbreaking and unrewarding work, in the last days of February, after completing the excavation of over two thirds of the valley, we came to an area where the rubble seemed to be intact: chips of beautiful white limestone, unaffected by weathering, which were still compact by not having been disturbed for centuries, without any mixture with bones or fragments of grave goods or furnishings, and which had probably been extracted from the depths of the mountain by workmen who

Fig. 53. Ernesto Schiaparelli.

Fig. 54. The shaft to the Tomb of Kha at the time of its discovery. Schiaparelli excavations, 1906. Museo Egizio Archive.

had dug a tomb. It was clear that if a tomb were found here, it would probably lie intact, and it also seemed likely that a tomb was not far away. Indeed, by continuing the excavations for another two days, the edges of an irregular opening appeared in the side of the mountain [Fig. 54]. It was completely blocked by rubble. Once the debris was removed, the entrance rapidly emerged and provided access to a fairly wide staircase which descended very steeply into the bowels of the mountain. As the white chips filling the whole of the staircase were hastily removed and carried away, a beautiful, large piece of carefully folded reed matting was discovered below the chips and on the steps of the staircase which had been roughly carved in the cliff. Going further down for several metres, there was a corridor sealed by a solid intact wall, built with stones and carefully faced with mud [Fig. 55].

As the evening approached, we thought of stopping; but although it was reasonable to suppose that we had reached the edge of an intact tomb – since, as it had been cut deep into the mountain, it was unlikely that robbers had entered from the other side – I still wanted

5. A house on the edge of the world: The tomb of Kha and Merit (TT 8)

to make sure. A small opening was made in the wall and the old Caliph, the head of the workmen, wriggled through: his immediate exclamation of joy reassured us that our hopes had not been in vain.

That night supervisor Benvenuto Savina watched over the staircase, leaning against the wall which sealed the entrance, and Count Alessandro Casati camped at the top of the staircase.[5]

When the flight of steps was cleared, Ernesto Schiaparelli was able to enter the tomb. At that time, the Inspector of the *Service des Antiquités* was Arthur Weigall, a young British archaeologist who collaborated with Flinders Petrie in the first years of his career. And so, Weigall joined Schiaparelli in this first exploration of the tomb, the account of which is given in his notes:

> The mouth of the tomb was approached down a flight of steep, rough steps, still half-choked with debris. At the bottom of this the entrance of a passage running into the hillside was blocked by a wall of rough stones [Fig. 55]. After photographing and removing this, we found ourselves in a long, low tunnel, blocked by a second wall a few yards ahead. Both these walls were intact, and we realized that we were about to see what probably no living man had ever seen before.[6]

Fig. 55. Cobbled wall, sealing the entrance to the Tomb of Kha. Schiaparelli excavations, 1906. Museo Egizio Archive.

The long corridor, with a total length of 13.40 metres, was divided into two sections, each one sealed by a cobble wall (Fig. 56). In the second section, Shiaparelli and Weigall found a large bed next to the entrance of the burial chamber (Fig. 57), which was barred by a wooden door. Weigall provides us a vivid account of this moment:

> The wood (of the door) retained the light colour of fresh deal, and looked for all the world as though it had been set up but yesterday. A heavy wooden lock held the door fast. A neat bronze handle on the side

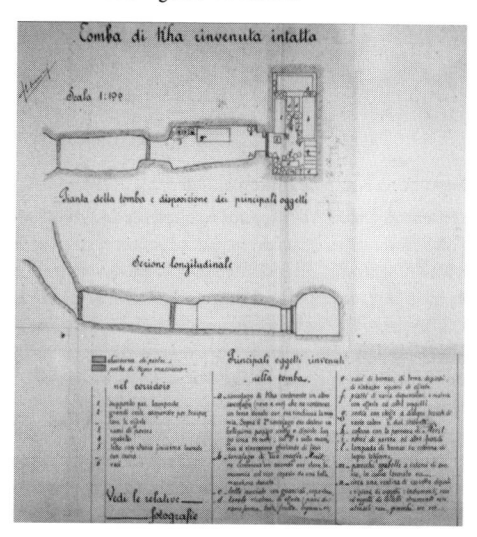

Fig. 56. Plan and section of Kha's tomb drawn by Francisco Ballerini. Museo Egizio Archive. Copyright of the Museo Egizio in Turin.

of the door was connected by a string to a wooden knob set in the masonry door post; and this spring was carefully sealed with a small dab of stamped clay. The whole contrivance seemed so

Fig. 57. The corridor preceding the funerary chamber of Kha at the time of its discovery. Schiaparelli excavations, 1906. Museo Egizio Archive.

modern that Professor Schiaparelli called to his servant for the key, who quite seriously replied, "I don't know where it is, sir."[7]

When the door was open the burial chamber was finally revealed, showing a perfectly undisturbed burial with two black rectangular coffins covered by linen sheets and a diversified array of everyday goods, including beds, stools, jars and boxes (Fig. 58). Everything had been left in perfect order. So much so that it was possible to see the

5. A house on the edge of the world: The tomb of Kha and Merit (TT 8)

Fig. 58. The funerary chamber of Kha at the time of its discovery. Schiaparelli excavations, 1906. Museo Egizio Archive.

traces left on the floor by the last visitor, who swept it before closing the door leaving behind a papyrus-column lamp-stand burning.

Only when the team began to examine the funerary goods, the identity of the owner of the tomb became clear. Schiaparelli describes the funerary equipment he found as follows:

> Along the wall opposite the door there was a large coffin of tarred wood which included an entirely gilded chest in the form of a mummy with the mummy of the wife of the deceased, Merit; the mummy of Kha was in another larger coffin of tarred wood which occupied the adjoining wall: it was sealed within two further coloured and gilded chests, and decorated with beautiful garlands of flowers and on which a papyrus fifteen metres long with beautiful miniatures containing prayers of the cult of the dead – which had been folded several times – had been placed. The marriage bed was situated along the other wall: opposite there was a small statuette of the deceased adorned with garlands and all around tables laden with all kinds of foods, flat breads and fruit, heaps of branches of sycamore and persea trees, boxes, clay and alabaster vases, furnishings, and all kinds of furniture crowded the room so much that they barely left a small passage in the middle.[8]

Fig. 59. The clearance of the tomb with the objects being transported to the Valley of the Queens. Schiaparelli excavations, 1906. Museo Egizio Archive.

5. A house on the edge of the world: The tomb of Kha and Merit (TT 8)

Unlike the usual pattern, the circumstances surrounding the clearance of the find had been extremely fortunate. Any object was removed from the site until the complete record of the find was achieved, giving us the rare opportunity of knowing with accuracy the original position of each object. Moreover, the tomb was documented in photography before any object had been removed, giving us a glimpse of how it looked when it was found by Schiaparelli. On the 18th, February the grave goods were transferred to the Tomb of Prince Amunherkhopeshef (Fig. 59), in the Valley of the Queens (QQ 55), before being shipped to Cairo.

Gaston Maspero, who held the post of Director of the Egyptian antiquities department granted Schiaparelli permission to bring Kha's entire burial assemblage to Italy, except for a lamp, some loaves of bread, three blocks of salt and nineteen clay vases,[9] which were left in the museum in Cairo. Since then, this unique assemblage has been kept in the Museo Egizio in Turin, preventing further dispersal of the objects.[10] Unlike the usual practice, the mummies had not been unwrapped upon their discovery. These exceptional practices in the early years of Egyptian archaeology, turned this find into one of the first sites to have been cleared after modern standards of scientific archaeology.

Funerary chapel

The funerary chapel of Kha (TT 8) was built on the northern terraces of the necropolis (Fig. 60). As usual, the chapel was set up inside a walled courtyard which was normally entered through a miniature version of a pylon. The chapel itself was shaped like a small mudbrick pyramid measuring 4.50 m on the side. Since the pyramid was no longer used in royal tombs, this model became available for private use. The structure was completed by a sandstone *pyramidion* which was found in 1923 in the courtyard of a nearby tomb and is now kept at the Louvre Museum.[11]

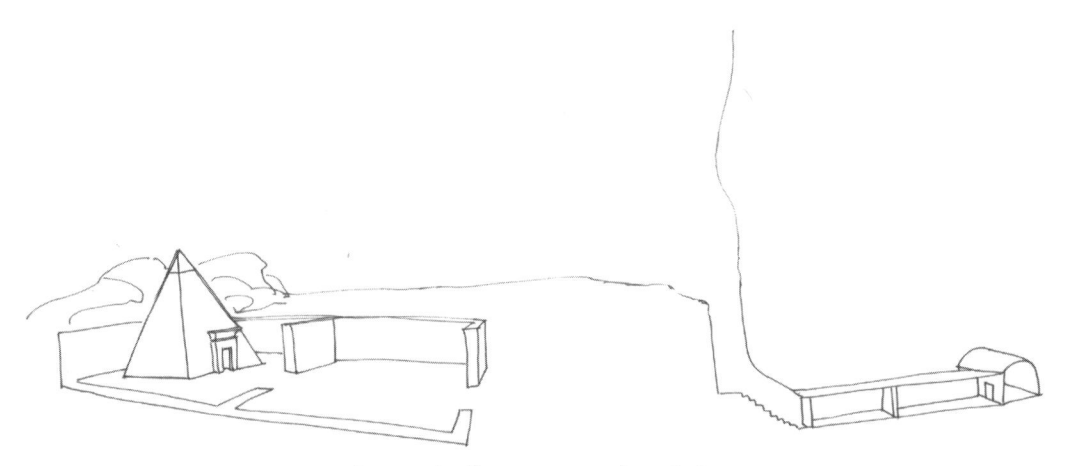

Fig. 60. The funerary complex of Kha.

Fig. 61. Pictorial decoration of the funerary chapel and the funerary stela of Kha kept in the Museo Egizio in Turin (C. 1618). Drawings from Vandier d'Abbadie, Jourdain 1939, Pl. III, IV and VIII.

The entrance of the chapel lies to the north-east. Inside, there is a small vaulted chamber entirely coated in painted plaster. The pictorial decoration is elegantly designed after the graceful style dating from the reign of Amenhotep III, with balanced composition and wealth of detail (Fig. 61).

On the right wall, an adoration scene is depicted with Kha and Merit presenting offerings to Osiris, who figures enthroned inside a canopy. The couple are escorted by their daughter and offering bearers.[12]

The left wall shows a banquet scene celebrated for Kha and Merit, who are seated in front of a table generously provided with food and flowers, mirroring the enthroned effigy of Osiris depicted on the opposite wall. The couple receive offerings from their son, while their daughter, Merit, approaches the couple affectionately to fasten her father's cloak. Behind the couple's offspring, musicians play and dance while servants take care of the guests who attend the banquet.

The rear wall of the chapel displayed the funerary stela of Kha. Now in the Museo Egizio, the stela was purchased by Bernardino Drovetti and reached Turin as early as 1824.[13] The stela shows the enthroned gods Osiris and Anubis worshipped by Kha (upper register) and the couple receiving offerings from their firstborn son. This stela was the central piece of the wall, which was painted with scenes showing Kha in adoration (second register) and the couple receiving offerings by the funerary priest.

Burial chamber

As we have seen, the shaft leading to Kha's burial chamber was located nearly 20 metres away from the chapel, at the foothill of the mountain. As was usual, the funerary chamber was undecorated. It measured 5.60 × 3.40 metres showing a slightly vaulted ceiling, 2.9 m high.

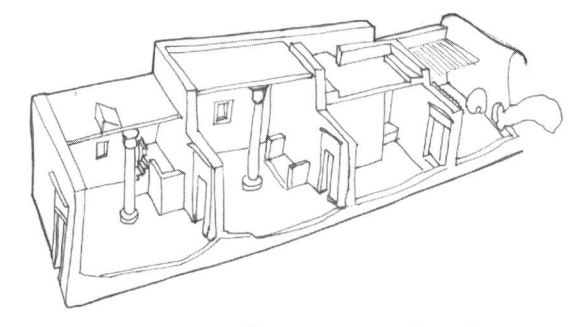

Fig. 62. A typical house in Deir el-Medina.

5. A house on the edge of the world: The tomb of Kha and Merit (TT 8)

In this small area, a vast collection of goods was stored in an orderly manner, revealing a unique glimpse of a private a house from Deir el-Medina (Fig. 62).

The funerary feast

Most of the objects included in the tomb had actually been used by Kha and Merit in their own house. An important part of these goods included food provisions. Tables made of wood or cane, such as those still used today by the villagers of the west bank, were laid up with all types of food, creating a full-scale banquet. In the tomb many kinds of bread were found (Fig. 63), as well as vegetables such as onions, lettuce, pumpkin, olives, and legumes including broad beans, chick peas, and lentils. Fruit was also found, such as grapes, tamarinds, figs, pomegranates, and dates. Naturally, Kha's feast included meat and fish, which were dried or salted.[14]

The table furnishings included elegant amphorae decorated with painted petals and flowers on the neck. The vases are rounded, with one or two handles and a long neck (Figs 64–66). They contained wine, a highly-prized drink used almost exclusively in wealthy households.

Fig. 64. Sealed jar (S. 8516).

Fig. 63. Cup with loaves (S. 8234).

Fig. 65. Wine jar with festive decoration and stand (S. 8224).

Fig. 66. Festive jars (S. 8619, 8620, 8621, 8622).

All these goods had been included in the Tomb of Kha as part of the funerary cult of the Ka which in this way could be sustained in the afterlife. The wooden statuette of the Ka stood on the deceased's chair of honour (Fig. 67), exactly as Kha himself had been seated on his own chair at the reception hall of his house in Deir el-Medina. In his statue, Kha is beautifully depicted as a young man, adorned with a garland on the shoulders and another one at his feet (Fig. 68). The inscription written on the base of the statue states:

> Offering which the king gives to Amun-Re, king of the gods, and to Osiris, the great god, ruler of eternity, so that they may give invocations-offerings in bread and beer, ox and fowl, alabaster and linen, incense and unguent, and all things good and neat, libations, wine and milk for the Ka of Kha, the justified, the good god.

The chair itself is also inscribed with offering-formulae designed to provide the Ka of the deceased with "all things good and neat". It was placed before the tables laden with food offerings exactly as in the banquet scene depicted on the chapel, which in turn would not differ much from the festive family gatherings that were held at Kha's house.

On festive occasions, the owner and his wife would have sat on similar chairs, flanked by their relatives and friends seated on foldable stools set up for the occasion, such as those that had been found in the tomb. Small tables laden with all kinds of foods stood before each guest. A larger larder was prepared in the room with the goods that would be served during the feast, exactly as it is depicted on the walls of

5. A house on the edge of the world: The tomb of Kha and Merit (TT 8)

Fig. 67. Funerary chair of Kha (S. 8333).

Fig. 68. The Ka statuette of Kha (S. 8335).

Fig. 69. Stand with a lustration bowl (S. 8222.2).

the chapel (Fig. 61). This larder included wine-jars and small tables provided with fruit, bread, vegetables, and meat.

These feasts would have been held at the reception room, the house's larger compartment. Small windows placed high up on the walls of this compartment provided filtered light and assured a cool atmosphere. A stand with a bowl containing water would be positioned at the entry hall for welcoming ablutions (Fig. 69). At night papyrus-column lamp-stands, such as those found in the tomb, illuminated the room (Fig. 70).

Fig. 70. Papyrus shaped lamp (S. 8628).

5. A house on the edge of the world: The tomb of Kha and Merit (TT 8)

The Tomb of Kha included goods which would be typically found in the storerooms of his house, such as baskets with spices including cumin, juniper, tarragon, and coriander (Fig. 71).[15] Onions and bunches of garlic and blocks of salt were also found, exactly as if they were stored at his home. In Deir el-Medina, the houses were provided with an open courtyard located at the back. The kitchen would be found here, as well as the underground storerooms hewn out of the rock.

Fig. 71. Basket (S. 8417).

Personal objects

Kha's bed was left on the corridor preceding the actual funerary chamber (Fig. 72). The bed is nicely crafted in sycamore wood with the base made of intertwined plant fibres reinforced by two slightly arched longitudinal planks. The bed is supported by four feet in the form of lion's paws.

Merit's bed was smaller than Kha's but it was carefully arranged in the room, opposite to her own coffin set (Fig. 73). The bed is beautifully painted in white with the base made of intertwined plant fibres. It rests on four feet in the form of lion's paws. It was covered with bed linen, including a fringed bedspread, and a padded headrest. Next to Merit's bed was found a wealth of women's toiletry objects, which had been used by Merit in her bedroom.

A large wooden container was designed to store Merit's long wig, which was made of locks of real hair, sewn and plaited to form the fashionable hairstyle of the period.[16]

Fig. 72. The bed of Kha (S. 8327) and stool (S. 8614).

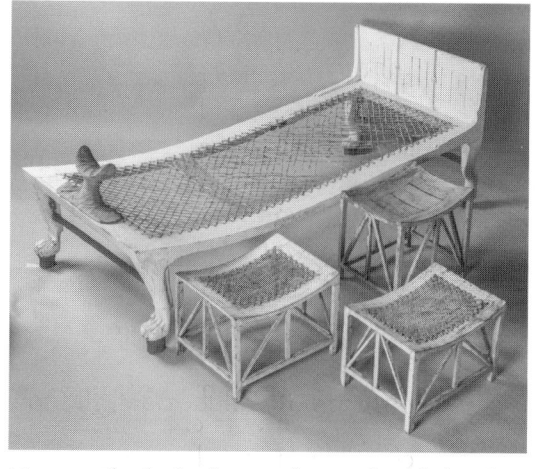

Fig. 73. The bed of Merit (S. 8629) with headrest (S. 8631) and stools (S. 8510, 8512).

Fig. 74. Cosmetic box of Merit (S. 8479) and broidered rug (S. 8528).

Merit's cosmetic box is a beautiful casket with a double flat lid, subdivided into inner sections (Fig. 74). It contained a charming collection of small vases made of alabaster or coloured glass. The vessels held traces of ointments and creams made from fat and a small *kohl* tube glass decorated with white and yellow festoons combined with a thin applicator. *Kohl* is a black paste made of charcoal and antimony and applied to the eyelids and eyelashes as a filter for the sun's rays and as a disinfectant.[17]

Fig. 75. Alabaster ointment vessels (S. 8322, S. 8445).

Kha also seems to have had his own collection of unguents. Thirteen alabaster vases, some sealed, contained various types of plant-based oils and scented concoctions that had been used to anoint the body (Fig. 75).[18] Some of them such as the "seven

5. A house on the edge of the world: The tomb of Kha and Merit (TT 8)

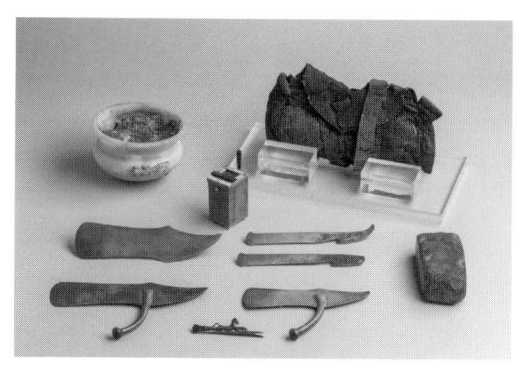

Fig. 76. Scissor, blades and grind stone.

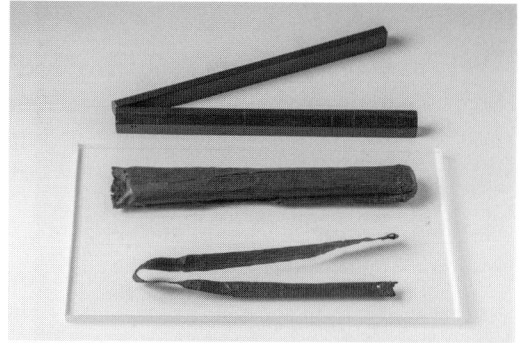

Fig. 77. Folding cubit (S. 8391).

sacred oils" had funerary connotations as they were used in embalming rituals, while others were used in everyday life. The objects used in Kha's toilette included knives, razors, and scissors (Fig. 76).

Amongst the personal belongings of Kha, work tools were included such as the folded cubit (Fig. 77), the scribe's palette (Fig. 78) and the boxes holding a variety of utensils including wooden smoothers for papyrus or perhaps pestles to grind pigments (Fig. 79). A manuscript purchased by Schiaparelli on the antiquities market was probably found and stolen by workmen during his mission's excavations. It contains the offering ritual for the deified pharaoh Amenhotep I. The text consists a series of formulae, aiming at keeping the god fed through the presentation of food and drink, which constituted an integral part of the daily cult performed in Egyptian temples every day.[19] It is likely that Kha used this book in his ritual duties performed in the Temple of Amenhotep I in Deir el-Medina. It is thus possible that Kha included a small collection of books in the "scriptorium" of his house.

Fig. 78. Writing tools (S. 8387).

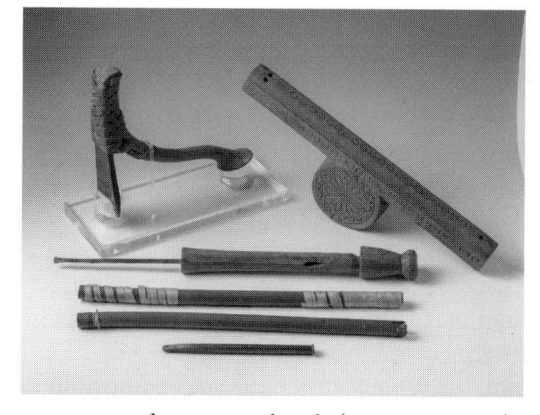

Fig. 79. Implements and tools (S. 8386, 8395–96).

Fig. 83. Gifts offered to Kha: scribe's tablet (S. 8388), senet game board previously belonging to Banermeret (S. 8451.1), cup with the cartouches of Amenhotep III (S. 8355), situla with the name of Userhat (S. 8231), royal cubit given to Kha by the Pharaoh Amenhotep II (S. 8647).

Two of the staves were inscribed, respectively with the names of Khaemwaset and Neferhebef, both "overseers of works", akin to Kha; they were clearly gifts from his colleagues, staves being a sign of authority, they must have been offered to Kha as a sign of respect and esteem.[25]

The same Neferhebef may have had a closer relationship with Kha, since both he and his wife Taiunis were included in the decorative programme of the funerary chapel of Kha, appearing on the banquet scene as guests. They offered a *senet* game board to Kha, one that had belonged to a son of Neferhebef's named Banermeret.[26]

Funerary objects

In the Tomb of Kha, objects from everyday life outnumber funerary objects. Curiously, on the same chair where the statuette of the Ka was standing, a pair of *shabtis* was found. One of them, carved in stone, was leaning against the back of the chair (Fig. 84), the other one was found inside a model black coffin, identical to the rectangular outer coffins of Kha and Merit (Fig. 85). The miniature coffin contained

5. A house on the edge of the world: The tomb of Kha and Merit (TT 8)

a wooden *shabti* and models of agricultural tools (a hoe and a carrying pole). These objects were of a different character than Kha's wooden statue. They referenced the imagery of the Book of the Dead and in fact were both inscribed with Chapter 6, alluding to the ability of these miniatures to work in the Field of Iaru instead of the deceased. They are thus allusions to the mythical landscape of the afterlife, where the deceased and his wife were supposed to be regenerated and fed by the mother goddess. Positioned together with the statuette of the Ka, one senses a subtle reinterpretation of the cult of the Ka at the light of the Osirian paradise that was offered to the justified ones.

Fig. 84. Shabti of Kha (S. 8337).

The coffin set of Kha

Kha was buried within a nested assemblage of two anthropoid coffins and an outer rectangular coffin (Fig. 86). The assemblage was found against the rear wall of the burial chamber, covered by a large linen shroud. The outer coffin was carved in sycamore wood and coated with pistacia resin.[27] Unlike the miniature model coffin (Fig. 85), which

Fig. 85. Models of tools and model coffin with shabti of Kha (S. 8338-8339).

Fig. 86. Coffin set of Kha: outer rectangular coffin (S. 8210), middle coffin (S. 8316) and inner coffin (S. 8429).

Fig. 87. Coffin set of Kha.

5. A house on the edge of the world: The tomb of Kha and Merit (TT 8)

Fig. 88. Book of the Dead of Kha (S. 8316/3=8438): Adoration of Osiris by Kha and Merit.

was inscribed with texts alluding to the four Sons of Horus and images of Isis and Nephthys, the outer coffin was undecorated. The arched lid evokes the Per-Nu shrine, a symbolic allusion to the mythical tomb of Osiris. The box rests on a sledge, alluding to the day of the funeral, when the bier was transported to the tomb.

The middle coffin of Kha is anthropoid, designed after the layout of the "black" type, in use during Kha's lifetime (Fig. 87). It was adorned with floral garlands, which were used during the mummification process to assure regeneration and rebirth. Folded over the coffin the magnificent fourteen metres long papyrus containing the Book of the Dead was found (Fig. 88–89).[28]

The craftsmanship of the middle coffin of Kha is superb. It is coated with gleaming dark pitch (pistacia resin), with the exception of the hieroglyphic bands and iconographic motifs, which are modelled in plaster overlaid with gold leaf.

Fig. 89. Book of the Dead of Kha (S. 8316/3=8438): The deceased in the form of Ba-bird.

The lid and the box are naturalistically moulded after the contour of the body. The fists are gilded and are shown crossed over the chest. The face is beautifully carved and gilded; the eyes are inlaid with alabaster and the eye lines are inlaid with blue glass. The deceased wears a striped wig with the lappets decorated with gilded terminals. The striated pattern continues onto the case. On the crown of his head the goddess Nephthys is depicted (Fig. 90), while Isis is shown on the reverse side of the footboard. As Osiris, the deceased is kept between the protective embrace of these goddesses.

The Broad Collar is decorated with falcon-headed terminals. On the abdomen, a vulture was depicted alluding to the mother goddess Nut summoned in the longitudinal band of text, where the sky goddess is addressed to place the deceased among the Imperishable Stars. Both the winged deity and the longitudinal inscription allude to the protective role of the lid as the embodiment of the heavenly goddess.

Four transverse bands of inscriptions spring from either side of the longitudinal band, running down the sides. The texts and images depicted on the sides refer to the positions

Fig. 90. Middle coffin of Kha (S. 8316): detail of the headboard.

Fig. 91. The scene of Duamutef on the inner coffin of Kha (left) and on the inner coffin of Merit (right).

5. A house on the edge of the world: The tomb of Kha and Merit (TT 8)

Fig. 92. Middle coffin of Kha (S. 8316): detail of the case.

of gods escorting the deceased. Thoth is featured twice on each side, opening the doors of heaven (at the shoulders and feet). These figures allude to Chapter 161 of the Book of the Dead, which refers to the triumph of the sun god Re over his enemy Apophis and to the opening of the sky by Thoth enabling the sun god to ascend to the heavens.[29]

On the left side Hapi, Anubis, and Qebehsenuef are depicted, on the right Imseti, Anubis and Duamutef are shown (Fig. 91). These scenes are drawn from the vignette of Chapter 151 of the Book of the Dead, showing these divinities grouped around the mummy to protect the deceased from Seth and assure his resurrection.

Finally, a pair of *wedjat*–eyes are depicted on the left side, at the level of the shoulders (Fig. 92). They are a faint reminder of the eye-panel that was once used to decorate the left side of rectangular coffins.[30]

The inner coffin of Kha was also adorned with floral garlands. The layout of the object follows exactly the same scheme detected on the middle coffin. However, there is one major difference to be recorded: the inner coffin is covered by thin gold leaf applied onto an extremely fine layer of plaster in which the figures and inscriptions had been previously modelled in relief (Fig. 87).[31] A coffin of this character observes the layout of the "black" type but makes extensive use of gilded foil instead of dark pitch.

From the symbolic point of view, the three nested coffins establish a progression from complete darkness in the outer coffin, to full "illumination" in the innermost coffin, the object which holds the mummy within. In between, lies the middle coffin were divine beings and sacred texts are already shown "solarised" against the overall black background.

The nested assemblage of coffins thus recreated the magical burial chamber of Osiris, the so-called "Chamber of Gold". In the secrecy of this realm, Osiris (the "Black one") unites with Re (whose light, like gold, shines eternally). From this union results the illumination of the corpse of Osiris, who irradiates with sunlight in the deep darkness of the netherworld. This solar interpretation of immortality imprinted a magical dynamism into the burial assemblage, with the different coffins showing distinct stages towards full illumination *i.e.* Osirian resurrection and solar rebirth.

The coffin set of Merit

The coffin assemblage of Merit comprised two nested coffins (Fig. 93). The outer rectangular coffin was found covered by a linen shroud. Pitch coat was unevenly applied over the walls. The lid is arched, as with the coffin of Kha, but the box does not rest on a sledge.[32]

The inner coffin is anthropoid and presents an interesting layout, with its two halves showing different decoration. The box is designed after the layout of the pure "black" type, with the sides covered with pistacia resin and the figures and inscriptions overlaid with gold foil, such as the middle coffin of Kha. However, the lid is entirely gilded, as with the inner coffin of Kha (Fig. 94). The two halves thus provide Merit with a "two in one" type of coffin, combining the layout of the middle and inner coffins of her husband.

The "economy" perceived in this shortened assemblage is matched in the quality of the craftsmanship, which is inferior: despite the use of gold, the texts are not moulded in plaster but incised on the wood, sometimes sketchily, and the deities are roughly depicted (Fig. 91). The rendering of the facial features is crude despite the use of inlaid eyes. The cheeks are large, suggesting a virile face. Moreover, the texts are not in the name of Merit but in that of her husband. These features, as well as the excessive size of the coffin, convinced Shiaparelli that it had originally been made for Kha but subsequently used for the burial of Merit, possibly to cope with an expected event such as the woman's premature death.[33] This interpretation is consistent with Merit's shortened coffin assemblage,

5. A house on the edge of the world: The tomb of Kha and Merit (TT 8)

Fig. 93. Coffin set of Merit: outer rectangular coffin (S. 8517) and anthropoid coffin (S. 8470).

Fig. 94. Coffin set of Merit.

where each half of the anthropoid coffin is used as *pars pro toto*, representing an entire coffin.

The mummy of Merit was equipped with a splendid cartonnage mask (layer of linen soaked in plaster), whose symbolic purpose was to protect the deceased (*i.e.* Osiris) from his enemies and to grant him his divine powers (Fig. 95). As in the case of the anthropoid coffins, the funerary mask depicts the deceased as a resurrected god. In terms of craftsmanship, the quality of the work is superb. The face is beautifully moulded, displaying a delicate nose and finely carved lips. The eyes and eyebrows are beautifully inlaid with glass paste and stone. The striped wig is gilded, inlaid with glass paste, while the Broad Collar is inlaid with turquoise and other semi-precious stones. Perhaps more significantly, the mask includes the vulture goddess on the chest, the same

Fig. 95. Mummy mask of Merit (S. 8473).

one depicted on the anthropoid lids. This motif is not a usual feature in the funerary masks from this period, showing that a magical association was already being established between the decoration of the funerary mask and the lid, a phenomenon which will eventually lead to the creation of the mummy-cover in the late Ramesside Period.

The mummies

Contrary to the usual procedures used at this time, Schiaparelli did not unwrap the mummies of Kha and Merit and for this reason they remained perfectly preserved (Fig. 96). Over time, the development of imaging techniques, such as X-rays and CT scans, have progressively made clear the anatomy of both corpses and the magnificent jewellery concealed under the linen bandages.[34]

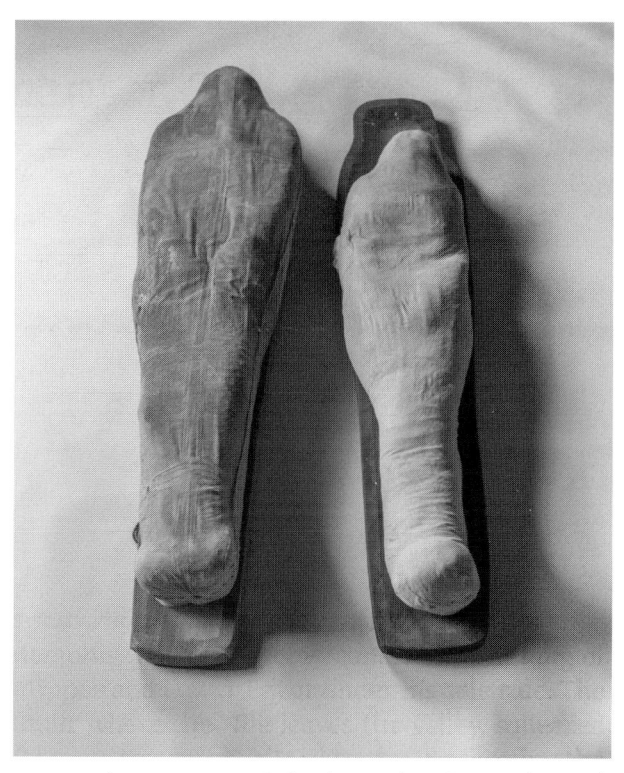

Fig. 96. The mummies of Kha (S. 8316) and Merit (S. 8471).

Kha lay in a supine position with his arms beside his body and his hands covering his genitals, the legs, parallel and the feet together. The body was wrapped in various layers of linen. An outer shroud was fastened by two superimposed bandages which run from the head to the toes while four more bandages were placed on them transversally to keep the body in the correct ritual position. Three-dimensional reconstruction has made it possible to view the gold jewellery on Kha's body.

Kha wears a necklace called a *shebyu*-collar, made of numerous disks through which a piece of twine was threaded (Fig. 97). Such collars were given by the

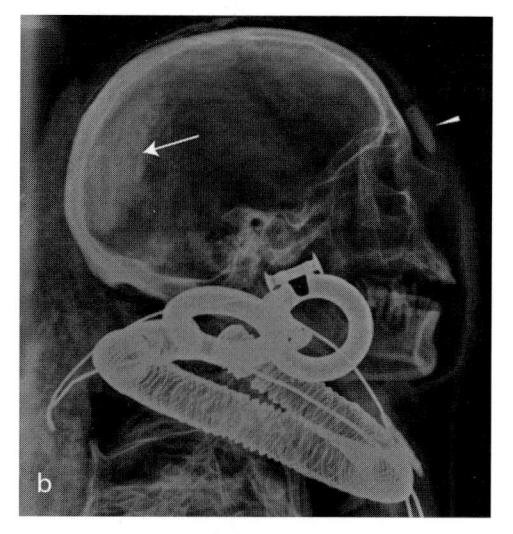

Fig. 97. X-Rays of the mummy of Kha: The head is adorned with a shebiu-necklace, large earrings and a snake-head amulet.

pharaoh as the "gold of honour". He wears other personal adornments such as five rings, two bracelets, and large earrings. A few amulets had been included, such as a *tjet*-amulet made of stone or faience on his chest, and a cornelian amulet portraying the head of a serpent on his forehead to protect him from snake bites or scorpion stings in the afterlife. The largest amulet found in the mummy was a heart scarab attached to a gold chain (Fig. 98).

Despite the sumptuous jewellery that adorns and protects the body, Kha seems to have undergone a process of mummification in which the internal organs were not removed. The analysis of the body revealed that Kha was about sixty years old when he died and must have suffered from arthritis. His height was estimated at 171 cm.

Merit's mummy lies in a supine position with her arms along her sides and her hands covering her genitals (Fig. 99). She wears gold rings on her left hand. Other pieces of jewellery are arranged on the body: a belt and earrings. Strangely, two gold rings were found near her head; they must have adorned her right hand but for some reason they were placed in an unusual position by the embalmers. Merit wears a magnificent Broad Collar made of seven rows of over 400 beads of various shape (Fig. 100).[35] The woman died young, showing several lesions that may have resulted by the careless handling of the mummy. The fact that it remained stored for a long time before the definitive burial took place might have caused the damage detected in the bones.

The mummy was placed in a coffin that was too large for her and for this reason folded linen fabric had been placed on the bottom to fill the gap between the body and the sides of the coffin, while eight long rolls of bandages surrounded the head and feet.

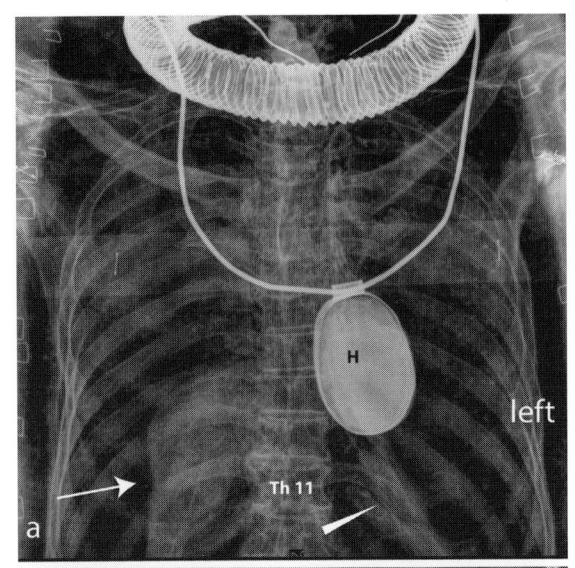

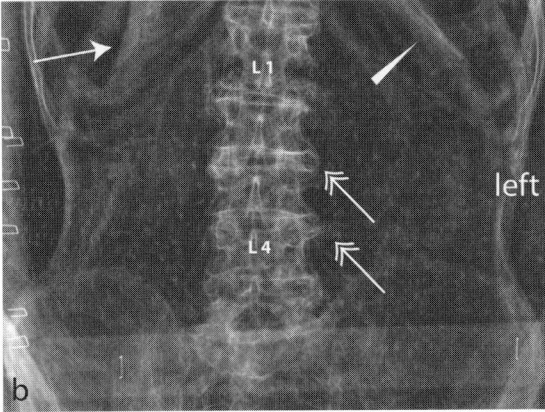

Fig. 98. X-Rays of the mummy of Kha: The thorax is protected by a finely carved heart scarab suspended on a wire.

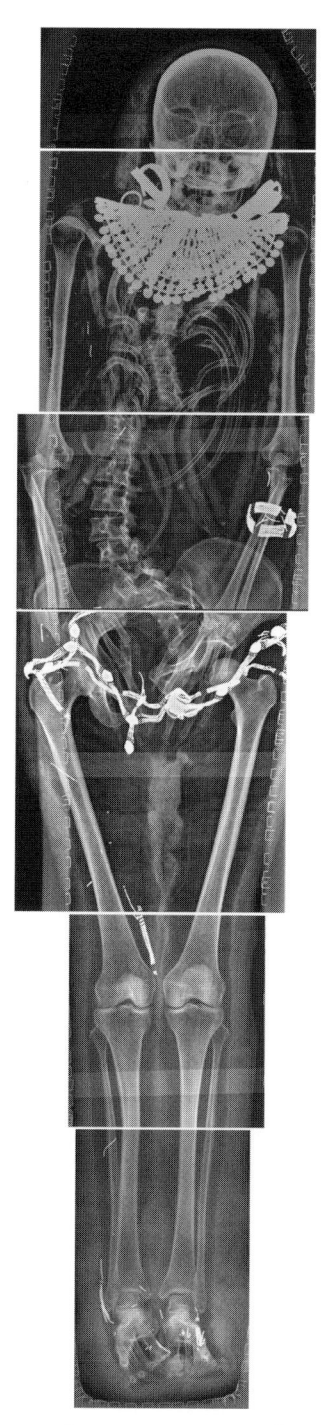

5. A house on the edge of the world: The tomb of Kha and Merit (TT 8)

Fig. 99. X-Rays of the mummy of Merit: The mummy wears a bracelet and a girdle around her waist. The bones present severe damage resulting from careless handling in antiquity.

The Book of the Dead

Perhaps one of the best artefacts found in the tomb is the papyrus providing one of the earliest intact assemblages of the Book of the Dead (Fig. 88–89). It consists of 38 sheets of papyrus joined together for a total length of 14 m.

Kha's Book of the Dead lists 33 chapters, proceeding from left to right. Many of these texts are illustrated by colourful vignettes. The introductory scene shows Kha and Merit adoring the enthroned god Osiris (Fig. 88). This beautiful vignette, the largest of the book, is similar to the scene depicted on his funerary chapel (right wall) and sums up the supreme goal of Egyptian funerary beliefs, the admission before Osiris, the king of the underworld, which supposes deification and immortality. Dressed up for the occasion, wearing the same type of festive garments collected in his tomb, Kha is escorted by Merit. The couple are depicted in the beautiful pictorial style of Amenhotep III's reign. Kha is shown with the gilded heart amulet, an object that seems to have been used as a royal decoration from the reign of Thutmose III to the reign of Amenhotep III.[36] Curiously, such an object was not discovered amidst Kha's belongings, nor in his mummy. This is one of the earliest occurrences of the heart amulet in an Osirian scene, a trend that will become increasingly important after the Amarna Period.

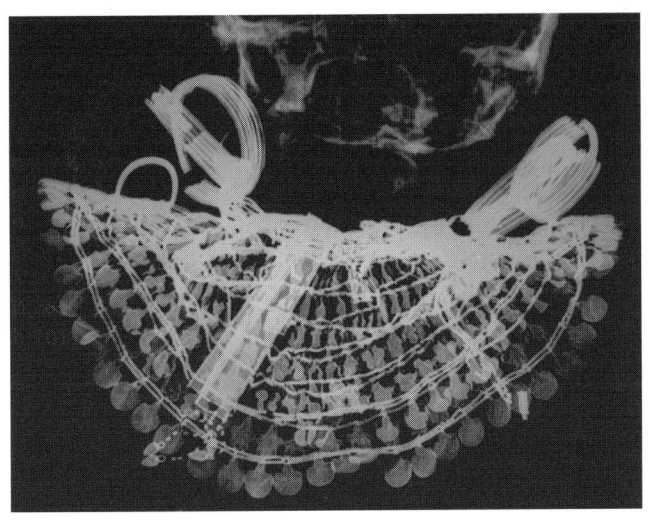

Fig. 100. X-Rays of the mummy of Merit: The mummy is adorned with large earrings and a large collar.

The papyrus includes vignettes featuring the procession that leads the deceased to his tomb and the "Opening of the mouth" ceremony (Chapter 1, 13) and many others designed to protect the deceased against dangerous animals – such as crocodiles (Chapter 31) and snakes (Chapter 33) – or to allow the use of magic amulets, such as the *tjet*-knot of Isis (Chapter 156) and the Djed-pillar (Chapter 155). However, the most important subject dealt with in this book is the ability of the deceased to move freely between the underworld and the earthly realm or, to use the original Egyptian expression, to "go forth by day" (*peret em heru*). It is in this context where we find the only depiction of the deceased as a Ba-bird (Chapter 77 – Fig. 89).[37]

The manuscript was folded over the middle coffin of Kha and this location is telling about its use as an extension of the anthropoid coffins, as if it opened to the resurrected deceased the itinerary to "go forth" to the daylight and join the cycles of the sun.

5. A house on the edge of the world: The tomb of Kha and Merit (TT 8)   87

Ritual objects

Some objects seem to have had a specific funerary meaning. This is the case of a selection of bread and loaves with an irregular shape, which in fact resemble the spots of the solar calf rising from the turquoise trees of the east in Chapter 124–125 (Fig. 101).[38] This young bull, who carries the star Sirius, alludes to the dawn at the summer solstice and these breads probably allude to a "communion" ritual.

Another item bearing an unsuspected significance is the stool carved in the form of the head of a goose, an animal (Figs 102, 103). A similar composition was found in a stove from the Tomb of Tutankhamun (KV 62), as well as one of his thrones,[39] both suggesting an association with the imagery of solar radiance, as if identifying the seated individual with the reborn solar child carried over by Geb, in his avian form.

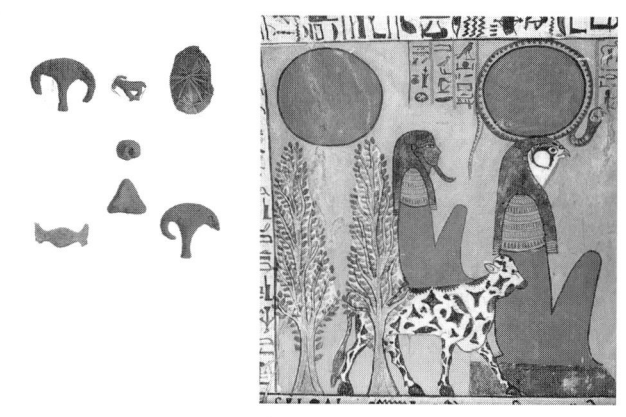

Fig. 101. Ritual loaves (S. 8259) and solar calf rising from the eastern horizon (Tomb of Sennedjem).

Fig. 102. Folding stool with goose shaped feet (S. 8509).

Fig. 103. Goose shaped feet of a folding stool. Broidered and painted patterns at the background.

Concluding remarks

The vivid decoration of Kha's chapel is consistent with the festive atmosphere of the compositions, illustrating the funerary banquet (left wall). The fundamental difference between this chapel and the mastabas of the Old Kingdom is noteworthy. Despite the joyful atmosphere and serene beauty, the chapel is much more than a "House of eternity" for the deceased's Ka. The divine realm is now visible and, in fact, the deceased is depicted in interaction with the king of the netherworld, Osiris. The tomb is now conceived as a sacred place, and for this reason, it is shaped like a temple, provided with its own pylon, courtyard and inner sanctuary, where Osiris is depicted.

When we see the objects collected in the burial chamber of Kha and Merit, it is clear that this is not just a random selection of artefacts. As a foreman of such a privileged settlement as Deir el-Medina, Kha had served in the construction of the royal tombs of Amenhotep II, Thutmose IV, and Amenhotep III. The importance of his merits is clearly displayed in the collar with which he was buried, the "gold of honour", which was given by the pharaoh to his most loyal officials. The royal gifts found in his tomb provide further evidence of Kha's high position.

Given his status, Kha certainly acquired some of his funerary goods in the royal workshops themselves. This is clearly the case with his Book of the Dead, which displays close similarities, both in style and in the sequence of spells, with the papyrus found in the Tomb of Yuya and Tuya (KV 46), the parents of Queen Tiye, wife of Amenhotep III.[40] In the largest vignette, both Yuya and Kha wear a golden heart amulet, before Osiris. This is a striking detail, since golden heart amulets were used after the reign of Thutmosis as a royal decoration,[41] and it is here for the first time associated with an Osirian context. This subject thus seems to have been highly praised in the workshop where both papyri had been produced.

The fine quality of Kha's anthropoid coffins also suggests a royal workshop. However, the inferior levels of execution of the inner coffin of Merit, betray a different workshop, perhaps an informal atelier. This difference is perhaps explained due to the fact that Merit's coffin was commissioned early in Kha's career, when he could not yet afford the most exquisite coffins. Later in his life, he eventually succeeded in obtaining more luxurious objects for himself.

Other clues suggest that preparing his tomb was a lasting enterprise that must have required his attention during most of his lifetime. The tomb itself is revealing of the efforts he spent in this endeavour. The pictorial work carried out in his funerary chapel recalls the graceful style from the reign of Amenhotep III, which is a late work, considering the span of Kha's life and career. It is thus likely that his burial chamber had been carved much sooner in his life. This hiatus may help to explain the unusual distance between the burial chamber and the funerary chapel. Perhaps much later in his life, he realised the danger of building a chapel so close to the mountain slope. It is, therefore, possible that he may have (re)built his chapel in a safer position. This circumstance became a most fortunate one, as a rock landslide eventually covered and sealed the burial shaft in antiquity, protecting it from tomb robbers until it was discovered in 1906.

Kha gained or purchased his funerary equipment in different episodes of his career. For example, the style and layout of the anthropoid coffins date from before the reign of Amenhotep III. This is the case of the vulture goddess depicted on the chest of the anthropoid coffins. During the reign of Amenhotep III, the depiction of the heavenly goddess Nut, with outstretched wings, became more common than the vulture. The *wedjat*-eyes depicted on the box also points to an earlier dating. During the reign of Amenhotep III it was depicted on the lid or not at all.

We already stated that the inner coffin of Merit, previously prepared for Kha, must have been a much earlier acquisition. It is interesting to speculate on the whereabouts of Merit's coffin set and the remaining burial equipment until the definitive sealing of the burial chamber. Was the coffin set of Merit buried immediately in the burial chamber or was it stored elsewhere?

The distribution of the coffin sets in the burial chamber suggests that the interments were deposited in a single event, with the largest set, that of Kha, positioned against the rear wall of the chamber, followed by the coffin set of Merit and other larger pieces of furniture, such as Merit's bed and Kha's chair. The remaining smaller objects would have been installed afterwards. It is thus logical to infer that all these objects had been stored elsewhere until they were carried to the tomb. This is obvious with most of the funerary objects. However, many items from this tomb had been used in Kha's house. Some of them received a funerary inscription, which shows that domestic furniture could have been summarily prepared for a funerary use, before they entered the tomb by simply adding a dedicatory inscription. Finally, it is also logical to assume that Merit's personal belongings had been stored after her death, which seemingly occurred many years before Kha's own death.

From the symbolic standpoint, the coffin sets from the Tomb of Kha are distinct from those used in previous periods. The "black" type was introduced during the reign of Hatshepsut. The rectangular outer coffins are designed to recreate the sacred burial chamber of Osiris. Spatial references, previously referring generically to the sky, earth, and cosmic orientations, are now entirely projected in the netherworld aiming at recreating an extraordinary event: the rebirth of Osiris. Therefore, the burial assemblage as a whole is designed to recreate a process rather than to perpetuate a result in time, as was the case during the Middle Kingdom.

In the burial of Kha, the three nested coffins are used with a clear sense of progression from a state of complete darkness (outer coffin) to full enlightenment (inner coffin). We can say that in the burial assemblage of Kha the progression towards the inner spheres of the nested assemblage recreates a path from darkness to illumination, but also from silence to speech, and from opaqueness to visibility. The three layers created in these nested assemblages have cosmogonic meaning. They suggest that this phenomenon is not confined to this particular corpse, reaching, on the contrary, the totality of the created cosmos, making the world begin anew.

This cosmic reading of the ultimate destiny of the deceased is the result of the full interpretation of the burial chamber at the light of the concepts conveyed in the Book of the Dead. Most of the funerary objects are decorated with images or spells from this composition. The new layout of the coffins is shaped after the imagery of Chapter 151 and Chapter 161. The heart scarab is inscribed with Chapter 30 B. The *tjet*-amulet used on the neck refers to Chapter 158, which summons the power of Isis to protect the mummy, and *shabtis* are inscribed with Chapter 6. But, of course, the richly illustrated papyrus, with its selection of spells provided in itself the itinerary of such extraordinary transformation.

This "contamination" of the funerary material culture by the imagery of the Book of the Dead is a major achievement, as in private tombs visual culture had always covered topics related to the earthly life. The traditional subjects depicted in tombs had always been the funerary banquet and the provision of the tomb. When funerary rituals started to be depicted, they could be seen as events from the world of the living, even if they were supposed to occur in the necropolis. With the vignettes of the Book of the Dead, visual culture embraced the sacred realm of the netherworld and made it visible.

However, it is interesting to see that, unlike many contemporary Theban tombs, where we may see a wealth of pictorial decoration showing these new topics, in the Tomb of Kha this phenomenon is contained within the thick walls of the rectangular coffins.

In fact, in his tomb, great importance is still given to the traditional cult of the Ka, *i.e.* to the imaginary of the afterlife as an extension of the earthly existence. The burial equipment included all the goods necessary for the Ka of the deceased. However, the way these goods were selected betrays a more sophisticated interpretation of this generic aspiration, suggesting the recreation of his home, where he once lived with Merit, his beloved wife. The fond memories of the life they had together echo through each object, in the manner of the verses of the *Harper's Song*:

> Follow your heart as long as you live!
> Put myrrh on your head,
> Dress in fine linen,
> Anoint yourself with oils fit for a god.
> Heap up your joys,
> Let your heart not sink!
> Follow your heart and your happiness,
> Do your things on earth as your heart commands!
> When there comes to you that day of mourning,
> Wailing saves no man from the pit![42]

Most of the burial equipment of Kha is composed of the contents of his own home, which were brought to the underworld, perhaps aiming at bringing back to life the memories of his long deceased wife. If so, the tomb as it was prepared by Kha provided the couple with nothing less than the home where they once lived, and where they could once again live forever, together, for all eternity.

Map 4. Deir el-Medina. Map of the site.

Notes

1. Bryan 2000, 240.
2. Ferraris 2015, 130.
3. Ferraris 2015, 130.
4. Ferraris 2015, 134.
5. Report published in 1927. In Ferraris 2015, 134.
6. Reeves 2000, 126.
7. Reeves 2000.
8. Report dated from February 20 to the Italian Ministry of Education. In Ferraris 2015, 134.
9. Objects numbered with the *Journal d'Entrée* references from 38647 to 38462.
10. Moiso 2016.
11. Andreu 2002, 305.
12. D'Abbadie and Jourdain 1939.
13. Ferraris 2015, 130.
14. Ferraris 2015, 148–149.
15. Ferraris 2015, 130.
16. Ferraris 2015, 146.
17. Ferraris 2015, 146.
18. Ferraris 2015, 148.
19. Ferraris 2015, 258.
20. Ferraris 2015, 238.
21. Ferraris 2015, 238.
22. Ferraris 2015, 147.
23. Ferraris 2015, 239.
24. Ferraris 2015, 150.
25. Russo 2012.
26. Ferraris 2015, 150.
27. Ferraris 2015, 140.
28. See also the coffin set of Amenhotep, in Reeves 2013, 25.
29. Taylor 2016, 53.
30. Sousa 2018a, 30.
31. Ferraris 2015, 143.
32. Ferraris 2015, 143.
33. Ferraris 2015, 143.
34. Bianucci *et al.* 2015; Ferraris 2015, 244.
35. Ferraris 2015, 249.
36. Sousa 2011.
37. Ferraris 2015, 258.
38. D'Abbadie and Jourdain 1939.
39. JE 62030. In Saleh, Sourouzian 1987, 181.
40. Ferraris 2015, 137.
41. Sousa 2011.
42. Lichtheim 1973, 197.

Chapter 6

The Garden of Heaven: The family tomb of Sennedjem (TT 1)

During the reign of Amenhotep III, massive construction works had been carried out in the Theban necropolis. Besides the royal tomb (KV 22) and the colossal Temple of Millions of Years built on the greenish floodplain, a royal palace served by an immense harbour was built in Malkata to hold the magnificent Sed festivals of the king. This frantic activity certainly had a huge impact on the villagers of Deir el-Medina, who were at the core of these projects.

When, later on, Akhenaten moved his capital to Akhetaten ("The Horizon of the Sun Disk"), in Middle Egypt, it is difficult to estimate the devastating impact of this decision in Deir el-Medina. Did the royal artisans move with the king to the newly built city or did they remain in Thebes, and consequently became "unemployed"?

The fact is that the royal tomb was built in Akhetaten, in the eastern desert *wadi*, with a new layout and a newly created iconographic repertoire, for which the highly experienced royal artisans from Deir el-Medina were certainly poorly prepared. In any case, during the short reign of Akhenaten, the villagers of Deir el-Medina were not only greatly impoverished as they would surely have felt miserable and helpless in face of the desecration of the Theban temples carried out by the agents of the pharaoh. The images of the god Amun had been chiselled away, his statues ritually "killed", his temples closed down and his beautiful festivals suppressed. Even the Beautiful Feast of the Valley, the most important celebration in the Theban necropolis, had been discontinued. In Thebes, these were times of resistance during which the supreme god Amun-Re could not find a better refuge than the hearts of his own devotees.

My heart longs for the sight of you,
O Lord of the persea tree,
When your neck receives garlands!
You grant satiation without eating,
And drunkenness without drinking.

...

Turn back to us, O Lord of the plenitude of time!
You were here when nothing had come into being,
And you will be here when "they" are at end.
You let me see darkness that you give –
Shine for me, that I might see you!

...

Oh, how good it is to follow you,
Amun, O Lord,
Great to find for the one who seeks him!
Drive off fear, place joy
In the heart of humankind!
How happy is the face that beholds you, Amun:
It is in festival day after day.[1]

This poem written during the period of persecution describes the situation of those who longed for the sight of Amun-Re. The inner experience of a divine presence had become detached from external signs, due to the absence of the divine festivals that could no longer be celebrated.[2]

The situation would eventually change when Akhenaten died and his young heir, Tutankhamun, ascended to the throne. The Court then moved to Memphis, but royal construction works did return to the Valley of the Kings, or perhaps more exactly to the Valley of the Monkeys (KV 23), a previously unused *wadi* of the Theban Mountain. Tutankhamun intended to start a new line of royal burials by excavating his tomb at this new location. Ironically, the premature death of the king dictated the return to the Valley of the Kings, where Tutankhamun was eventually buried in a much smaller tomb (KV 62).

This did not prevent Memphis from becoming the main artistic centre of Egypt, which suggests that most of the royal artisans from Amarna had moved there, originating an exceptional development in Memphite funerary arts.

Only when the 19th Dynasty was founded and Seti I started his ambitious building programme in Thebes, a real volte-face occurred in Deir el-Medina, which saw the village return to its full activity, as it was again enlarged to accommodate new settlers. At its peak, during the reign of Ramesses II, the community contained around sixty-eight houses spread over a total area of 5,600 m^2.

One of these new settlers was Sennedjem. His title, *sedjem ash em Set Maat* ("Servant in Set Maat", *i.e.* worker of Deir el-Medina) was modest but he succeeded in achieving the rare prowess of building a magnificent tomb on the southern edge of the mountain slope (Fig. 104), not far from the house where he actually lived, located in the new quarters of the village added in the southern sector. Here, in the last house of the

6. The Garden of Heaven: The family tomb of Sennedjem (TT 1)

Fig. 104. The Tomb of Sennedjem in the southern sector of Deir el-Medina.

settlement, he lived with his wife, Iyneferti (Fig. 108).[3] They were both engaged in the cult of Hathor (Fig. 105), the fertility goddess of the Theban necropolis, who provided rebirth, love and joy. Sennedjem is mentioned as "Servant of Hathor, the Mistress" and Iyneferti held the title "Great Chantress of Hathor, the Mistress of the West".[4] Perhaps his own name, Sennedjem, meaning the "Sweet Lover",[5] might be an homage to the great goddess. The fact is that they had at least ten children. Some of them pursued the footsteps of their father as royal artisans and a few lived in the neighbouring houses.

This was the case of Khabekhnet, the eldest son. He had the same title as his father and worked during the reign of Ramesses II. His tomb (TT 2) lay next to that of his father, and his beautifully decorated burial chamber was designed in the so-called "monochromatic" style.[6] Khabekhnet married Sahte, the daughter of another artisan from Deir el-Medina, the sculptor Piay. They had many children, all mentioned in his tomb and also in the tomb of his father.[7]

Khonsu, another son of Sennedjem, achieved a successful career. He had the same title as his father, "Servant in Set Maat" and served under the reign of Ramesses II, eventually becoming foreman in Set Maat. Khonsu married Tamaket, with whom he had three sons and one daughter, Isis, who seems to have married her uncle, Khabekhnet, the eldest brother of Khonsu.[8] Interestingly enough, Isis was not buried in her husband's tomb but in her grandfather's burial ground.

Little is known of most of the remaining sons and daughters of Sennedjem and Iyneferti. Many of them are mentioned and depicted on their relative's tombs and certainly some of them were buried with Sennedjem in his burial chamber.

Discovery

The undisturbed tomb of Sennedjem, perhaps one of the finest ever found in Deir el-Medina, was discovered in 1886 by the villagers of Gurnah in a pristine state of preservation. With the permission of Gaston Maspero, the French Director of the *Service des Antiquités*, Salam Abu Duhi and three other *gurnawi* villagers carried out excavations in Deir el-Medina, looking for old tombs.[9] After seven days of hard work, they found an undisturbed shaft, at the bottom of which a short gallery was found leading to an undecorated vaulted chamber. On the floor of this room, next to the northern wall, they found a slab hiding a smaller second shaft, leading to another chamber hidden by a beautifully painted door. The door displayed an intact seal featuring the head of Anubis moulded in clay. In the light of this discovery, Salam told Maspero immediately, who visited the site on the 1st February, with Urbain Bouriant, from the French archaeological mission in Cairo.

Fig. 105. Log sculpted with the effigy of Hathor. Egyptian Museum in Cairo (JE 25630).

When the team opened the door, a profusely decorated chamber was revealed filled with hundreds of objects. Several mummies and coffins were piled up against the west wall. On the opposite side of the room, the team found two large disassembled funerary shrines, together with a variety of different objects:

> Eight canopic boxes, forty small boxes with funerary statuettes, a hundred charming limestone figurines, twenty painted vases, funerary beds… In addition, a beautiful chair (…) two stools with canvas backdrop imitating red leather, a folding stool, bouquets of flowers, a cubit, an ostracon containing a very curious novel, although very short. Insinger and Toda have photographed the chamber and are going to photograph some of the objects.[10]

Jan Herman Insinger was a Dutch banker who came to Luxor to benefit from a climate that could ease his tuberculosis. He became a close friend of Maspero, who used his services as a photographer during his inspections.

As for Eduard Toda i Güell, the Consul of Spain in Egypt from 1884 to 1886, he was bond to Maspero by a close friendship, which led Maspero to entrust him with the important responsibility of clearing the newly discovered tomb.

Fig. 106. Eduard Toda on board of the dahabeya, with the antiquities cleared from the Tomb of Sennedjem.

Assisted by seven workers, Toda transferred the objects to *Boulaq*, the *dahabieh* of the *Service des Antiquités* based on the west bank. However, the harsh conditions faced along the way damaged many objects, which were broken or lost. The unconfined mummies were so deteriorated that only the skulls were kept.[11]

Once the shipment was concluded, Toda carried out the inventory of the find, listing more than 165 objects on board (Fig. 106).

The preliminary examination of the objects revealed that this tomb was used as a family burial ground. Besides Sennedjem it had been used to bury at least 19 other individuals.

Eleven of them were unconfined, while nine others were buried in exquisite coffins, sometimes forming double sets, finely decorated and varnished. The main burials of the tomb belonged to Sennedjem (Fig. 107) and his wife, Iyneferti (Fig. 108). Some of their sons had also been buried in the tomb, such as Khonsu and his wife Tamaket, and other sons such as Parahotep, Taashsen, Ramose, and Hathor. Grandsons had also been buried in the tomb, such as Isis, daughter of Khonsu. Two unborn children were found in small boxes painted in yellow. Therefore, at least three generations were identifiable in the tomb, but it is possible that it was used by further descendants of Sennedjem.

All the antiquities were transported to the Boulaq Museum in Cairo. Despite the pristine condition of the objects, they were seen by Maspero as less valuable when compared with the tomb itself. In his letter to his wife Louise, dated from the 3rd February, he says:

> (The tomb) was filled to the top with coffins and objects, eight adult mummies, and two child mummies (...) the mummies are exquisite, of a beautiful red varnish with much elaborated depictions, but they are only the least interesting part of the find.[12]

Perhaps this helps to understand why, at this point, a decision was made to keep a selected sample of the objects and sell the remaining collection. In his letters, Gaston Maspero explains this decision:

> It goes without saying that we bought the fellahs the half that would belong to them. It costed us 46 guineas. Once we have chosen all that was good for the Museum, the sale of

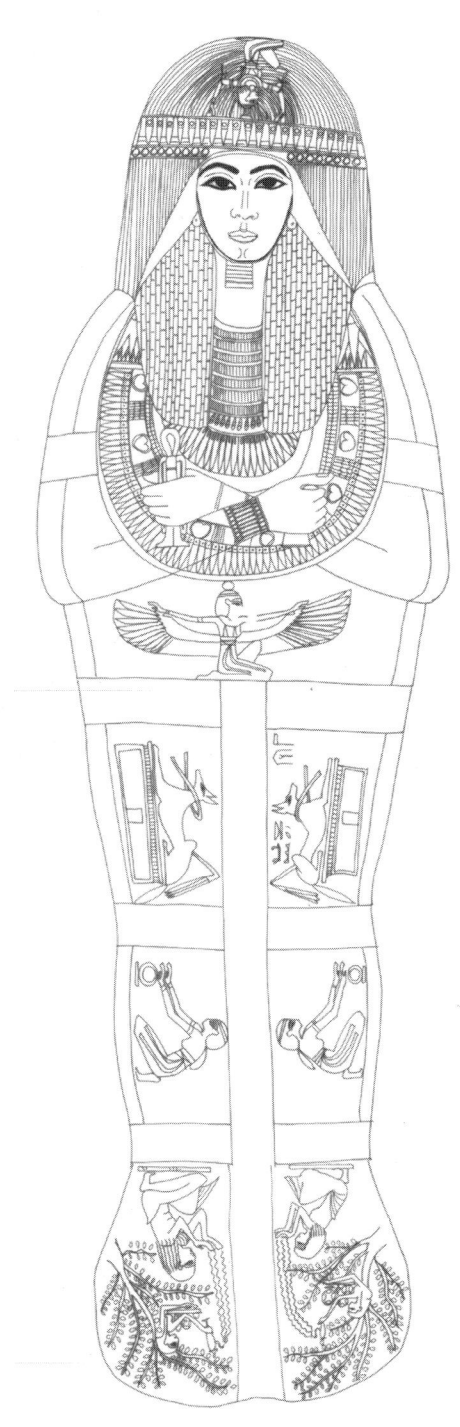

Fig. 107. Sennedjem's lid.

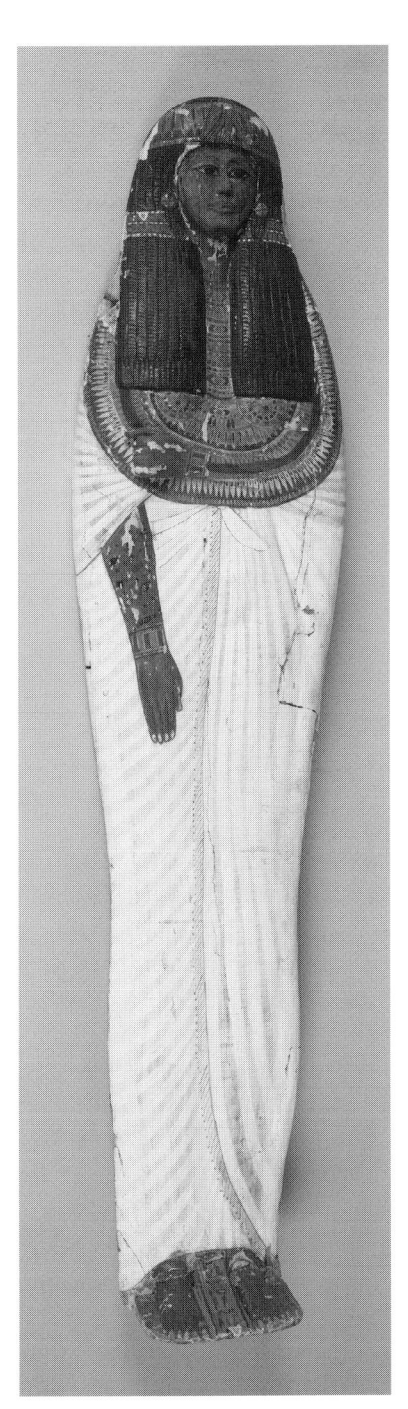

Fig. 108. Funerary plank of Yeneferti. Metropolitan Museum of Art (86.1.5c).

the superfluous mummies and objects will bring us back at least 60 guineas, or maybe 80, which will be used in the excavations of Luxor and the Sphinx. It will be a good deal in every way. Good from the scientific perspective, since it gave us monuments of which we had no specimen, and good from a financial point of view: not only, in the end, these objects did not cost us anything, as we will earn money enough to engage in further excavations.[13]

The exquisite coffin set of Sennedjem remained in Cairo, as well as the burial assemblage of his granddaughter Isis, and a selected sample of the objects considered to be "unique", or "more representative". A significant part of the collection, including the burial assemblages of Sennedjem's wife, Iyneferti, and his son, Khonsu, was bought by the Metropolitan Museum of Art in New York, which prevented the complete pulverisation of the find. The burial assemblage of Tamaket, the wife of Khonsu, was bought by the Egyptian Museum in Berlin but it was eventually destroyed during World War II. Other objects can be found in a variety of Museums, but sadly the location of some of them can no longer be traced.

The tomb complex of Sennedjem

Despite the disappointing fate of the collection found in the tomb, the funerary complex of Sennedjem remains an exceptional discovery, providing a rare glimpse of a completely preserved funerary complex dating from the Ramesside Period, comprising a funerary chapel and its courtyard, a shaft, and underground chambers, one of them beautifully decorated and perfectly preserved containing an intact burial equipment. Such rare circumstances allow us to understand the interrelation between tomb decoration and burial equipment, probably better than any other site.

The tomb of Sennedjem is located on the southern edge of the necropolis, within a walled rectangular terrace that served two other chapels, all of them shaped like pyramids (Fig. 109). The largest and the oldest of the three is the southern one, built in mudbrick.[14] At the centre stands the pyramid of Sennedjem, and on the northern part of the terrace, the chapel of his son Khonsu. These two were built in stone and mudbrick as was usual during the 19th Dynasty. Since it was the last to be built, the pyramid of Khonsu is the smallest of the ensemble. The shortage of space dictated its peculiar layout, comprising straight vertical walls topped by a small pyramid. Despite that, this chapel is the only one to preserve vestiges of painted decoration.[15] However, Khonsu did not build a burial chamber for himself and together with his wife, Tamaket, he was buried in his father's tomb.

The open courtyard would have been flanked by a small pylon on the east side. A mudbrick wall divided the courtyard, separating the southern pyramid from the chapels of Sennedjem and Khonsu. The courtyard provided the appropriate setting for the performance of funerary rites, such as the Opening of the Mouth ceremony, and for family gatherings on the occasion of the Beautiful Feast of the Valley. For this reason, a low mudbrick bench was set up against the north wall to hold the funerary offerings on festive occasions.[16]

Fig. 109. Sennedjem's funerary complex.

Originally, the pyramid of Sennedjem was 4.5 m wide and 6.85 m high. The structure was topped by a limestone *pyramidion*, fragments of which had been found showing Sennedjem in adoration to the sun god.[17] The sides of the pyramid were plastered and painted white. The entrance to the chapel was open on the east side. The lintel shows Sennedjem and his wife in adoration to Sobek. Above, in the niche, a stela featured the deceased adoring the rising sun.[18]

Inside the chapel, no trace of decoration was found in the small vaulted chamber. The west wall was excavated on the mountain slope in order to provide the ritual contact with the western mountain. Vestiges of a funerary stela had been found in this location.

The shaft leading to Sennedjem's burial chamber was excavated in the courtyard, 1.70 m away from his pyramid (Fig. 110). The shaft is 6 m deep with small niches carved at regular intervals in order to allow the descent to the burial chamber without need for a ladder. On the west wall, a passage leads to a large undecorated vaulted chamber. This is the central room of the underground galleries of the tomb, providing communication with three other chambers, each one accessible from pits excavated next to each wall. In antiquity, this room was probably used to store provision of food in baskets and pots, which the modern excavators most likely found too unimportant to collect. On the south wall, a small storeroom is found, while to the west, an undecorated room is reachable by a flight of stairs. Positioned along the axis of the tomb, this room was probably intended as the main burial chamber but, for unknown reasons, it

6. *The Garden of Heaven: The family tomb of Sennedjem (TT 1)* 101

was abandoned and another chamber built next to the north wall. This room, the main burial chamber, was accessible by a shaft excavated on the pavement of the undecorated room, concealed under a slab of stone.[19]

At the bottom of the shaft, the entrance to the burial chamber was protected by a profusely decorated gate (Fig. 111). The lintel shows Sennedjem adoring the god Atum on his barque and the doorjambs display inscriptions. The wooden door was beautifully decorated on both sides. The exterior displays two registers. The upper one shows the deceased with his wife and his daughter Irunefer before the enthroned god Osiris and Maat. The lower register shows seven of his sons in adoration before Ptah-Sokar-Osiris and Isis.

Fig. 110. Sennedjem's tomb. In Bruyère 1959, Pl. VII.

Fig. 111. The door of the burial chamber (exterior and interior views). Reconstruction by John Hirst.

The burial chamber

The beautiful scenes displayed in Sennedjem's burial chamber were not painted directly onto the bedrock. Mudbrick walls had been built along the sides of the chamber and then coated with whitewash or plaster. Over the surface created in this way, the multicoloured scenes were painted against a yellow background. The floor was painted red, creating a vivid contrast with the yellow walls (Fig. 112).[20]

In this small area, a fascinating pictorial narrative is unfolded along the walls and the vaulted ceiling of the chamber. The story starts on the side walls of the entrance, follows to the long sides of the chamber (south and north walls), and progresses to the short sides (east and west walls), before reaching the ceiling and coming back to

Fig. 112. The burial chamber (general view).

the passage leading out of the chamber.

The side walls of the entrance and the interior face of the wooden door allude to scenes borrowed from Chapter 17 of the Book of the Dead. The door shows a single vignette featuring Sennedjem and his wife seated under a pavilion playing the *sennet* game. The game, which means "passing over", symbolised the preparations for entering the next world. It was played in the earthly life, but in the funerary setting alluded to the challenges the deceased had to face to reach immortality. On the left side of the entrance, the solar disk rests on the horizon flanked by the lions Aker, named "Yesterday" and "Tomorrow". This is the depiction of the sunset and alludes to the beginning of the nightly journey of the sun in the netherworld.

When entering the burial chamber, the narrative progresses on the left side. Again, another representation from Chapter 17 is found, with the mummy of Sennedjem lying on a lion-headed funerary bed, hidden under a pavilion flanked by Isis and Nephthys in avian form (Fig. 113).

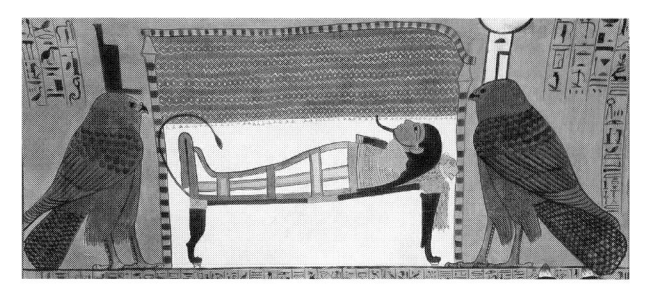

Fig. 113. Isis and Nephthys in avian form watching over Osiris lying on the funerary bed (south wall).

Fig. 114. Anubis embalms Osiris lying on the funerary bed (north wall).

On the opposite wall (North) a similar scene is shown, now with Anubis embalming the deceased within the mummification tent (Chapter 151). The jackal-headed god rests his hands over the chest of the mummy, bringing the deceased back to life (Fig. 114).

The following scene on the north wall shows the deceased escorted by Anubis, who guides him to the court of Osiris (Fig. 115).[21] This alludes to the judgement of the dead (Chapter 125). The weighing of the heart is not depicted, but the structure of the scene is similar, including the double depiction of Sennedjem, always showing respect and reverence as it was expected in the court of Osiris. It is noteworthy that before Osiris, the deceased shows grey hair, perhaps alluding to his status as an elderly "wise man".

Fig. 115. Judgement scene (north wall).

Fig. 116. Sennedjem and his wife before the Guardian deities of the underworld (south wall).

The shrine of Osiris is depicted at the centre of the north wall, facing the entrance directly. When approaching the tomb, the visitor thus faces the effigy of Osiris as if entering his holy shrine (Fig. 111). This visual effect expresses the Osirian significance of the burial chamber, as a whole.

Our visual story progresses to the right side of the south wall (Fig. 116), with Sennedjem and his wife addressing ten guardian deities of the underworld

Fig. 117. The Fields of Iaru (east wall).

(Chapter 145–146).[22] If they are found pure, the guardians would allow them to pass over these gates and enter the paradisiac Fields of Iaru (Chapter 110), featured in the east wall (Fig. 117).[23] The imposing scene of the Fields of Iaru is prefaced by the solar barque. It shows an aquatic landscape presenting a profusion of islands and waterways arranged in several registers. In the first register, Sennedjem and his wife kneel on the sand adoring the divine triad of Re-Osiris-Ptah followed by two unnamed gods. One of their sons, Parahotep, navigates on the barque, while another son, Khonsu, performs the Opening of the mouth ritual on the mummy of Sennedjem.

In the second island Sennedjem and his wife work on the fields. They harvest the fields of wheat and linen and plow the fertile soil. Perhaps resulting from this hard work, Sennedjem is presented with a generous meal in the neighbouring piece of land. The island has a pleasant garden lushly planted with palm trees and sycamores.

The third island is represented as a narrow piece of land planted with flowers, such as poppies, cornflowers, and mandrakes. Finally, out in the waters, a tiny island is shown where the barque of Re-Horakhti is docked.

On the opposite wall, the necropolis is depicted (Fig. 118). Under the protection of the jackal gods, Sennedjem and Iyneferti unite with Osiris, Re-Horakhti, and their suite (Chapter 190).

Fig. 118. Sennedjem and his wife address the gods of the underworld (west wall)

Once reaching the west, the narrative progresses on the ceiling, which is arranged in two longitudinal partitions (Fig. 119).[24] On the south partition, from the east to the west, we see the vignette of Chapter 109, showing the solar disk rising from the turquoise trees. A young bull representing the sun comes forth, carrying the star Sirius, an allusion to the dawn at the summer solstice. The scene is completed with the effigy of Re-Horakhti-Atum (cf. West wall). In the following scene, Sennedjem is depicted in adoration before underworld deities (Chapter 112). Next, a vignette shows Sennedjem before a cosmological scene featuring a snake, perhaps Sa Ta (meaning the "Son of the Earth") twisted over the horizon, and a mummiform god seated under the sky (Chapter 126). This partition is concluded with Sennedjem in adoration before a triad headed by the god Thoth (Chapter 116).[25]

From the east to the west, the North partition is decorated with the tree goddess Nut feeding Sennedjem and his wife featured on their own tomb (Chapters 59). In the following vignette, Sennedjem and his wife adore a group of five gods depicted against the nightly sky, showing seven stars and the solar disk, an allusion to the Imperishable Stars and the nightly form of the sun (Chapter 135).[26]

There follows another allusion to the nightly journey of the sun: the solar barque carrying the Benu bird, and the god Re-Horakhty-Atum (Chapters 100, 133). The Great Ennead escorts the sun god, here used instead of the *shemsu*-sign, meaning "Followers".

6. The Garden of Heaven: The family tomb of Sennedjem (TT 1)

Fig. 119. The decoration of the ceiling.

The partition is concluded with Sennedjem opening the doors of heaven, depicted over the horizon (Chapter 68). The scene alludes to going forth to the daylight, a subject that is continued on the ceiling of the entrance.

Back to the entrance, the ritual slaughter of Apopis, the enemy of Re, is depicted on the right wall. The "Great Cat", the manifestation of the solar god, kills the serpent before the dawn of the New Year, with the sacred tree of Heliopolis depicted at the background.

On the ceiling, the long arms of the goddess Nut rise from the eastern horizon with the reborn sun disk. The cycle is completed and the sun rises from the underworld going forth by day.

Contrasting with the highly theological character of these compositions, all borrowed from the iconographic repertoire of the Book of the Dead, a secondary cycle is summarily featured along the lower edge of the south wall, which in this tomb provides the contact with the world of the living. Here we find a banquet scene showing Sennedjem and his family gathered in a joyful celebration. From both sides of the entrance, they face and salute those who enter the tomb.

On the left side of the wall, from the west to the east, figure Sennedjem and Iyneferti receiving the funerary cult from their son, Bunakhtef. A boy, Ranekhu, and a girl, Hotepu, are featured next to their parents. The parents of Sennedjem are depicted next, with a girl at their feet, receiving the symbol of the breeze, the north wind. The third group is formed by Khabekhnet, the eldest son of Sennedjem, and two ladies.

On the opposite side of the wall several sons, cousins, and nephews of Sennedjem, are depicted, the eldest ones are seated, while the younger ones are standing (Fig. 116).

This family gathering alludes to the festivities taking place during the Beautiful Feast of the Valley when families went to their relatives' tombs on the Theban west bank to celebrate the renewal of life. In this mind-set, the tomb's garden played a particular role, bringing the mythical Field of Reeds to the realm of the living.[27] However, in the Tomb of Sennedjem, a reversed phenomenon seems to occur, with the earthly family gathering being transposed to the afterlife, where Sennedjem and his descendants meet on the banks of the Fields of Iaru. Sennedjem's burial was thus literally conceived as a garden of heaven where life is recreated anew.

The burial equipment

When it was found, the burial chamber was crowded with furniture. Some of the objects alluded to the earthly life

Fig. 120. Jewellery box. Metropolitan Museum of Art (86.1.8).

6. The Garden of Heaven: The family tomb of Sennedjem (TT 1)

and included jewellery boxes (Fig. 120), baskets, beautifully decorated jars (Fig. 121),[28] boxes containing linens and food. Some of them look worn, indicating that they had been used in life, such as Sennedjem's chair and stools. Some artefacts belonged to other individuals. Two stools belonged to his wife, Iyneferti, and another to the grandson Mes, son of Khabekhnet.

From the nine jewellery boxes found in the tomb, two of them are inscribed for Sennedjem's wife, Iyneferti. Two others carry the name of Khabekhnet, and another one that of Ramose, also a son of Sennedjem. Four other boxes remained uninscribed.[29]

The jewellery of Sennedjem's family included three pectorals for Sennedjem, two pectorals and one necklace for Khonsu, two rings for his mother, and one pectoral without any associated name. It is likely that other personal adornments have been taken away from these boxes by Sennedjem's own descendants.[30]

An interesting group of artefacts is formed by Sennedjem's personal objects. His tools included a royal cubit rod, a triangular level (Fig. 122), and two plumb levels. Some of these tools may have been used by Sennedjem in his work. However, some of them have been converted for funerary use. The triangular level, for example, may have been used in Sennedjem's lifetime as it was found broken. However, it is inscribed with funerary texts addressed to Ptah and Re-Horakhty-Atum-Hemiunu, asking for benefits in the afterlife for Sennedjem, which clearly shows a funerary purpose.[31]

The funerary use of this object is perhaps better understood in light of the beliefs regarding the weighing of the heart. During the Ramesside Period, a new type of heart amulet adopted the shape of the plumb bob, in order to show that one's heart guides us to overcome mistakes and reach perfection[32]. The triangular level, making use of the same plumb bob, alluded to the correct use Sennedjem had made of his heart to reach perfection in his works.

Fig. 121. Festive wine jar. Metropolitan Museum of Art (86.1.10).

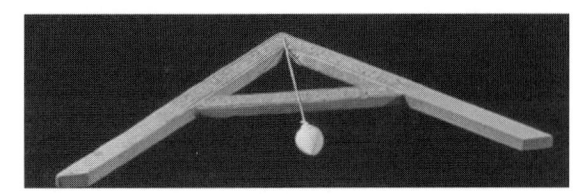

Fig. 122. Sennedjem's tools: triangular level. Egyptian Museum in Cairo (JE 27258).

110 Gilded Flesh

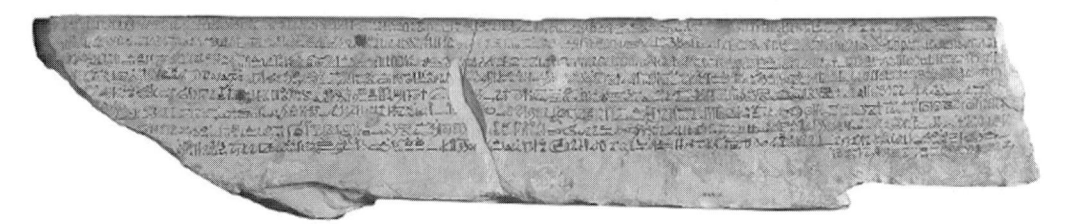

Fig. 123. The ostracon with the beginning of Sinuhe's Tale. Egyptian Museum in Cairo (JE 27419).

Another object that is telling of Sennedjem's interests is the large ostracon inscribed with a fragment of the *Story of Sinuhe*, perhaps the most celebrated tale of Egyptian literature (Fig. 123). The *ostracon* is 106.5 cm large, one of the largest ever found, providing a copy of the beginning of this tale written in hieratic script.[33] It was found along with Sennedjem's coffin set. It is clear that Sennedjem took this story much as one takes a favourite book when moving to a new home. Another ostracon provided a list of working material, which shows the personal engagement of Sennedjem in his work.

A wide range of statuettes was included in the tomb. One of them shows the Ka of Sennedjem, depicted in festive garments and wearing a long wig (Fig. 124). The white garments had been covered with gleaming varnish. His arms fall along the body flanking a column of text reading:

> Everything which goes forth upon the offering table of Amun in Apet-Sut, for the Ka of Sennedjem, the justified, happy in peace.[34]

This is a rather unusual offering formula, as it expresses the wish of Sennedjem's Ka to feed himself from the divine offerings presented in the great temple of Karnak, a motif which would more likely be expected in the context of Amarna's funerary religion.

A wide range of *shabtis* belonging to several individuals had been found in the tomb. The role of these figurines is directly related to the Fields of Iaru depicted in the tomb. The *shabtis* were crafted to work on the fields instead of their owners. Some of them are inscribed with Chapter 6, while others bear a short inscription only.[35]

Amongst the *shabtis* included in the tomb were found objects belonging to individuals that were not actually buried in the tomb, as in the case of the *shabtis* inscribed for Khabekhnet.[36] They were probably included as gifts, intended to provide extra help in the Fields of Iaru.

Fig. 124. Ka statuette of Sennedjem. Egyptian Museum in Cairo (JE 27221).

6. *The Garden of Heaven: The family tomb of Sennedjem (TT 1)* 111

Fig. 125. Shabti box and shabtis. Metropolitan Museum of Art (86.1.14-related).

It is, therefore, interesting to note how important this imagery was in strengthening family bonds, as if Sennedjem and his sons expected to find themselves together in the lushly green islands of the netherworld.

Most of the *shabtis* are mummiform,[37] but a few of them display festive garments, or mix aspects from both models (Fig. 125).[38] As *shabtis* tend to adopt the shape of the anthropoid coffin in use, at this stage, these differences point to the coexistence of two types of anthropoid coffins, one mummiform and the other showing the deceased in festive dress, as we effectively see in the coffins of the tomb.

The coffin set of Sennedjem

When Maspero entered the burial chamber, he found two richly decorated wooden shrines disassembled and laid over the south wall, on the left side of the entrance. These funerary shrines were used as outer coffins by Sennedjem and his son, Khonsu, but as generations succeed, the lack of space in the burial chamber required the disassembling of these large coffins in order to accommodate more burials.

Fig. 126. Sennedjem's funerary shrine. Egyptian Museum in Cairo (JE 27308).

Mounted on a sledge provided with wheels, the funerary shrine of Sennedjem was probably used to transport the mummy from the place of mummification to the tomb. It was furnished with a curved lid, imitating the roof of a *naos* with a cavetto cornice (Fig. 126).

This shape is that of the Per-Wer, the archaic shrine of Upper Egypt, typically used to contain images of divine beings in a temple's precinct. A subtle change of meaning is implied in this new form of body container when we compare it with the typical Per-Nu form, associated with the mythical tomb of Osiris. The Per-Wer is used in divine temples to hold the statue of the god. Its use in the funerary context suggests the association between the sarcophagus and a shrine where the divine image of Osiris is identified with the mummy.

Sennedjem's funerary shrine is richly decorated with images and texts depicted against a yellow background, an evocation of the gold leaf used in royal shrines.

6. The Garden of Heaven: The family tomb of Sennedjem (TT 1)

In fact, this object was clearly crafted imitating royal archetypes as we see in the Tomb of Tutankhamun (KV 60), covered in gold leaf and decorated with images and texts taken from the Books of the Amduat. Private coffins were not allowed to use these royal compositions, and so the decoration of Sennedjem's shrine makes use of the imagery of the Book of the Dead.

The short sides are decorated with the goddesses who defend the mummy. On the north side is Selket and Neith, who were responsible for protecting the deceased's head. On the south side are Nephthys and Isis who are charged with protecting the deceased's feet.

The long sides are arranged in two registers.

The first register alludes to the usual decoration scheme detected on the cases of the "black" coffin types. The east side shows Thoth, together with Hapy, Anubis and Qebehsenuef. On the west side Thoth is depicted, this time with Imseti, Anubis and Duamutef.

On both sides, the second register is decorated with motifs taken from the vignette of Chapter 17 of the Book of the Dead, some of them clearly based on the vignettes featured on the burial chamber. The lid was profusely decorated as well (Fig. 126), displaying two partitions as seen on the ceiling (Fig. 119).

The coffin set of Sennedjem would have been positioned inside this funerary shrine, lying on a funerary bed (Figs 130, 137). This bed, inscribed for Sennedjem, was found associated with the coffin set of Khonsu instead, showing that as the tomb was being used by the following generations, the original burial equipment was rearranged. The sides of Sennedjem's bed are decorated with long snakes painted yellow with black markings and outlines. The two mythical snakes face each other on the headboard, while the tails overlap on the footboard, protecting the corpse from danger. This motif is a subtle allusion to royal Book of the Amduat, namely to the Sixth Hour of the night, when two snakes surround the sun god to protect him.[39]

The anthropoid coffin of Sennedjem presents an interesting mixture of features (Fig. 130). Despite being painted in yellow, the case shows the layout of the "black" type. This is explained because it imitates the gilded coffins typically found with the "black" type. The striped headboard and the bands of text slightly moulded in plaster are conspicuous features of the "black" type scheme. The long sides also show the usual layout of the "black" type, with Thoth, Anubis and the four Sons of Horus.

Nothing in this scheme is particularly new, except for the use of varnish that covers the object, including the inscriptions and images.

Varnish was first used in the Ramesside Period as a substitute for black pitch and gold leaf, which were previously the materials of choice to provide gleaming light to the coffin.[40] From an artistic standpoint, this technical innovation offered unlimited possibilities for the development of coffin decoration as varnish had the enormous advantage of adding gleaming light, without hiding the pictorial work, as did black pitch. This transparency effect given by varnish allowed pictorial decoration to be further elaborated and, in fact, the outstanding development in coffin decoration that occurred from the Ramesside Period (1295–1069 BC) onwards could only be possible with this technical innovation.

The coffin set of Sennedjem documents the first steps of this process, particularly on the lid, which shows the deceased in mummiform guise as it would be expected in the gilded versions of the "black" type (Fig. 107). In fact, some of its features are evidently borrowed from the "black" scheme, such as the effigy of Nephthys depicted at the crown of the head, and the goddess Isis on the reverse side of the footboard.

However, other features have a different provenance. The headboard of the lid does not show the deceased adorned with the striped divine wig as "black" coffins do. It shows the subject wearing the wig of natural hair traditionally used on the occasion of divine festivals. The braiding motifs of the hair are carefully carved in relief, and the ears are not featured, remaining hidden under the heavy masses of hair.[41] Moreover, Sennedjem wears a short beard, typically used in earthly life. A naturalistic detail was added to the "portrait" of Sennedjem: two curved lines on the chin, suggesting a dimpled chin.

The depiction of the deceased as shown in Sennedjem's coffin is borrowed from the so-called "festive dress" type, a type of anthropoid coffin probably originating in Amarna as a funerary response to the Osirian beliefs no longer in use during the reign of Akhenaten.[42] In this revolutionary vision, the anthropoid coffin depicted the deceased as living, dressed up in festive garments so to join the sacred festivals performed in the Temple of Aten in order to celebrate the light and eternal life granted by Aten. This, and not the Osirian resurrection, was the vision of immortality put forward by Akhenaten.

Other pieces of evidence unearthed in the South Tombs Cemetery at Amarna strengthen this idea. Although much destroyed, a few anthropoid coffins are decorated with images of human offering bearers on the long sides, instead of the traditional gods,[43] a feature which only in the late Ramesside Period would again be reintroduced in the so-called "yellow" coffins.

Despite the failure of Akhenaten's reform, the new model of coffins depicting the deceased as living was not forgotten, and during the reigns of Tutankhamun and Horemheb, a synthesis between the two former models was essayed with coffins and sarcophagi blending the layout of the "black" type with the "festive dress" type. This phenomenon is particularly well attested in the necropolis of Saqqara during the late 18th Dynasty.

The burial assemblage of Sennedjem includes a life-sized funerary plank featuring the deceased in festive dress, exactly as he would be depicted in a "festive dress" type of coffin (Fig. 127).[44] He is depicted as a younger man than in the coffin lid, with a long wig and short beard. His torso is naked, adorned with a large floral collar, and his arms are shown lying alongside the body. Sennedjem wears a long-folded kilt of white linen. It is noteworthy that such a depiction of Sennedjem is consistent with the way he is featured on the wall paintings of his tomb, *i.e.*, as a justified god. His coffin set therefore, provides a new interpretation of the "festive dress" type, which

6. The Garden of Heaven: The family tomb of Sennedjem (TT 1)

embodies the deceased as a divine agent of the cult, thus in perpetual interaction with the deities of the netherworld.

This scheme follows the Memphite models, pursuing the synthesis between the solar layout put forward in Amarna and the Osirian "black" scheme. In Sennedjem's set, the "festive dress" was fully preserved in the mummy plank and residually maintained in the coffin lid, which preserved the portrait of the deceased as living.

However, the remaining layout of the lid attests to new and major steps in this pursuit. At first sight, the "black" type scheme seems to be fully back in favour, as the lid is reshaped after the Osirian mummiform guise (Fig. 107). Nevertheless, the lid is now carefully arranged in five distinct sections, each one of them decorated with a repertoire of its own.

The upper section is delimited by the contour of the forearms, which are crossed over the chest. Sennedjem has clenched fists and holds religious emblems, such as the *tjet*-sign.

The abdomen is decorated with a transversal panel featuring the winged goddess outstretching her wings over the deceased, and the lower section covers the legs, and displays two longitudinal partitions decorated with the jackal god Anubis and the mourning goddesses Isis and Nephthys. All these motifs are borrowed from the Osirian repertoire of the "black" type.

Nothing, except the formal arrangement of these sections is particularly new. The most important novelty is found on the footboard, showing vignettes depicting the deceased under the tree-goddess. On the left partition, the deceased is shown as a young man, but on the right, he is depicted as an elderly man, with grey hair, a contrast also used in the judgement scene featured on the north wall of his burial chamber (Fig. 115). These small vignettes reveal a new phenomenon as, for the first time the deceased is integrated into the pictorial programme of the coffin. This step represents a breakthrough in coffin decoration, which from then onwards

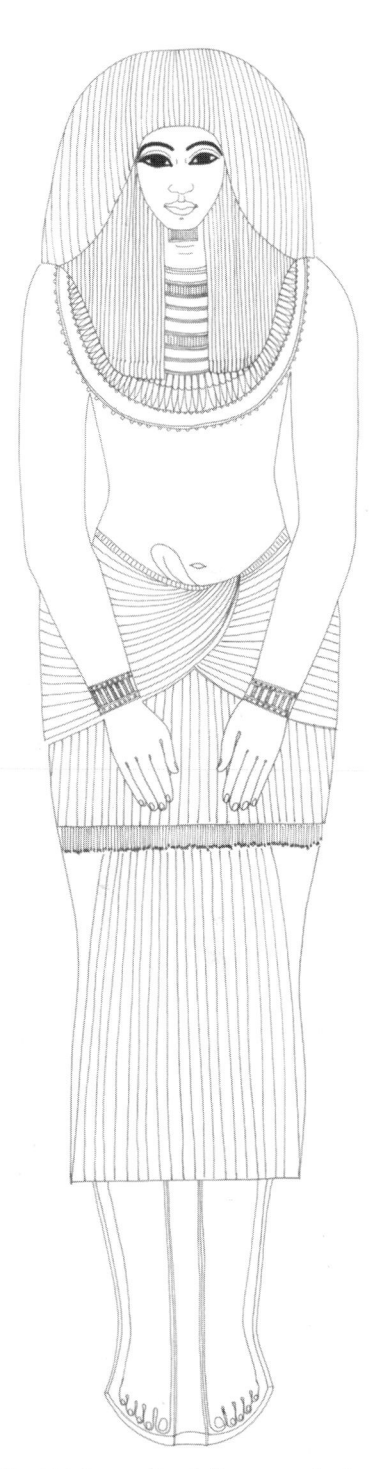

Fig. 127. Sennedjem's funerary plank.

would fully explore the possibilities offered by this new resource. With that, the full synthesis between the "festive dress" type and the "black" type was achieved. The mummiform body of the deceased was fully used as a background to show him as a living god celebrating the afterlife as an ongoing interaction with the cosmic deities of the netherworld.

The coffin set of Sennedjem included a funerary mask (Fig. 128). The object kept in the Egyptian Museum in Cairo has been identified as the mask of Sennedjem. However, the soft rendering of the almond-shaped face and graceful smile shows a greater affinity with the coffin set of Khonsu. Moreover, this mask is decorated with a bunch of lotus flowers over the head, a detail also found in the coffin set of Khonsu. Conversely, the mask kept in the Metropolitan Museum of Art, identified as the mask of Khonsu, shows the same austere expression and long face that we see in Sennedjem's coffin. On both objects the lotus bunch is missing. Therefore, since the objects are uninscribed, it is possible that the masks have been changed, if not in antiquity, then perhaps by the excavators themselves.

Fig. 128. Sennedjem's mask. Metropolitan Museum of Art (86.1.4).

6. The Garden of Heaven: The family tomb of Sennedjem (TT 1)

The coffin set of Khonsu

Crafted just one generation after the coffin of Sennedjem, the double coffin set of Khonsu shows fully how the new motifs impacted on coffin decoration in the Ramesside Period.

Khonsu achieved a higher status in the community of Deir el-Medina than his father, reaching the position of foreman. The exquisite quality of his coffin set is telling about his success.

Like his father, Khonsu prepared for himself a large funerary shrine to hold his double coffin set (Fig. 129). The shrine includes almost the same repertoire of scenes than his father's and it is likely that it had been used as a model. However, in the shrine of Khonsu the scenes were rearranged in such a way that the global composition is even more impressive than in Sennedjem's shrine. On the long sides, this was achieved by mingling the two registers in one, creating a single panel with larger figures. In this scheme, the vignettes of Chapter 17 were depicted between the effigies of Thoth and the Sons of Horus. The style is smoother, with the images elegantly designed.[45]

Inside, the double coffin set was laid on Sennedejem's funerary bed (Fig. 130), suggesting that Khonsu disassembled the funerary shrine of his father in order to accommodate his own. When this operation took place the funerary bed of Sennedjem was then used in the burial assemblage of Khonsu. As we have stated, this was not a minor

Fig. 129. Burial assemblage of Khonsu.

Fig. 130. Sennedjem's burial set. Egyptian Museum in Cairo (JE 27308).

artefact, as it was the only one in the tomb to show an explicit royal motif borrowed from the Book of the Amduat, which in theory was still out of reach for commoners.

The double coffin set of Khonsu does not involve a funerary plank featuring the deceased in festive garments. The outer coffin shows the deceased wearing the striped divine wig and his beard is long and curled as worn by the gods of the netherworld (Fig. 131). The clenched hands crossed over the breast hold a wooden *tjet*-symbol for "protection", and a *djed*-symbol for "stability". Osirian multicoloured bracelets, similar to those found in the mummy of Senebtisi, adorn the fists.

Several sections of the lid show further developments regarding the use of the deceased in the iconographic programme of the coffin. The lower section, in particular, shows that the transversal arrangement of the scenes detected on Sennedjem's coffin gave place to a longitudinal one, which makes these vignettes independent from those featured on the case.

Besides the jackal deities and the mourning goddesses, we now see Khonsu in adoration before Osiris. The footboard follows the model provided by Sennedjem's coffin, featuring the tree goddess pouring the water of life for his wife Tamaket, and for the Ba-birds of Khonsu and his wife. The layout of the case remained unchanged showing Thoth, Anubis, and the Sons of Horus in their usual positions.

The burial assemblage of Khonsu includes an inner coffin with a similar design and exquisite levels of craftsmanship (Fig. 132). Unlike the outer coffin, which depicts the deceased as an Osirian god, it shows the subject as living, depicting the long,

6. The Garden of Heaven: The family tomb of Sennedjem (TT 1)

Fig. 131. Outer coffin of Khonsu. Metropolitan Museum of Art (86.1.1a-b).

Fig. 132. Inner coffin of Khonsu. Metropolitan Museum of Art (86.1.2a-b).

Fig. 133. Canopic chest of Khonsu. Metropolitan Museum of Art (86.1.3a-b).

festive wig, and the short goatee beard. The central panel also reveals an unexpected anomaly, featuring the winged goddess facing the right side, thus breaking an almost universally observed rule: every central marker faces the left side.[46] This odd occurrence could be explained by a mistake introduced by an inexperienced painter, but the high skill of execution makes it unlikely. The lower section shows several scenes with Khonsu and his wife in adoration before Anubis, Osiris, Isis and Nephthys.[47] On the footboard solar scenes are featured alluding to the rising and the setting sun: on the right side, the sun disk is raised by the sun god Khepri, while on the left it is held by the arms of the sky goddess Nut.

The burial assemblage was completed with the funerary mask, now kept in the Egyptian Museum in Cairo, and a Canopic box kept in the Metropolitan Museum of Art (Fig. 133). The mummy was transferred in 1933 to the Peabody Essex Museum. The examination of this mummy revealed that Khonsu died between fifty and sixty years of age.

Altogether this burial assemblage is the only one in this tomb to recover the idea of the nested set of coffins, which is a usual practice in the "black" type. For these reasons, this is the coffin set where the synthesis between the "black" type and the "festive dress" type was most accomplished.

Coffin of Isis

Isis was a daughter of Khonsu and Tamaket and she seems to have married her uncle Khabekhnet, the eldest son of Sennedjem. Her husband owned his own tomb (TT 2) but, despite that, she was buried with her parents in the tomb of her grandfather.

She was buried in a single coffin displaying puzzling features when we consider the late dating of her burial. The lid reproduces the image of the owner prepared for eternity in the pose of the living. She is depicted as a beautiful slender figure exuding a timeless grace and youth (Fig. 134).

She wears an elaborately pleated dress bordered by a fringe and tied under the breast; one hand is held by the side and the other flexed across the breast holding a clump of ivy which gracefully falls along her body.[48]

A heavy wig with fine tresses is tied with a large diadem, whose front is decorated with a lotus blossom. Rings and pearls are beautifully fixed to the tresses. A magnificent *wesekh*-collar masks the entire breast; the bosom, shaped in relief, is decorated with rosettes. Charming bracelets, chains, rings and bands ornament the forearms.

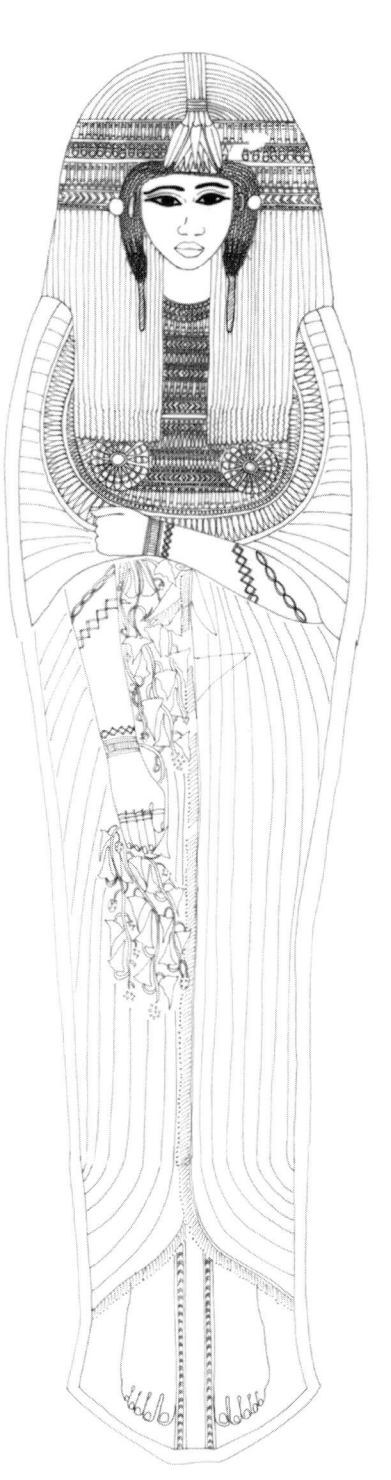

Fig. 134. Lid of Isis.

The layout of the sides is designed after the "black" type, featuring the usual figures of the four Sons of Horus and Thoth alternating with bands of text (Fig. 135).

Unlike the coffin set of her father, which was designed after the latest developments of his time, the coffin of Isis is surprisingly "archaic". Its layout follows exactly the same hybrid scheme observed on anthropoid sarcophagi from the late 18th Dynasty. The anthropoid sarcophagus of Ramesses I (1295–1294 BC), carved when he was still a vizier under the King Horemheb makes use of a similar combination of features.[49] The lid depicts Ramesses as living, wearing his ceremonial costume as vizier, with his arms displayed along the body and the feet crudely carved in the round. As in the coffin of Isis, the layout of the sides is designed after the "black" type.

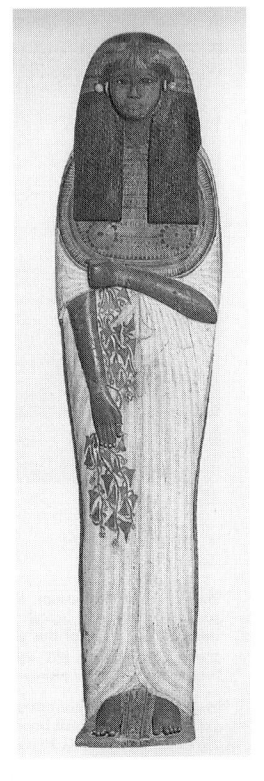

Fig. 135. Coffin of Isis. Egyptian Museum in Cairo (JE 27309).

On purely stylistic grounds, the coffin of Isis is the oldest of the group found in this tomb, showing the simple juxtaposition of the two types of coffin previously in use.

The mummy of Isis was wrapped in a mat of reeds. The craftsmanship of the mummy mask reveals a poor sculptural work, showing a crude treatment of the face, painted in dark red. The depiction of Nephthys at the back of the mask points to an early dating of the object.

Such an archaic layout of the burial equipment of Isis might suggest either that she was awarded a coffin that was considered "obsolete", or that her coffin was reused from an earlier burial. Given the late dating of the Isis burial, the archaic layout of her coffin set presents an inherent riddle.

Concluding remarks

Despite his apparently humble position as a servant in Set Maat, Sennedjem managed to accomplish a remarkable work not only in the decoration of his tomb, but also in the preparation of his own burial equipment. This accomplishment is even more striking when we think that the workers of Deir el-Medina only had one day each decade to rest.

Not only was there a huge amount of work involved in setting up the buildings and the underground galleries of the funerary complex, but the decoration of the tomb and the funerary equipment reveals the knowledge of a mastermind.

In all probability, Sennedjem was a craftsman from Memphis who, at the time of Seti I, was encouraged to move to Deir el-Medina. Probably his ancestors may have been active in Amarna and in Memphis, where they became well acquainted with the new imaginary of the afterlife put forward by Akhenaten, which revolved around the eternal and ongoing celebration of light. Telling in this respect is his small Ka statuette depicting the deceased wearing a ceremonial dress, entirely covered in varnish (Fig. 124).[50] The inscription that runs vertically down Sennedjem's dress expresses the ideal afterlife as an eternal engagement of the deceased in the sacred festivals performed in the Temple of Karnak. Although adapted for the Theban context, such vision of the afterlife derives directly from Akhenaten's reform.

The important role played by the "festive dress" type in the layout of the coffins of Sennedjem and his family reveals his deep engagement in integrating and adapting the ideas originated in the Amarnian reform into the traditional Osirian framework. This concern pervades the religious culture of his time, and it is detected even in the highest spheres. For example, under Seti I, the plan of the royal tomb adopted the same longitudinal layout first put forward by Akhenaten in his tomb of Amarna.

Illumination and radiance were sought as the ultimate expression of a glorious afterlife. In terms of coffin decoration, this goal was reached by adding the gleaming coating provided by varnish. A few *shabtis*[51] found in the tomb show further evidence of this trend, as they bear the inscription *sehedj Osiris N.* ("To make shine the Osiris N.") pointing out to the solarisation of the Osirian afterlife and depicting the deceased as a solarised god.

The burial equipment found in the tomb of Sennedjem, spanning several generations, provides an unrivalled corpus to understand this phenomenon. Of primary importance in this process was the integration of the deceased himself in the repertoire of coffin decoration, which had a deep impact in terms of the symbolism associated with coffins. The repertoire of the "black" type recreated the assembly of gods escorting Osiris in his burial chamber and in this context the deceased is identified with Osiris lying on his bed, thus playing a passive role. The "festive dress" type shows a new vision of the afterlife as an eternal interaction with the gods, and the deceased is featured as a performer of rites, thus playing an active role. The integration of both models essayed immediately after the reign of Akhenaten would eventually originate a new type of anthropoid coffin, the so-called "yellow" type, which only achieved its full expression by the end of the Ramesside Period. The 19th Dynasty and early 20th Dynasty bore witness to an experimental process where attempts were carried out with the goal of achieving the full synthesis between both models. We integrate these coffins into the "proto-yellow" type, which shows an unstable and highly experimental scheme of decoration. The "yellow" coffins are the result of this process, which transformed the "Chamber of Gold" featured in the "black" type into a multidimensional "building" featuring the landscapes of the netherworld. In this process, coffin decoration absorbed the repertoire of tomb decoration.

The inspiration for this phenomenon may have been provided by royal sarcophagi. The anthropoid sarcophagus of Seti I is entirely decorated with scenes taken from the Book of the Amduat, which were typically used in the decoration of the royal funerary chambers.[52] This is one of the earliest occurrences of the explicit use of the repertoire of royal tombs in the decoration of anthropoid sarcophagi. With its extensive depiction of the nightly journey of the sun, this sarcophagus may well have been the model for the new type of decoration witnessed in the tomb of his servant, Sennedjem (TT 1).

Prevented from using the compositions of the Amduat in his tomb, Sennedjem used the visual resources of the Book of the Dead instead. The quality of the work he achieved is outstanding both in his coffin set and in his burial chamber. However, besides the obvious beauty of the paintings, which betrays the work of accomplished artisans, the narrative character of the scenes shows a deep understanding of the imagery of the Book of the Dead and not just a naïve assemblage of scenes.

Moreover, the layout of the tomb scenes, particularly those displayed on the ceiling, reveals a new interpretation on the burial chamber, which in fact is designed after the layout of a sarcophagus. On the ceiling, the longitudinal and transversal bands of inscriptions are borrowed from the layout of the sarcophagus' lid, as they refer to the same deities usually mentioned on coffins: Thoth, Anubis and the Sons of Horus.[53]

On the other hand, Sennedjem's coffin was revolutionary by including the deceased himself in the iconographic programme of coffin decoration, which is a novelty of this period. With it a magical link was established between the coffin and the burial chamber, triggering the "download" of iconographic repertoire from tomb decoration to its burial equipment (Fig. 136).[54]

In Sennedjem's tomb, the decorative programme of coffin and tomb are so intimately intertwined that we may actually "see" the flow of iconography between them. This process established a magical continuum between the ceiling of the funerary chamber, the lid of the anthropoid coffin, the funerary plank, and eventually the mummy itself (Fig. 136).

In this way, in the tomb coffins of Sennedjem, lids and tomb ceilings were designed exactly under the same inspiration, providing the deceased with several transitions, one could almost say "layers", between the innermost sphere – the wrappings of the mummy itself – and the netherworld. In this context, the anthropoid coffin was seen as a transitional object linking the mummy to the cosmic sphere.

The personal engagement of Sennedjem's family in this process makes it even more meaningful. The Tomb of Sennedjem makes clear that, in a few generations, the layout of the lid evolved continuously. The sharp contrast between the parsimonious coffin set of Sennedjem and that of his son, Khonsu, shows that the concepts introduced with the "festive dress" type opened up coffin decoration to the exploration of the iconographic resources previously used in tomb decoration only. This was the key to the tremendous success achieved by the emerging model. The lids of the coffins

6. The Garden of Heaven: The family tomb of Sennedjem (TT 1)

Fig. 136. Burial chamber and funerary assemblage of Sennedjem. Diagram of Sennedjem's Tomb in Farid, Farid 2001. Courtesy of Hany Farid.

were decorated with miniature scenes featuring the deceased in (ritual) interaction with the gods of the netherworld. These scenes clearly empowered the deceased and enhanced his/her godlike status.

As a royal craftsman, Sennedjem was clearly familiar with the ideas revolving around the king's immortality. Despite the interdiction that prevented his use of royal imaginary, he dared to craft his funerary bed after the mythological model taken from the Book of the Amduat, which associated him with the dead king and Osiris (Fig. 137). By doing so, it is clear that Sennedem was versed in funerary compositions, which should not surprise us, given the remarkable consistency revealed in the decoration of his tomb and coffins. Moreover, it is clear that his intellectual interests were wide in scope, versing literature as well, as the Sinuhe's *ostracon* reveals.

All these elements show that Sennedjem was acquainted with the most updated developments in terms of funerary iconography and that his own background, firmly rooted in the Amarnian short-lived experience, challenged him and his descendants to pursue a new synthesis, a process in which they excelled.

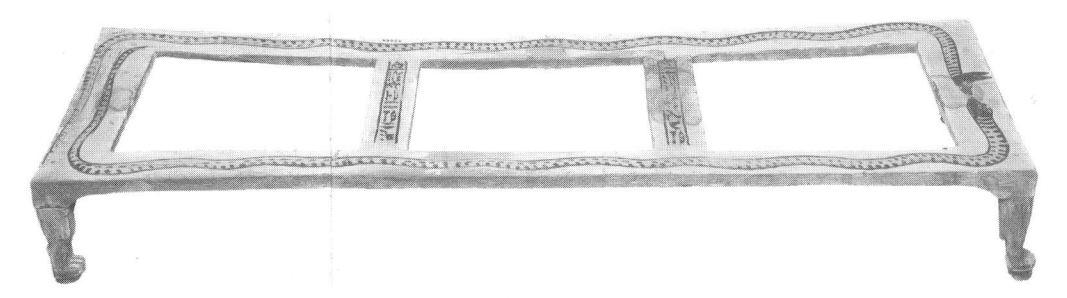

Fig. 137. Sennedjem's funerary bed. Egyptian Museum in Cairo (JE 27254).

The awareness of the importance of this mission probably contributed to strengthening the family bonds between the Sennedjem and his descendants. Khonsu, who built for himself a finely decorated chapel did not want to construct a burial chamber, preferring to be buried in his father's tomb instead. Nevertheless, he did prepare an outstanding coffin set, which included a funerary shrine, which stand out as a masterpiece of pictorial art.

Also his daughter Isis, despite being married to Khabekhnet, was buried in her grandfather's tomb, next to her parents and in a coffin so outdated in style that it could already be seen as a relic of old. Her marriage is also intriguing, as Khabekhnet, the eldest son of Sennedjem, was much older, suggesting that Khonsu and Khabekhnet kept a strong bond between them, which is also attested in their chapels. Despite having his own chapel, Khonsu shared with Khabekhnet, the latter's chapel from TT 2.

Besides the incredible wealth provided in terms of visual culture, both in the burial chamber and in the coffins, the Tomb of Sennedjem offers a rare glimpse of a particular family whose role in this process seems to have been rather crucial.

Notes

1. Assmann 2001, 223–224.
2. Assmann 2001, 223–224.
3. Bruyère 1959, 6.
4. Iyneferti dedicated a stela to Hathor, which was found next to the Ptolemaic temple of the goddess. Bruyère 1959.
5. The word *sen* means "brother", but it was often used with romantic connotations, meaning "lover", particularly in the love poems dating from this period.
6. Bruyère 1952.
7. Bruyère 1959.
8. On the lid of the sarcophagus of Khonsu, Khabekhnet appears with Isis in front of Khonsu and his wife Tamaket. Hornung, Bryan 2002, 146.
9. Bruyère 1959, 1.
10. *Lettres d'Égypte*. Maspero, 2003 (translated from French).
11. Bruyère 1959, 1.
12. *Lettres d'Égypte*. Maspero 2003.

6. The Garden of Heaven: The family tomb of Sennedjem (TT 1)

13 *Lettres d'Égypte.* Maspero 2003 (translated from French).
14 Bruyère 1959, 8.
15 The *pyramidion* is today kept in the Museo Egizio in Turin. Andreu 2002, 304.
16 Bruyère 1959, 11.
17 Bruyère 1959, 16.
18 Bruyère 1959, 18.
19 Bruyère 1959, 21–23.
20 Shedid 1994.
21 Bruyère 1959, 39–43; Farid and Farid 2001, 5.
22 Farid and Farid 2001, 4.
23 Bruyère 1959, 35–39.
24 Bruyère 1959, 27–32; Farid and Farid 2001, 2.
25 Bruyère 1959, 29.
26 Bruyère 1959, 31.
27 Assmann 2001, 285–318; Williams 2018, 12.
28 Saleh and Sourouzian 1987, 219.
29 Hayes 1959, 403.
30 Hornung and Bryan 2002, 150.
31 Hornung and Bryan 2002, 148.
32 Sousa 2011, 12–14.
33 Saleh and Sourouzian 1987, 220.
34 Hornung and Bryan 2002, 144.
35 Unpainted limestone figures carved of limestone bear short inscriptions giving in one instance the name of Iy-neferty (shortened to "Iy-ty") and in the two others that of Mose, probably a son or grandson of Sennedjem.
36 Andreu 2002, 298.
37 Andreu 2002, 298.
38 For the *shabtis* found in the tomb, see Mahmoud 2011.
39 Hornung and Bryan 2002, 149.
40 Sousa 2018a.
41 The anonymous "festive dress" funerary plank 1 (Michael Carlos Museum in Atlanta) presents a noticeable exception, displaying ears.
42 Sousa 2018a.
43 Stevens 2018, 150.
44 Delvaux and Therasse 2015, 72.
45 Saleh and Sourouzian 1987, 216.
46 Personal communication by René Van Walsem.
47 Hayes 1959, 417.
48 Saleh and Sourouzian 1987, 218.
49 Cairo Egyptian Museum. Saleh and Sourouzian 1987, 218.
50 Cairo Egyptian Museum (JE 27221). In Hornung and Bryan 2002, 144.
51 *Shabti* of Khabekhnet, from TT 1. See Hornung and Bryan 2002, 143.
52 Taylor 2017.
53 Bruyère 1959, 25.
54 Sousa 2018a.

Chapter 7

The healing light: The burial assemblage of the priestess Tabasety

During the reign of Ramesses III the Mediterranean world was about to collapse. A major movement of people spreading from the East destroyed the Hittite empire and caused the fall of Mycenae, generating a surge of displaced people, complete with women and children, seeking new homes.[1] Like a tidal wave, this devastating mass of people, a nation on the move, eventually broke upon the shores of the Nile Delta, forcing their way into Egypt. In Year 8 of Ramesses III, the "Sea Peoples", attacked by both land and sea. This invasion was smashed by the pharaoh, and the account of this battle is recorded on the walls of Ramesses' great funerary temple at Medinet Habu in Thebes. Despite the victorious overtone of the scenes, in fact, they witness the Egyptian loss of supremacy in the East, and in the long run, the beginning of the insidious infiltration of "Libyan" peoples in the Delta. Ceasing the conquest of Egypt, these mercenaries developed into a military aristocracy that would eventually take over the pharaonic throne.

As the long reign of Ramesses III came to an end, the massive displacements occurred in the Mediterranean basin eventually affected the pharaonic administration, as they destroyed the international network of trade and distribution. Internally, this resulted in the increasing impoverishment of the Egyptian population, in famine and social unrest.

By the end of the 20th Dynasty, the crisis deepened further, particularly in Thebes. The "year of the hyenas", occurring during the reign of Ramesses XI, bore witness to starvation, tomb robberies and thefts in the Theban necropolis. In Deir el-Medina the situation was so critical that the villagers abandoned the village and moved to the former Temple of Ramesses III in Medinet Habu, forming a new settlement inside its walls, the town of Djamet (Fig. 138).

To help him cope with this crisis, Ramesses XI encouraged the Libyan military cast to take control of the Temple of Amun-Re and a new theocratic political system was implemented in Thebes.[2] From the beginning, the main goal of the new high priests

7. The healing light: The burial assemblage of the priestess Tabasety

Fig. 138. The Temple of Millions of Years of Ramesses III at Medinet Habu. Aerial view.

of Amun was to deny the Theban necropolis from the wealth of funerary goods that had been stored in tombs during the New Kingdom. The necropolis had grown so incredibly rich that it was extremely difficult to control in times of scarcity and social instability. Besides the royal tombs, the Theban hills were roamed looking for old tombs, and marks were left by the scribes of the necropolis, stating the condition of each tomb.[3] These operations were not seen or recognised as a concerted operation of robbery but rather as a necessary operation used by the high priests of Amun to stabilise the area. A little before these operations had taken place, an earthquake caused landslides on the Theban mountain, burying temples and funerary structures set up along the foothill. This catastrophic event hid some of the tombs, such as the Tomb of Kha, preventing them from ransack during the 21st Dynasty.

The new burial ground chosen by the high priests of Amun to hold the burials of the Theban elite was now confined to the area around the former Temple of Hatshepsut (Fig. 139). Small undecorated tombs were excavated on the neighbouring cliffs, each one holding a limited number of burials. The burial set of the priestess of Amun, Tabasety, was probably found in one of those caches during the 19th century (Fig. 140–142).

Fig. 139. The Temple of Millions of Years of Hatshepsut at Deir el-Bahari.

The discovery

The modern history of the coffin set of Tabasety begins in the first half of the 1940s, when the archaeologist and ethnographer Werner Jacobsen was invited to a reception at the home of Ivan Lystager, an industrialist living in Lyngby, North of Copenhagen. On his way to Lyngby, Werner saw an Egyptian mummy at an antiquities shop. It was part of a burial assemblage including a coffin and a mummy-cover. The coffin had been previously restored and the mummy presented visible traces of plundering. Despite that, the burial assemblage was still impressive and Jacobsen suggested that Lystager should acquire these antiquities. The objects and the human remains were then moved to his residence and literally became part of the family. So much so that, when Lystager got divorced, it is said that Tabasety and her coffin set was placed in the bedroom of his former wife.[4]

In November 1950, P.J. Riis, Professor of Classical Archaeology at Aarhus University was contacted by the National Museum in Copenhagen announcing that Lystager wished to donate the coffin set of Tabasety to the University.

7. The healing light: The burial assemblage of the priestess Tabasety

Fig. 140. The coffin of Tabasety (lid). Antikmuseet in Aarhus.

Fig. 141. The coffin of Tabasety (right side). Antikmuseet in Aarhus.

When the mummy arrived at the museum, it was still wrapped in linen bandages. Some of the bandages had, however, already been removed, particularly in the area of the abdomen, revealing that it had been previously desecrated. The bandages that covered the face had also been removed, exposing the frontal part of the skull. These actions probably took place when the coffin was found.

Abundant clues left in this burial assemblage shows how it was dealt with by antiquities dealers. Probably not long after it was discovered, the burial assemblage found its way to the antiquities market. Here, the dealers "carefully" cut off the headboard of the mummy-cover, suggesting that its face was an attractive work of art that could be easily sold separately.

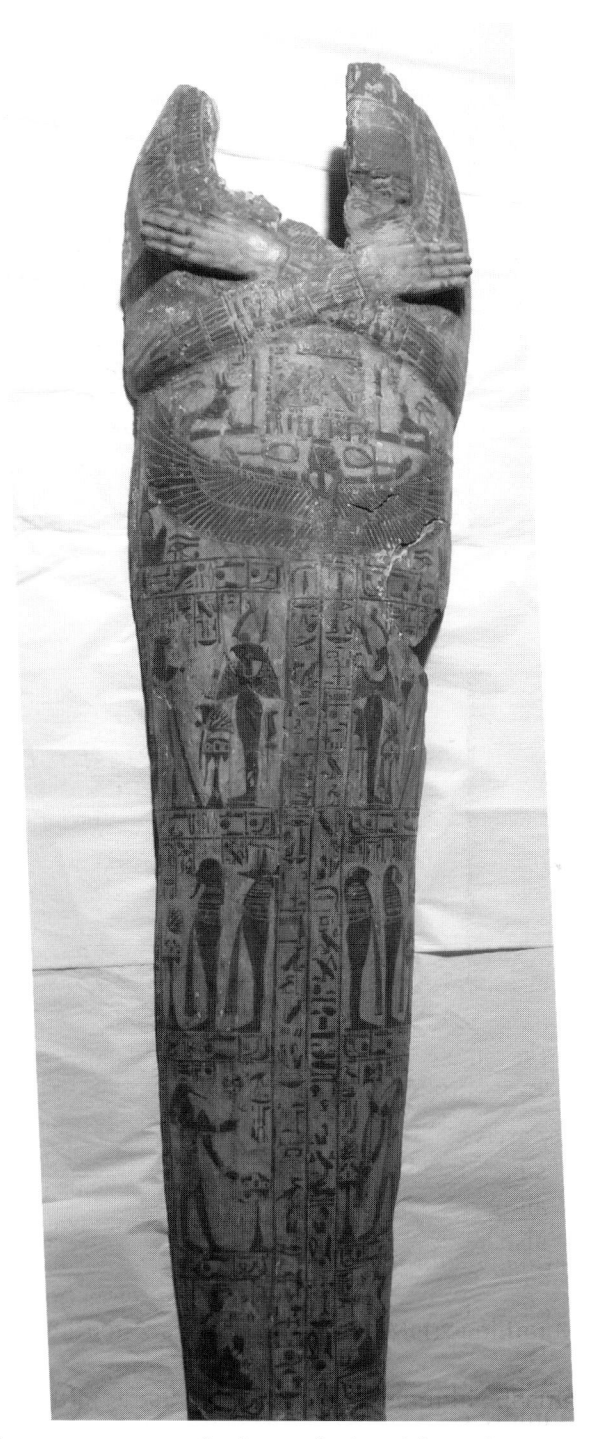

Fig. 142. The mummy-cover of Tabasety (right side). Antikmuseet in Aarhus.

With the headboard of the mummy-cover ripped out, the head of the mummy became fully visible, revealing some parts of the skull behind the disturbed wrappings of the mummy. At this point, someone had the idea to "embellish" the ensemble by cutting off the wrappings of the head in order to fully show the skull. This was done to enhance the visual and emotional impact of the assemblage on a potential buyer.

Aiming at the same result, the coffin underwent a "restoration" process. Careless handling and exposure to the air resulted in the loss of material, particularly on the edges and borders of the objects. The restorer added plaster where the original decoration had collapsed and did not hesitate to add fake inscriptions and iconographic details. To complete his work, the restorer outlined the beautiful scenes of the coffin to enhance the visual impact of the deities. The traces of this intervention are abundantly documented on the eyes, the contour of the fingers (usually over numbered) and limbs. Sadly, the lid was covered with wax to "stabilise" the pictorial decoration, which resulted in melting the vivid pigments.

Clearly, the restorer was aiming at impressing an acritical audience who was only able to relate with these antiquities from an aesthetical point of view. No Egyptological knowledge was thus expected to mediate the interaction with these objects. Such expectations point to a relatively early date for this operation. It is likely that the burial assemblage, as a whole, might have reached Europe during the early or mid-19th century, where it was eventually bought by a private collector.

The fact that only in 1940 it had been officially found is most likely related to the turmoil triggered by World War II. The coffin set was either confiscated or sold during this period and it eventually found its way to the antiquities shop where Werner Jacobsen, fortunately, saw it.

During the 1950s the mummy received considerable attention. Its examination was carried out by Carl Krebs at Aarhus Kommunehospital, using X-ray. This non-invasive methodology allowed Krebs to see the interior of the mummy. This examination showed that the bones had been heavily disturbed, probably by tomb robbers while searching for funerary artefacts within the mummy. The X-rays also revealed that the deceased was a woman and that no objects remained in the mummy.[5]

In 1983, a new exhibition of the Aarhus Egyptian collection was designed by Hans Erik Mathiesen. The coffin set and the mummy were the highlights of the exhibition, placed at the centre of the room together with texts, casts of a number of Egyptian sculptures, as well as a small collection of antiquities surrounding the central pieces. It was perhaps during the preparation of this exhibition that Hans Erik Mathiesen was inspired to have the mummy analysed again.

In 1988, the coffin set and the mummy were taken to the Forensic Department at Aarhus Kommunehospital. As the X-ray photographic plates from 1953 could not be found at that time, new X-rays were taken by Bent Madsen on both the coffin and mummy. This examination showed a chaotic picture with the bones from the upper part of the vertebral column lying diagonally across the chest. The thoracic vertebrae were placed on the right side close to the humerus. Several vertebrae were spread

7. The healing light: The burial assemblage of the priestess Tabasety

confusingly through the area from the throat down to the pelvis.

In the same year, a decision was made to unwrap the human remains and the linen wrappings were further cut, allowing all the bones and organic remains (Fig. 143), with the exception of the skull and the feet, to be removed and investigated in detail.[6]

Since then, the linen bandages and the human remains have been stored inside the coffin trough.

The autopsy was carried out by Markil Gregersen (Fig. 144) and photographed by Mikkel Randlev Møller.

Later on, in 1992, radiocarbon analyses were undertaken by Jan Heinemeyer of both the coffin and the mummy. The coffin was dated to 1301–1035 BC, while the mummy to 1320–910 BC.

In 2016, the author of these lines and the Director of the Antikmuseet in Aarhus, Vinnie Nørskov, carried out a new examination of the assemblage aiming to integrate the forensic results with Egyptological knowledge (Fig. 145). Quite providentially, Mikkel Randlev Møller assured again the photographic record of the new examination.

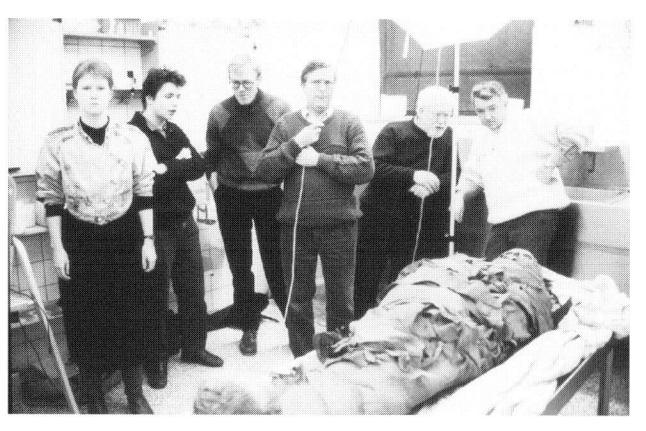

Fig. 143. Examination of the mummy at Aarhus Kommunehospital by Bent Madsen and his team, in 1988. Photo by Mikkel Randlev Møller.

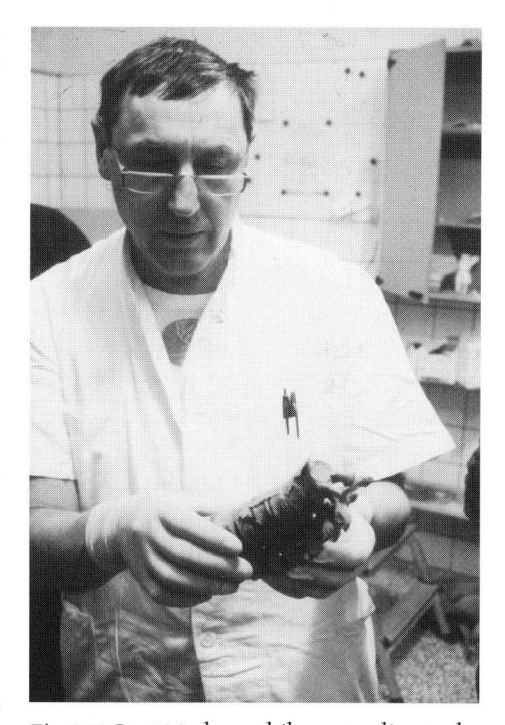

Fig. 144. Bent Madsen while proceeding to the examination of the mummy. Photo by Mikkel Randlev Møller.

The burial equipment

The coffin set of Tabasety is a typical assemblage belonging to the early phase of the so-called "yellow" type. By the end of the 20th Dynasty (1186–1069 BC), two new decisive inputs were eventually added to coffin decoration, originating a new type of anthropoid coffin. For the first time, the decorative scheme of the case – which during most of the Ramesside Period was

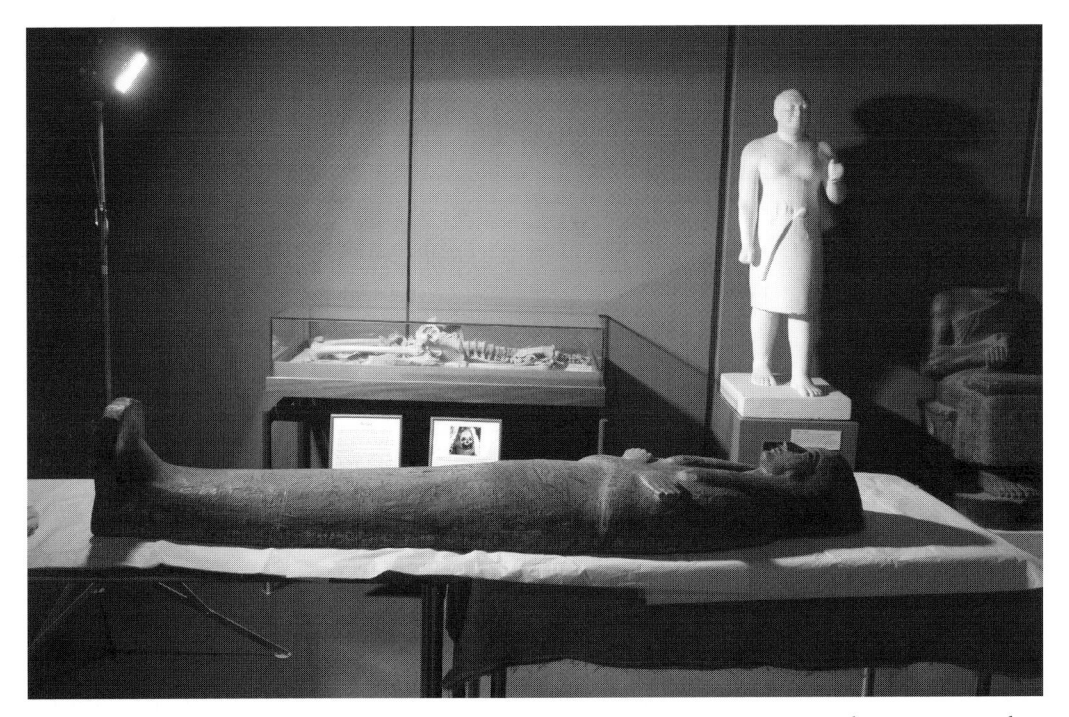

Fig. 145. The burial assemblage of Tabasety during its examination in 2016. Antikmuseet in Aarhus. Photo by Mikkel Randlev Møller.

designed after the "black" type – was challenged. The new artistic input already detected during the early years of the Ramesside Period, depicting the deceased in the decorative programme of the lid, was eventually extended to the decoration of the case.

Moreover, a new funerary object was created, the mummy-cover. From the magical point of view, this object became an unexpected interface between the interior and the exterior of the mummy. The headboard borrowed the features of the mummy-mask and projected outwards the image of the deceased as a living god, while the lower section was designed after the layout of the open-work boards, whose purpose was to protect the mummy itself, where the Osirian regeneration took place. It is not by chance that, once created, the mummy-cover became the defining object of the "yellow" type. Not surprisingly, when a new model of coffins emerged, in the beginning of the 22nd Dynasty (945–715 BC), the mummy-cover disappeared from the archaeological record too.[7]

Unlike the "proto-yellow" coffins, the decorative scheme of the "yellow" type is carefully codified, displaying a stable set of key-features that shaped both the lid and the case. This scheme comprises "autonomous" pictorial areas, combined in a global layout that forms a carefully planned "topography" with the following sections:[8]

Headboard – On the lid, this area includes the head and the wig, while on the case, it is normally composed of a tripartite panel.

Upper section – On the lid, this section is delimited by the contour of the forearms or the floral collar. On the case, this section is decorated as a whole scene, where the deceased witnesses important mysteries of the underworld;

Central panel – This tableau only figures on the lid and it is specific from the "yellow" type. The transversal panel illustrates the rebirth of the sun god under the protection of his heavenly mother, as well as his mysterious union with Osiris that takes place in the Duat;

Lower section – On the lid, the lower section displays longitudinal partitions decorated with cult scenes. Similarly, on the case, the lower section is decorated with scenes showing the deceased before a variety of deities;

Footboard – On the lid, the vignettes are depicted in reversed direction and they are consistently associated with mourning rituals or solar scenes. On the case, this area is seldom decorated but sometimes it shows a large *tjet*-knot at the centre.

The definition of these pictorial areas originated an unprecedented growth in complexity in coffin decoration, with each section evolving separately and absorbing an increasing number of key-features ruling its composition. This phenomenon created an evolving line towards complexity which is specific from this corpus of coffins. Using the sequencing method, it is, therefore, possible to estimate the relative date of a "yellow" coffin, even if we do not have any information regarding its archaeological context.[9]

The decoration of the coffin set of Tabasety reveals a number of key-features dating from the beginning of this process.[10] Particularly telling of this early dating is the single block-frieze adorning the upper edges of the case, as well as the direction of writing adopted on the transversal bands of the lid and mummy-cover, which are aligned with the case (Fig. 141).[11]

The coffin set of Tabasety reveals excellent levels of craftsmanship both in terms of the carpentry work and of the pictorial decoration. The style is naturalistic, reminiscent of Ramesside painting. The priestess is gracefully depicted wearing beautiful white garments, fastened with long branches of ivy issuing from her waist (Fig. 141 – compare with the coffin of Isis from the Tomb of Sennedjem, Fig. 135). At times, she is elegantly adorned with a red folded scarf on her shoulders. Her beauty is highlighted with transparent garments, reminiscent of the voluptuous forms typical of the Amarna Period.

In terms of pictorial art, the coffin of Tabasety, like those of contemporary women, present a break with the Ramesside tradition of tomb decoration. Once family based, the subjects depicted on "yellow" coffins became strictly focused on the individual. During the Ramesside Period, women are always depicted with their husbands, most of the time playing a passive role, escorting them and supporting them. The coffin of Tabasety, shows the deceased on her own, but the typical secondary role performed by women is still maintained, as she escorts the god Thoth (Fig. 141). As in Ramesside scenes, Tabasety always keeps a passive role, playing the *sistrum*, and she is never involved in offering scenes.

Despite that, the coffin provides a dynamic view of the afterlife in many ways similar to the pictorial programmes that used to decorate Ramesside burial chambers. In fact, as we said, the "yellow" coffin is a "topographic" object, divided into different symbolic zones.[12] It is a multidimensional object in which the decoration serves the purpose of creating several "places" within the object. In other words, the "yellow" coffin recreates a "building".[13]

The purpose of creating such a symbolic "building" was to provide the deceased with a dummy decorated burial chamber where she could live in eternal interaction with the deities of the underworld. The coffin of Tabasety is no exception to this principle, displaying the structure of a Ramesside burial chamber. In this scheme, the tableaux decorating the upper sections of the case show the paintings that were supposed to be found on the east and west walls, while the lower sections show the scenes that would be expected to be found on north and south walls.

Given this structure, we can now look at the coffin of Tabasety from a different angle, as if entering into a burial chamber (Fig. 146).

On the eastern wall of this chamber we would find the scene depicted on the upper section of the left side. Here we see Tabasety entering in the underworld playing the *sistrum* and making adoration to Re-Horakhty and the goddess Maat, the goddess of Truth and cosmic order. On the north wall, we would find the scene depicted on the lower section of the left side, where an abbreviated version of the judgment scene is shown with Horus, "the avenger of his father", addressing Osiris on behalf of the deceased. There follows the depictions of the two Sons of Horus and Thoth, typical motifs from Chapter 151 of the Book of the Dead.

The west wall would be decorated with the scene featured on the upper section of the right side, where Tabasety is introduced by Thoth to the god Osiris, enthroned over his stepped burial mound. As Re-Horakhty on the opposite wall, Osiris is escorted by Maat. There follows the god Shay, "Destiny", and the sacred Ram of Amun. This wall is flanked on both sides by Thoth, opening the Gates of Heaven.

The south wall would show the scene depicted on the lower section of the right side, where primordial gods are shown, such as Geb, the god of earth, the god Benu (the Greek "Phoenix", who rises anew from death), and Anubis. These deities protect the deceased when she goes forth by day.

It is noteworthy that this programme includes motifs from Chapter 151 of the Book of the Dead (Thoth, the Sons of Horus and Anubis), which used to decorate the cases of the "black" type, but their role is no longer as prevalent as before. Consequently, the Osirian "burial chamber"[14] featured on the coffin walls unveils before our eyes a wider spectrum of scenes, combining Osirian subjects with others with solar significance, showing a dynamic view of the afterlife exactly as Theban tombs did during the Ramesside Period.

7. The healing light: The burial assemblage of the priestess Tabasety 139

Fig. 146. The magical "burial chamber" of Tabasety after the design of her coffin set.

As for the lid, it shows the decoration of the ceiling of Tabasety's "burial chamber". The lower section is designed after the layout of the doors of a shrine,[15] showing the deceased before funerary deities (Osiris, Ptah-Sokar, four Sons of Horus and others). This sacred gate is headed by a "lintel" alluding to the solar rebirth, showing the heavenly mother and the solar child. This heavenly gate opened not only to the interior of the "burial chamber" (*i.e.* the coffin), seen as the territory of the Duat, but to the interior of the corpse itself, where the mystery of the regeneration of the sun takes place.

The upper section of the lid depicts the deceased as a justified goddess. Some of her bracelets are Osirian (compare with the bracelets of Senebetisi) while others are depicted with gods, showing that her body is sanctified and filled in with the divine presence. On her chest, a winged scarab is shown, alluding to the sunrise and to her own rebirth. The rebirth of the sun god and the resurrection of Osiris are also suggested by the effigies of Re and Osiris on her arms. These mysteries are experienced by the deceased herself, one could truly say, "in her own flesh". Her skin is yellow to suggest gold irradiating sunlight, so we can say that the yellow background of the coffin shows the "gilded flesh" of the deceased, as if her body irradiated sunlight. A similar significance would be found in the Ramesside burial chamber, where the yellow background suggests solar radiance shining from the depths of the earth, as it is seen in the Tomb of Sennedjem. The gilded flesh of the deceased and the "Chamber of Gold" are thus closely intertwined in the "yellow" type.

The coffin set, as a whole, was prepared as a sacred chamber to hold the sun god during his nightly journey, from where he emerges as if from the very body of the deceased. The scheme of decoration of the coffin as a whole results from two juxtaposed images: the body of the deceased and the sacred "burial chamber". This process is not new in Egyptian art, reminiscent of the layout of the Ramesside block-statues, where a shrine is juxtaposed with the legs of the individual. This type of composition makes clear the personal relation, one could almost say "physical" or even "intimate", between the owner of the statue and the divine shrine where his personal god took residence. The "yellow" coffin therefore, alludes to the personal engagement of the owner with the deities ruling the underworld, conveying the powerful idea that the deceased's body is the sacred chamber where they rest.[16]

In this scheme what would be then the symbolic purpose of the mummy-cover?

Coffin decoration also revolved around ritual aspects and the mummy-cover seems to have played an important role during the funerary rituals. This is detected in the way varnish was selectively applied over the inscriptions and vignettes of the mummy-cover of Tabasety.[17] This procedure aimed at providing gleaming light to selected motifs and was probably carried out during the funerary rituals.[18] The varnish was so abundantly applied over the winged goddess of the central panel that it poured down the cover in thick drops. It seems likely that this procedure took place during the mourning rituals themselves and not at the workshop: the crude way the varnish was applied on the mummy-cover contrasts vividly with the high levels of craftsmanship detected in this equipment, suggesting that this gesture was performed by a different actor, obviously not concerned with the technical or aesthetical aspects of the operation. Moreover, the object remained in standing position long enough to dry off the varnish, preventing the change of course of the varnish drops.

The mummy-cover was designed as a ritual and symbolic interface between the mummy and the "burial chamber" (*i.e.* the coffin), connecting the interior of the mummy with the netherworld. Also, designed as a sacred gate, the mummy-cover "opens" its doors to the interior of the Duat (*i.e.* the mummy) where the ultimate mystery of the solar-Osirian union takes places.

Mummy

The mummy measured 153 cm in length. The linen wrappings had been cut off on the abdomen. The bandages that covered the face have also been removed, fully exposing the frontal part of the skull (Fig. 147).

The arms were found placed in front of the pelvis and the hands crossed over, resting between the legs. No traces of hair were found. The nose cave (*conchae*) was found intact, suggesting that the brain was not removed during the mummification. Inside the skull, dusty deposits of organic material were found at the back, probably resulting from the decomposition of the dehydrated brain.

There are no teeth on the upper part of the mouth, or visible holes for them, clearly indicating that this woman became toothless many years before she died. The jaw has no holes for the teeth either, with the exception of two small holes observed on the left side preserving remains of dental bone. The skull lines were examined with an endoscope, suggesting an age at death of between 40–60 years old.

The bones of the skull did not preserve the skin. In fact, with the exception of the forearms and hands, most of the skeleton did not preserve any tissue at all.

Inside the body cavity, the ribs were placed all over within the thoracic and abdominal cavities, lying in different directions. In the thorax, several flakes of dried tissue were found. The lungs, in particular, have desiccated completely and were found intact inside the body cavity while other organs seem to have simply turned into dust. Since no trace of wrapped organs was found, it seems that the corpse was dehydrated, but that evisceration was not carried out at all. The total loss of soft tissues on the skull and limbs suggest that the corpse may have been overexposed to natron during mummification, which probably occurred whilst avoiding the decay of the unremoved viscera.

After drying off the corpse, the limbs and the head were covered with a layer of mud. This "cosmetic" procedure seems to have played an aesthetical if not ritual purpose, contributing to restoring the lost tissues of the body and probably aimed at the regeneration of the body, given the symbolic association between the mud (Nile flood) and regeneration.

This exceptional procedure might have been related to the actual physical condition of the deceased. The forensic examination of the mummy revealed that she would have been significantly disabled for most of her life. In fact, the severe

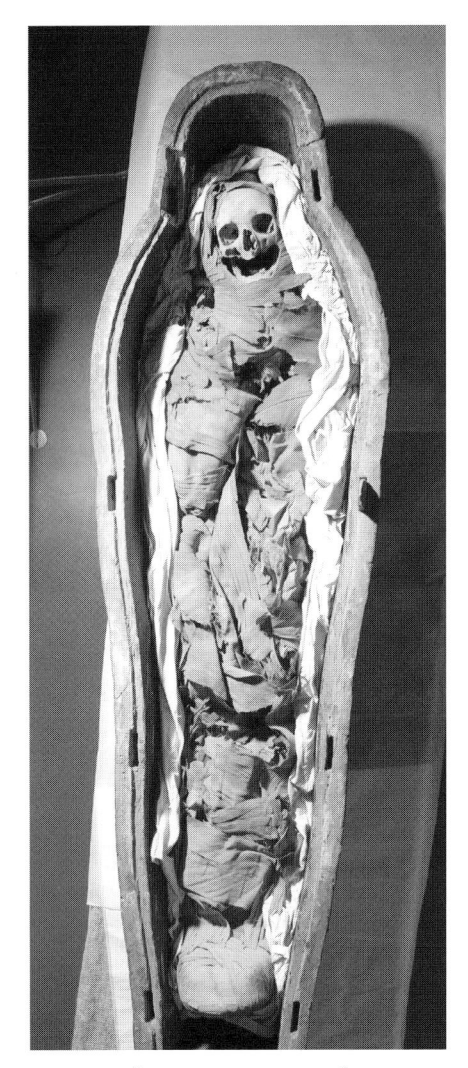

Fig. 147. The wrappings. Antikmuseet in Aarhus.

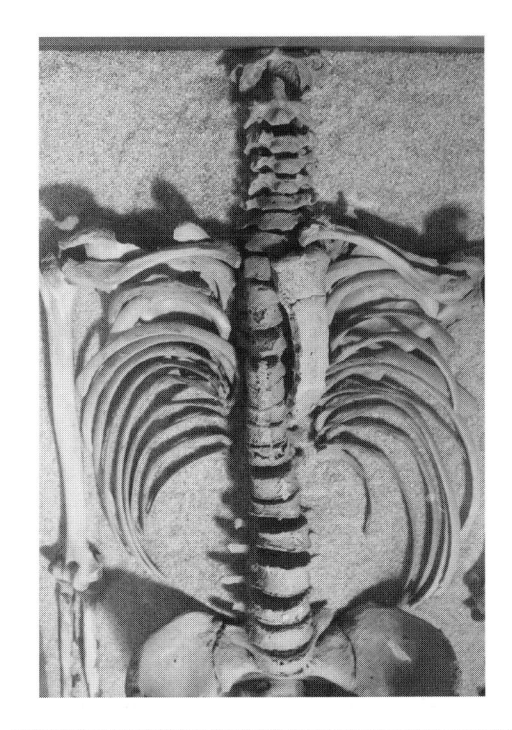

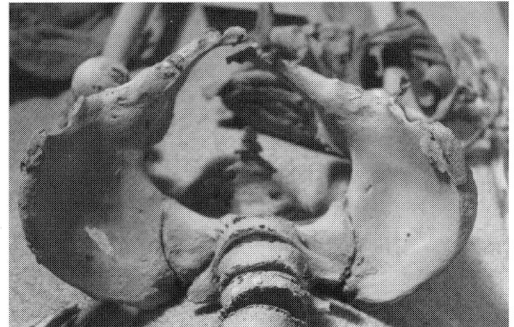

Fig. 148. The human remains. Antikmuseet in Aarhus.

fractures detected in the pelvic area occurred early in her life and some of them, such as a fracture detected in the sacrum, actually never healed.

As a result, a complete dissolution between the two pubic bones occurred, causing the development of arthrosis in the joint between the sacrum and the right part of the pelvis and in the left hip. There could have been a rupture of the joins between the sacrum and the hip bone too (Fig. 148).

Given the lack of other major injuries in the remaining bones, it seems that the severe fractures on her pelvis and sacrum bones resulted as a consequence of a single traumatic event, which happened early in her life, probably at the end of her childhood.

Small lithic structures found in the body cavity have been identified as urinate tract stones probably resulting from the deformation detected on the pelvis.

All these problems undoubtedly disabled this woman severely and made her suffer from chronic pain. Indeed, she must have experienced unbearable levels of pain even when performing the simplest acts of life. Walking must have been particularly painful. The two urinary stones may have been caused by the lesions that made urinating difficult, which also caused cystitis. Additionally, the deformation of the sacrum would have made her unable to bear children. The fact that she had a long life suggests that she never got pregnant otherwise she would have surely died in childbirth.

Severe signs of osteoarthritis were found in the backbone. These lesions must have appeared several years before her death. Based on measuring the long bones in the leg and arm it was calculated that this woman was 160–165 cm tall. However, because of the damage in her backbone, she was stooped during the later years of her life, reducing her effective stature to between 150–155 cm.

Concluding remarks

Despite the severe levels of disability, this woman had a relatively long life and it is clear that this was only possible due to the social support that she enjoyed. The fact that she was toothless many years before her death clearly reveals that someone was taking care of her, providing food that she was able to eat.

Her mummification and her burial assemblage are also telling of the special social status of this lady. Despite the poor levels of mummification itself, the way the corpse was wrapped in mud recalls the role that the Nile's flood played in rebirth and deification. The addition of "new flesh" therefore, seems consistent with the purpose of healing this woman from the painful life that she had. The mummy of the priestess was therefore, literally regenerated with new flesh, looking for healing and rebirth.[19]

The coffin set includes the state of the art of the iconographic novelties available at the time of its craftsmanship. Visibly, the object was crafted in a skilled workshop under learned supervision. The name of the deceased is mentioned in the main inscriptions of the lid, case, and mummy-cover. She is depicted six times on the lid as a justified goddess (lower section), twice on the case (Vignettes 2 and 7) and twice again on the mummy-cover (first register). In these depictions, her name is always added, clearly showing that the coffin was crafter under commission to be used by Tabasety, Chantress of Amun-Re in the temple of Karnak.

The poor state of preservation of the human remains – mainly reduced to the skeleton – is misleading in terms of the original configuration of the mummy. The careless handling by tomb robbers, antiquity dealers, and previous forensic examinations caused severe damage and most of the dried organic remains had been simply reduced to dust. It is likely that the mummy had been adorned with a few amulets, such as a heart scarab or a pectoral featuring a winged deity, as often found in mummies dating from this period.[20]

The stylistic criteria detected in coffin decoration point towards the end of the Ramesside Period and the first decades of the 21st Dynasty as the most suitable date of the coffin set. These dates are consistent with the results of the C-14 analysis of the wood, which dates the coffin from 1301–1035 BC. The dating obtained in the examination of the mummy is too wide to be conclusive (1320–910 BC).

Although we cannot be sure whether the deceased found in the coffin is Tabasety or not, we did not find any particular reason to challenge this identity in the burial assemblage. No evidence of reuse was found and the dating of the human remains is consistent with the coffin set. Therefore, it seems likely that the burial of Tabasety remained undisturbed during antiquity.[21] The mummy itself does not follow the usual layout known from later burials, involving exterior decorated shrouds with images of Osiris.[22] However, the quality of the linen wrappings is very good and they remain very well preserved.

Without further documentation regarding the life of Tabasety, one can only speculate about the traumatic event that occurred during the later years of her childhood. Whatever it was, this event changed her life dramatically. Given her condition, it is likely that she never got married, although the title "Lady of the House" is often accepted as labelling a married woman. If she did, it would be unlikely that she would have survived pregnancy. Without a family of her own, it is, therefore, surprising to find the title "Lady of the House" in her burial equipment.

On the other hand, her position as "Chantress of Amun" helps us to understand her status as a member of the Theban priesthood of Amun. Given the severe levels of disability she experienced, it is clear that Tabasety only managed to live a long life with the support provided by the temple of Amun itself.

The fine quality of her burial equipment and the fact that it was crafted under commission provide important evidence regarding the social status of this lady in the priestly community of Thebes.[23] Another interesting clue strengthens this idea. The longitudinal inscriptions of the lid are eroded in the area next to the footboard. In this area – and only here – the hieroglyphs had faded away as if someone repeatedly passed his (right) hand over and over again. This erosion might have occurred during the mourning rituals, with the attendants passing their hands over the lid, as it can be seen in the Ramesside funerary scenes. It is noteworthy that such critical levels of erosion are not usually seen in other coffins from the same period. The mourning rituals also involved the application of varnish on the mummy-cover. The traces of varnish left on the object show that it was left leaning over the coffin for a while.

It is clear that this severely disabled elderly woman held an important status in the priestly community of Thebes. Her name, Tabasety, is so far unattested elsewhere,[24] and it could have been used as an honorific title, perhaps alluding to her Northern origins, as it means "She who belongs to the goddess Bastet" or, more likely, "She who belongs to the city of Bastet", thus suggesting that the traumatic event that occurred during her childhood might have in fact happened in Bubastis, in the north. The fact that she was able to spend most of her life in Thebes is consistent with the close connection that existed between the kings settled in the Delta and the theocratic state of Amun.

Having lived in the transition between the 20th and the 21st Dynasty, it is, therefore, likely that Tabasety had been buried in an undecorated cache tomb in Deir el-Bahari, following the usual trend detected during this period. In this highly impersonal burial context, her coffin performed the role of the tomb itself, providing the decoration she needed for her burial chamber. However, the "yellow" coffin provides the deceased with much more than a building of eternity. It fully develops the vision that had been first put forward by Akhenaten, folding around the mummy wrappings of light where the deceased lives as if in perpetual celebration with the gods of the underworld. There is a strong contrast between the interior and the exterior of the coffin. The interior, painted in red, symbolises the earth, while the exterior coated with gleaming yellow, provides the realm of light. In this scheme, the mummy is hidden inside an earthly shrine protected by a sacred gate (the lid) which the deceased crosses to join the realm of light, engaging herself in the blissful experience of playing for the gods.

Notes

1. Taylor 2000, 328; Clayton 1994, 162.
2. Sousa 2018d.
3. Reeves and Wilkinson 1996, 205–206.
4. Sousa, Nørskov (forthcoming).
5. Holm-Rasmussen 1983, 99–102.
6. The forensic examination was performed under the supervision of Markil Gregersen. The team included Mathiassen (Classical Archaeological Institute), Professor Philipsen (Dentist School), his photographer, Mikkel Randlev Moeller, the Veterinarian Hansen, among others. Sousa, Nørskov (forthcoming).
7. Sousa 2018a.
8. Sousa 2017b.
9. Sousa 2018a.
10. Sousa 2018a.
11. For the general layout of the decoration of the "yellow" coffins see Van Walsem 2014, 18–19.
12. This process known as the architectonisation of coffin decoration is rooted in the deep change of patterns that affected the Theban necropolis (Van Walsem 1997, 359). From the Ramesside Period onwards the increasing scarcity of material resources led to a deep decline of tomb commissions (Cooney 2011, 3–44)
13. Van Walsem 1997, 358–359.
14. Taylor 2010, 114–115. The use of these motifs is standard in the scheme of decoration of "black" coffins and in the Ramesside "yellow" coffins. See Taylor 1989, 9–10.
15. Naville 1896, Pl. XXVI.
16. Sousa 2018a.
17. Evidence of the ritual significance of varnish when applied selectively on particular motifs has been recently pointed out. See Guichard, Pagès-Camagna, Timbart 2017, 177.
18. This procedure also reveals that the yellowish colour of these objects is the direct result of the use of varnish. See Loring 2012, 208–213.

19 Evidence is found of the use of mud in the decoration of the coffins. See Sousa 2017a, 126–129.
20 Aston 2009.
21 Later on, earlier coffin sets have been removed from the original burial grounds and became available for re-use, see Cooney 2014b.
22 Aston 2009.
23 On the relation of the burial equipment with the social status of the deceased see Cooney 2014a, 48.
24 The name Tabasety is not listed in Ranke 1935.

Chapter 8

The divine brotherhood: The tomb of the Priests of Amun

In the beginning of the first millennium, Egypt was split into two kingdoms. The 21st Dynasty ruled in Tanis, in the north, while generals of Libyan ascent took over the office of high priest of Amun heading the Theban theocratic state. From the beginning, one of the main purposes of this Libyan military elite was to control social instability in the Theban necropolis. The royal tombs from the Valley of the Kings had been open, emptied, and their goods transferred to safer deposits. The same strategy was applied all over the necropolis, which had been thoroughly and methodically dismantled.[1]

Emptying the tombs provided the Temple of Amun with enormous material gains which were used to consolidate the high priests' position in the Theban kingdom. The royal mummies, with the aura of sanctity they possessed, became an unrivalled source of political charisma. Under the powerful High Priest Pinedjem I, most of the royal mummies, rewrapped and docketed, were kept within a handful of easily guarded caches such as the Tomb of Seti I (KV 17), the Tomb of Amenhotep II (KV 35), and the Tomb of Horemheb (KV 57).[2]

Meanwhile, the new interments of the Theban elite were located in the area of Deir el-Bahari. Until the mid-21st Dynasty, this necropolis was composed of a network of small undecorated caches. However, despite the efforts to stabilise the area, at some point, the Theban necropolis was again under pressure and evidence of illicit usurpation of funerary goods shows that this remained a problem. A mummy-cover in the British Museum testifies to the illicit appropriation of funerary artefacts, with an inscription recording the restoration of the lid to its rightful owner after necropolis officials had removed it from the tomb and re-inscribed it for another individual.[3]

The situation must have grown to such an extent that perhaps during the pontificate of Menkheperre, it was decided to open the small caches at Deir el-Bahari and rescue their funerary goods and mummies in order to put them in a safe location.

Fig. 149. The Temple of Millions of Years of Hatshepsut at Deir el-Bahari with the Tomb of the Priests of Amun at the North-East corner of the temple's precinct.

A few of these caches, such as the tomb where the coffin of Tabasety was found, managed to escape this "rescue" operation.

It is possible that the materials removed from these caches had been transferred to Medinet Habu, which was now the main settlement on the west bank. Such a rescue operation demanded a massive storage of goods. For the sake of efficacy coffins and mummies were separated and stored in different magazines within the walls of Medinet Habu.[4]

Given this unstable situation, it is likely that new interments ceased to be carried out. Thus, newly prepared mummies probably joined the same magazines where the rescued mummies from the first half of the Dynasty were stored. During this length of time, mummies were "restored" by adding wrappings or inscribed dockets, after the usual practice detected in royal mummies.

A few generations later, by the end of the 21st Dynasty, a new phenomenon took shape and collective tombs started to be prepared. The Royal Cache (TT 320) received the interments of the High Priest Pinedjem II, of his family, and his ancestors, including some of the pharaohs of the New Kingdom. Perhaps at the same time, a new burial ground of gigantic proportions started to be excavated next to the former Temple of Hatshepsut at Deir el-Bahari (Fig. 149). This tomb, one of the largest ever built in the Theban necropolis, aimed to hold the burials of the priesthood of Amun that remained stored in the magazines of Medinet Habu. When the tomb was ready, a large logistic operation was carried out to move the burials from Medinet Habu to Deir el-Bahari. The tomb, today known as the Tomb of the Priests of Amun, was sealed with 153 coffin sets buried within its galleries. It was so well protected that it managed to elude tomb robbers for more than 3000 years. It was found in pristine condition in 1891, providing us with the largest undisturbed site ever found in Egypt.

Discovery

The Tomb of the Priests of Amun (also known as Bab el-Gasus, after the original *gurnawy* expression Bab el-Gasawsa, meaning the "Gate of the Priests") is located on the north-eastern corner of the Temple of Hatshepsut in Deir el-Bahari. The site was first spotted by Mohammed Ahmed Abd el-Rassul.[5] In January 1891 Eugène Grébaut was the head of the *Services des Antiquités*. At that time, when Grébaut was involved in the clearance of the uppermost part of the temple, Rassul approached him and revealed his suspicions about the existence of a previously unnoticed tomb in the area next to the first courtyard of Hatshepsut's temple.[6]

Following his advice, Grébaut started to clear the area and it soon became evident that Rassul's instinct had proved correct. Beneath a multi-layered pavement of limestone slabs and mudbricks, a shaft was found filled with rock debris to a depth of about 11 metres.[7] At the bottom of the shaft, the excavators found a doorway in the southern wall sealed with mudbricks.[8]

At this stage, Grébaut called his younger colleague Georges Daressy, who was then working at the Luxor Temple, to assist him in exploring the tomb. The impressions recorded by Daressy provide a vivid account of his exploration of the tomb. The doorway of the tomb was opened on 4th February 1891, revealing a long corridor filled with scores of anthropoid coffins, most oriented south, arranged against the walls, usually in pairs, with one coffin set over the other, leaving a space in between for easy access to the innermost areas of the tomb. However, next to the entrance, barriers were formed by putting three sets of coffins side by side and three others on top of them.[9] Between the coffin sets, in no apparent order, there were wooden Osiris statues, vessels, and canopic jars. The floor was littered with the remains of floral garlands and fruit, broken *shabtis* and fragments of coffins. *Shabti*-boxes with one or two compartments were located randomly in the galleries, sometimes far from the original burial assemblage. Some collections of *shabtis* were found in baskets, while others had simply been left on the floor.[10]

On February 5th, 1891 the archaeologists started to clear the tomb by removing the funerary goods outside (Fig. 150). This process was performed in two steps. Inside the galleries, Daressy numbered the coffin sets with labels glued to the headboard

Fig. 150. The clearance of the tomb. Illustration by Émille Bayard published on the cover of the n° 2510 of L'Illustration on the 4th of April of 1891 (with thanks to Dik van Bommel). Eugène Grebaut is depicted below the tent leaning against the balustrade. Georges Daressy is recording the objects.

8. The divine brotherhood: The tomb of the Priests of Amun

Fig. 151. Eugène Grebaut, Mohamed Abdel Rassul and Georges Daressy standing between the burial sets unearthed from the tomb on the 5th of February. Archives of the Collège de France.

(the numbers form the later A-list)[11] according to the position they occupied in the tomb, beginning with the ones closest to the entrance.

Outside, a gang of workmen lifted the finds up from the shaft, under the supervision of Eugène Grébaut and Urbain Bouriant, the Director of the French archaeological mission in Cairo. When receiving the objects, Bouriant assigned a serial number to each one (later the B-list).[12]

A rare photo recently found in the archives of the Collége de France, shows Grébaut, Daressy and Rassul standing amidst the coffin sets removed from the tomb, with the workmen in the background. It is the only photographic record so far known of this major archaeological discovery (Fig. 151).[13]

In a third step, the objects were loaded onto the steamer of the Giza Museum anchored on the banks of the Nile. Twice a day, a procession of bearers carried the finds across the flood plain, to be loaded onto the boat (Fig. 152). Émile Bayard, a French traveller visiting the site – and the only outsider allowed to enter the tomb[14] – witnessed the impressive cortege of 200 men carrying 30 coffins. With the objects divided between the steamer and the others remaining in the tomb, Grébaut had to assure the protection of both. He thus employed armed guards as well as the crew of the steamer to assure the safety of the finds. Daressy took personal care of the

Fig. 152. Procession of bearers carrying the coffins towards the steamer. Illustration by Émille Bayard published on the n° 2510 of L´Illustration on the 4th of April of 1891 (with thanks to Dik van Bommel).

security of the tomb and, during this period, he slept in a tent near the entrance to the shaft.[15]

The clearance of the tomb was done quickly. It took only 9 days (from the 5th to the 13th of February). With its precious cargo finally secure on board, the vessel could then set off downriver to Cairo, arriving at the Giza Museum in the beginning of May. Here, the material was registered in the *Journal d'Entrée*, creating a third serial list of numbers (the JE-numbers).

In 1892, Jacques de Morgan was appointed Director of the *Service des Antiquités*, replacing Eugène Grébaut.[16] At this moment, the diplomatic agenda of the period would play a decisive role in the ultimate fate of the antiquities found in the tomb, namely during the coronation feast for the Khedive Abbas II Hilmy. The crowded conditions at the Giza Museum – bearing in mind that this wonderful palace now contained 254 newly arrived coffins just one year after its opening in 1890 – was the pretext for offering a portion of this find to the representatives of the diplomatic missions present in Cairo for the festivities.[17] As a result, a selection of the Bab el-Gasus coffins was retained for the Giza Museum and the rest of the objects were divided into groups each containing 4 or 5 coffins, nearly 90 *shabtis*, and one or two *shabti*-boxes. The ambassadors then drew lots to determine who would be awarded which group of coffins.[18]

In 1893, these lots were sent to the 17 countries involved in this diplomatic operation.[19] During the following year, the foreign lots reached their destinations. Originally seventeen museums profited from the Khedive's gift, but subsequently the objects were reallocated. Once more, diplomacy would play an important role in the further dispersal of the collection, with these antiquities being used to reinforce political alliances or display the power of a particular regime. In Scandinavia, for instance, King Oscar II decided to divide Lot XIV between Sweden and Norway, which were still joined in a political union.[20] Lot VI would be drastically dispersed throughout the vast territory of what would be the USSR.[21] In Switzerland, Lot IX was divided to allow several cantons an equal share of the collection.[22] The French lot is also one of the most scattered of the discovery. Today at least 35 museums are known to house objects from it.

The tomb

The entrance to the tomb had been sealed with a multi-layered system of large stones protruding from the surface and concealing a pavement of limestone slabs. Under these slabs, a thick layer of mudbricks covered yet another stone pavement sealing the top of the shaft, which was filled with rock debris to a depth of about 11 metres.[23]

A burial chamber was excavated into the northern wall of the shaft, eight metres below the surface.[24] At the bottom of the shaft, a doorway was open on the southern wall. This opened to a long undecorated corridor hewn out of the rock, 1.70 to 1.90 metres wide, and of a similar height. This corridor was 93 metres long and led south, to the main burial chamber. The secondary burial chamber was excavated to the east wall (Fig. 153).

At a short distance from the main chamber (76.2 metres from the entrance) a second, nearly perpendicular passage was carved at a lower level, two metres below the floor of the main gallery. It is 52.4 metres long and 1.50 metres wide (Fig. 154). This transverse gallery was left unfinished.[25]

The galleries of the Tomb of the Priests were finely carved. Despite the undecorated walls, the tomb shows rather sophisticated solutions from an architectonic standpoint. It was provided with what seems to have been an efficient lighting system. Along the longitudinal gallery, seven niches were cut into the east wall for lamps (Fig. 154).[26] These niches were carved at 1.50 m from the floor and still showed vestiges of white wax which had melted and run down

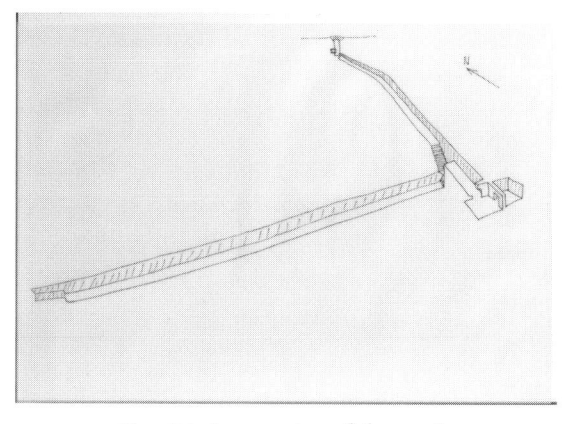

Fig. 153. Perspective of the tomb.

the wall. The transverse gallery presented four niches cut into the north wall for lamps. The main burial chamber was also provided with a niche for a lamp carved into the west wall.

However, by far the most interesting feature of the tomb consists of the sophisticated defensive device created to protect the funerary chambers. On approaching the transversal gallery, the corridor leads to a stairway, which abruptly narrows to half the width of the longitudinal gallery, creating a deep shaft on the west side (Fig. 154). If he would not fall into this trap, the potential intruder would eventually walk down the stairway finding himself before the transverse gallery.In this way, the funerary chambers would remain hidden to plain sight.

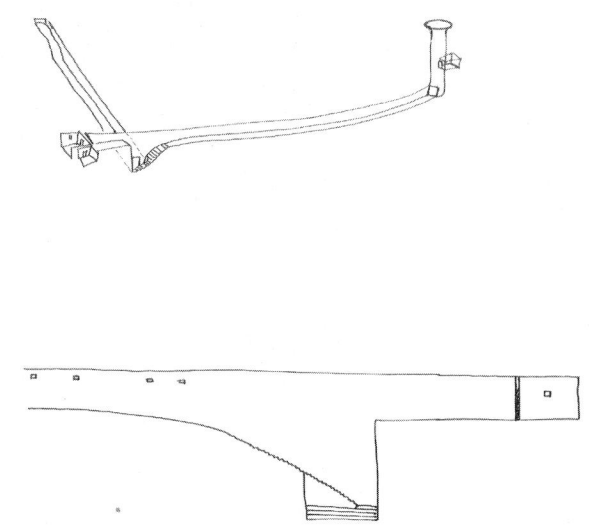

Fig. 154. The stairway connecting with the transverse gallery.

The burials

Probably during the pontificate of the High Priest Psusennes,[27] a decision was made to fill in the tomb. At this stage, the individuals responsible for the management of this burial ground had to decide who would be buried in the tomb. The burials found in the funerary chambers are clear in showing that the most important individuals belong to the family of the High Priest Pinedjem II, namely his brothers Tjanefer and Hori, his niece and even one of his daughters, Maatkare.

The burials of Pinedjem II's brother, Tjanefer A and his wife and sons were found piled up in the small burial chamber. The prominence of the titles held by Tjanefer certainly contributed to the notion of it as the main burial of the tomb. However, when we look at the archaeological evidence a different picture emerges.

The main burial chamber presented the coffin sets of two brothers, Hori and Ankhefenmut, together with other interments.[28] In this chamber, the statues of the divine mourners, Nephthys and Isis were found. Their role as mourning goddesses requires their "physical" relation with the main burial, which had to be located next to them, with these statues standing at its head and feet, as they are often depicted in the vignettes of Chapter 151 of the Book of the Dead.

If that was the case, then the burial of Hori (A.143) is the most likely to have performed this role, as in fact, it stands out as one of the most magnificent found in the tomb (Fig. 155). One of the most intriguing features of this burial assemblage

8. The divine brotherhood: The tomb of the Priests of Amun 155

Fig. 155. The coffin set of Hori and the possible relation with the statues of Nephthys and Isis.

is the depiction of the royal sceptres, an attribute missing in the coffins from the "yellow" corpus. We should note here that not even the coffin set of Pinedjem I displayed these attributes.[29] Another striking feature is the composition of the coffin set, which presents three wooden coffins, with the innermost of them replacing the mummy-cover.[30] To our knowledge, this is unique in the "yellow" corpus. In any case, during the 21st Dynasty, the absence of the mummy-cover in high elite coffin sets is only recorded amongst the royal burials in Tanis. Therefore, in many aspects, the burial of Hori suggests a royal "aura" and this remains a riddle, given the relatively modest titles presented in his equipment.

The use of three anthropoid coffins is clearly borrowed from the imagery of the royal nested assemblages from the New Kingdom. Despite this retrograde look, the layout of the coffin set of Hori stands out as one of the most elaborated, not only making use of a sophisticated programme with esoteric allusions to the imagery of the Books of the Amduat, as integrating the latest trends of coffin decoration. In many ways, the design of this coffin set can be considered the foundation stone for the development of the new layout of coffin decoration during the 22nd Dynasty.[31]

Last but not least, the gilded outer coffin of Hori was left undisturbed, while the inner coffins were plundered and their faces and hands were ripped off to remove the gilded foil, a practice also attested in the Royal Cache. However, it is important to mention that the outer coffin of Hori was the only gilded coffin found intact in the Tomb of the Priests, which somehow suggests the boldness of his charisma.

The examination of the mummy of Hori revealed that it was plundered in antiquity. For unknown reasons, its examination by Daressy was not completed. When listing the results of the examination of the mummy of Hori, Daressy states that *"le démaillotement n'a pas été términé"*, without referring to the reasons for such an unexpected and awkward occurrence.[32] Knowing how methodical Daressy used to be, this circumstance is deeply disturbing. Another intriguing fact regarding this coffin set is that it was never given general catalogue numbers, which perhaps prepared its oblivion on behalf of someone's collection.[33] These intriguing facts perhaps explain why this exceptional coffin set was never fully acknowledged with the boldness it deserves.

Besides the entourage of Pinedjem II, the tomb included a vast number of other interments. In all, 153 burials were unearthed in the tomb, revealing a similar composition of men and women. Many of these mummies may have been rescued from the caches previously emptied in Deir el-Bahari.

The picture provided by the examination of the mummies revealed that the community of individuals buried in Bab el-Gasus, the elite of the Theban society of this period, was heterogeneous, including both humble and luxury burials.[34]

The 153 individuals buried in the tomb provided a transverse coup of the Theban elite, revealing something like a "priestly community" exactly in the way that it could be expected to be found in a burial ground of this kind. In this context, the burial of Hori stands out as the "king" of this community, a status difficult to understand in light of our present knowledge.

Burial equipment

Once the mummies were selected, it was necessary to refurbish them with new funerary equipment, which could involve a double coffin set, a *shabti*-box, an Osiris figurine with a Book of the Dead, and a stela (Fig. 156). The examination of the burial assemblages from the tomb reveal different ways to form a coffin set. In general, the inner coffin and the mummy-cover were taken from an original funerary ensemble.[35] However, other assemblages are formed using objects without any connection between them, as if taken hazardously out of the available resources in a given storeroom. This explains the eclectic combination of cases, lids, and mummy-covers, as we often detect in the burial assemblages found in the tomb.[36] When a burial assemblage was formed, the available objects in the storerooms may have been combined according to practical reasons, often involving opportunistic choices. From this perspective, in most of the internments, the association of a particular mummy with a certain coffin set occurred long after the death of the individual.

Fig. 156. A typical burial assemblage from the late 21st Dynasty: outer and inner anthropoid coffins, mummy-cover, shabti-box with shabtis, Osiris statue with Book of the Dead, stela. The mummy is wrapped in a shroud sketched with the image of Osiris. Between the legs is found an Amduat papyrus. The heart scarab and a pectoral featuring a raptor are relatively common. The embalmer's incision is protected by the wedjat-plaque and inside the thoracic cavity wax figurines of the four Sons of Horus are found.

The same pattern of reuse is detected in other funerary artefacts such as the cloths that wrapped the mummies. Trying to identify the mummy using the information found in these sources can be misleading, as in some burials cloths were found inscribed with different names, suggesting that textiles had also been recycled from previous burials.[37]

Moreover, it is not certain that the quality of the funerary equipment can be used to assess the rank of the individuals. Our judgement on this aspect is affected by the dispersal of the find. However, the few reports left by Daressy show that a rich coffin set could be associated with a poor mummy,[38] and sometimes a good mummy could be found within a poor coffin set.[39]

A variety of artefacts was found between the coffin sets, namely 77 wooden statuettes of Osiris, most of them beautifully painted and hollowed out in order to contain a papyrus scroll with a short selection of spells from the Book of the Dead. The total number of scrolls found in the tomb reaches 123 papyri (77 scrolls were found in the Osiris statuettes, while 46 were found in the mummy wrappings), which can actually be seen as one the largest libraries from the ancient world ever found.

Nearly 110 *shabti*-boxes were found, each one containing dozens of *shabtis* modelled in glazed "faience". This new type of *shabti* alludes to the quintessential quality of "yellow" coffins, which was their gleaming light.[40]

Only eight wooden stelae were found. Normally they are decorated with an adoration scene showing the deceased before Osiris and an offering formula. The use of funerary stelae in the underground chambers of the tomb contrasts with the previous pattern of use during the New Kingdom, where they were positioned in the chapel.[41]

During the 21st Dynasty, the viscera are normally kept inside the mummies and so the use of canopic boxes decreases. However, it is noteworthy that four Canopic boxes had been found.

Nearly 30 baskets were found containing food (meat and fruit) or floral garlands, as well as ten vases.

Coffin decoration

From the 153 burial assemblages found in the tomb, more than one hundred burials comprised two nested coffins, while 52 were single. The total number of coffins unearthed in the tomb exceeded 250. The Tomb of the Priests therefore, provides the largest corpus of "yellow" coffins so far found on a single burial ground. Most of them show signs of having been redecorated during the second half of the 21st Dynasty.

The seriation method we use, allows us to estimate the moment when a certain coffin was decorated.[42] This analysis had shown that among this huge sample, we can find coffins dating from the late Ramesside Period to the late 21st Dynasty.[43]

During this period, at least three main stages can be detected in the evolution of the "yellow" type, each one displaying a stable set of features pointing out to a symbolism of its own.

Basic scheme. This stage is visible from the late Ramesside Period to the first half of the 21st Dynasty (Fig. 157). The basic scheme preserves a naturalistic style,

Fig. 157. The Basic scheme. Lid of Tabasety. Museum of Ancient Art in Aarhus.

8. The divine brotherhood: The tomb of the Priests of Amun

with large figures clad in white folded garments. The composition is light with the space between the figures left empty or inscribed with short label-inscriptions. From the symbolic standpoint, the outer walls of the case provide the decoration of a burial chamber, as it was conceived during the Ramesside Period. The most important section of the lid is the lower section, arranged in longitudinal partitions displaying funerary deities (Osiris, Ptah-Sokar, four Sons of Horus and others) and the deceased is shown actively involved in rituals. The resulting design of the lid suggests the layout of the doors of a shrine (Fig. 158).[44] The upper section depicts the deceased as a justified god. In all, the basic scheme features the deceased in the threshold of the underworld, from where he/she emerges as an active performer of divine rituals.

Fig. 158. Left: the lid as a sacred gate (Basic Scheme). Right: Gate in the Tomb of Nefertari.

Classical scheme It is typically found in coffins dating from the mid-21st Dynasty (Fig. 159). The style is increasingly schematic and the main figures are smaller. The composition is heavy with the space between the main figures filled in with liminal elements. Liminal elements are sacred or heraldic emblems originally depicted inside the troughs in symbolic relation with the mother goddess featured on the floorboard. From the middle of the 21st Dynasty onwards, these symbols had been integrated into the decoration of the outer walls of the coffins, filling in the object with the same sacred atmosphere that was associated with the interior.

The depiction of the deceased also changes: instead of the festive white garments used in divine festivals, he/she wears dark and tight clothes of uncertain significance. The variety of subjects decreases on the lid, which is mainly concerned with Osirian scenes, while the scenes featured on the case increase in complexity and diversity. From the symbolical standpoint, the outer walls of the case suggest the decoration of the funerary chapel, as it was conceived during the Ramesside Period, an architectonic setting for the display of ritual and/or mythological scenes. The layout of the lid evokes the plan of a royal tomb alluding to the nightly journey of the Sun god,[45] and to the union of Re with Osiris (Fig. 160).[46] At the same time, the deceased depicted on the headboard and upper section is now featured, with his/her arms partially hidden under the large floral collar. In this scheme, the deceased is figured as an Osirian and lethargic god.

Complex scheme. The growth in complexity evolved into such levels that by the end of the 21st Dynasty, new layouts were designed. There is a heavy uniformisation of subjects and motifs, all of them associated with an Osirian imagery.

The case now resembles a sacred chamber, often showing long registers extending themselves all along the sides. On the lid, the most important section is now the upper section, with the the Broad Collar reaching the abdomen (Fig. 161). The central panel displays three or more registers heavily decorated with liminal elements. In some objects this panel extends down the footboard (Fig. 162), reminiscent of the ceilings of the funerary shrines and temples, where a succession of vultures or winged sun disks can be seen flying along the longitudinal axis of the temple (Fig. 163). Once again, the lid alludes to the Sun's journey through the netherworld.

The role of liminal elements is even more increased, as well as the size of the large floral collar. Both features literally embraced the deceased alluding to mummification and regeneration provided by Hathor, the mother goddess who presided over the Theban necropolis.[47] Similarly, the depiction of the mummy braces introduced in the late 21st Dynasty alludes to the lethargic state in which resurrection takes place.[48]

The deceased is increasingly concealed underneath the heavy decoration provided by the

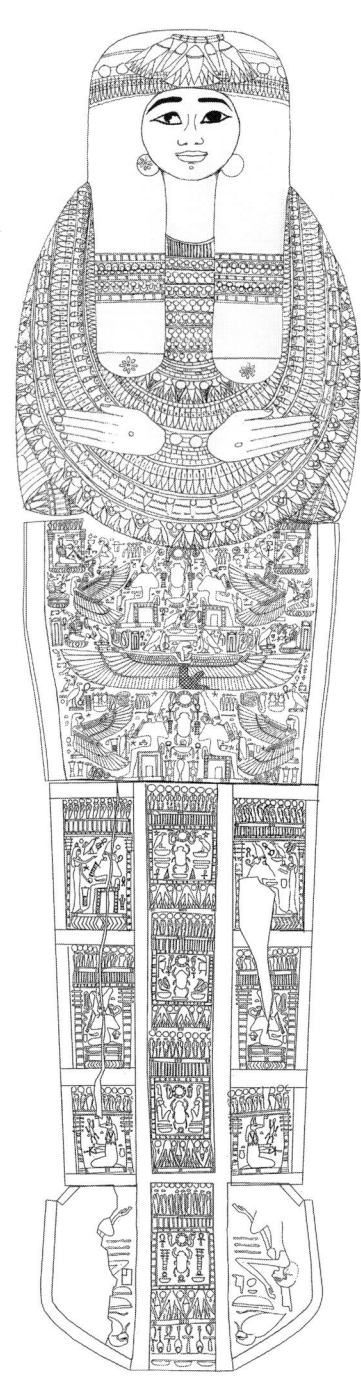

Fig. 159. The Classical scheme. Lid of Djedmutiuesankh. Geographical Society of Lisbon.

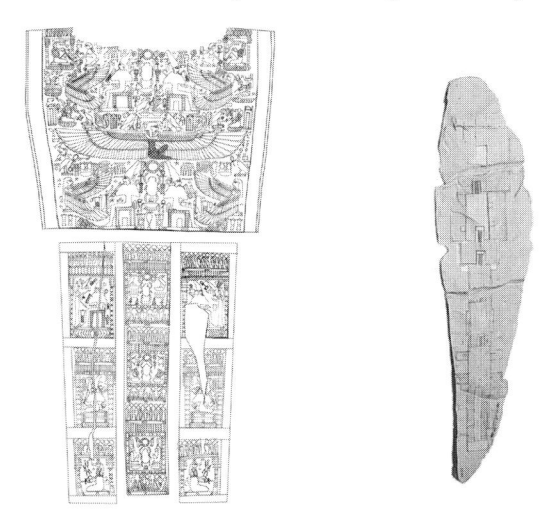

Fig. 160. Left: the lid as a royal tomb (Classical Scheme). Right: Ostracon with the plan of a royal tomb.

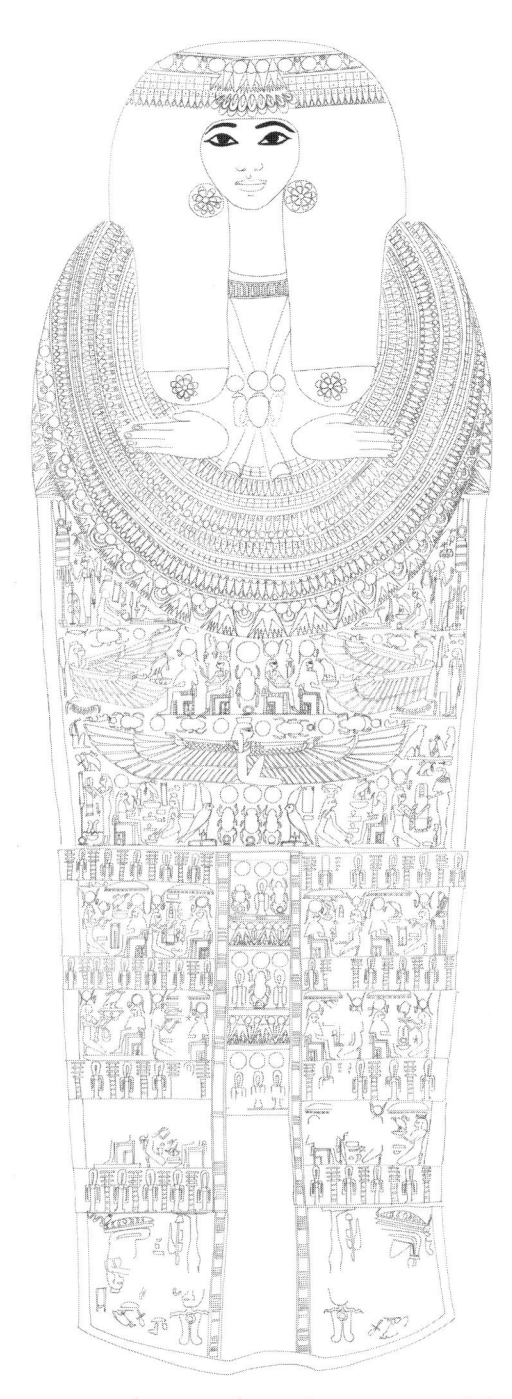

8. The divine brotherhood: The tomb of the Priests of Amun   161

Fig. 161. The Complex Scheme. Outer lid of Butherkhonsu. Kunsthistorishes Museum in Vienna.

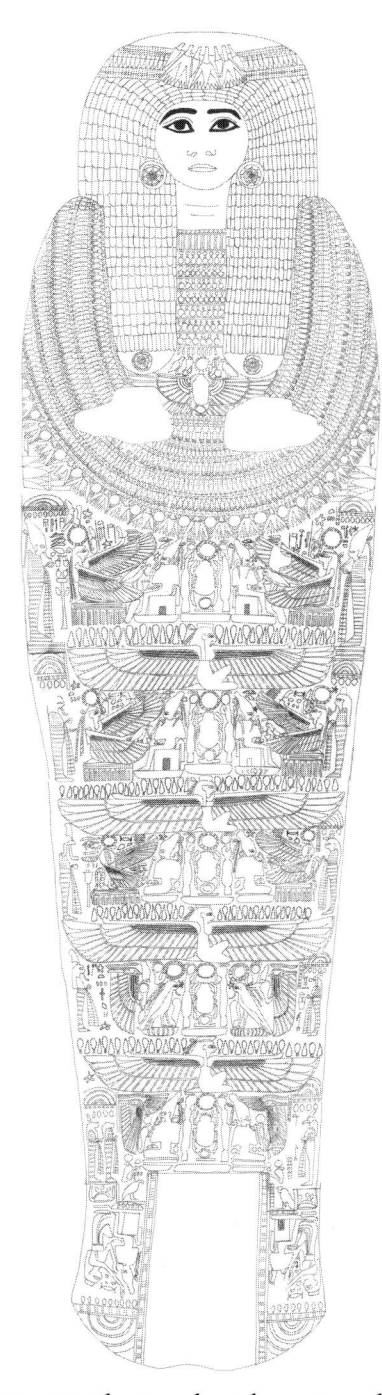

Fig. 162. The Complex Scheme. Inner lid of Djedmutiuesankh. Egyptian Museum in Florence.

floral collar and the myriads of liminal elements. Both the floral motifs and the liminal elements conveyed to the coffin the sacredness of the Duat and surrounded the deceased with the divine presence of Hathor, as if the deceased had entered into the goddess' realm to be regenerated under her protection. Therefore, late coffins of the "yellow" type depict the deceased as a lethargic Osirian deity of the underworld, literally embraced by the life-giving flowers, plants and magical symbols of the "Mistress of the West". Such embrace is figured inside the troughs, which are decorated with a large effigy of the mother goddess with her arms open holding the mummy within (Fig. 164). The mummy, on the other hand, is normally wrapped in a shroud sketched with the effigy of Osiris, the divine son of the heavenly goddess. Coffin and mummy thus convey the idea of the union between mother and son, from which a new life will rise anew.

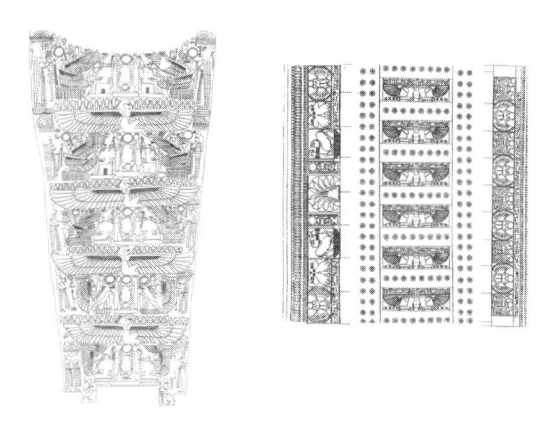

Fig. 163. Left: the lid as a sacred ceiling (Complex Scheme). Right: Funerary cover of Asetemkhebit, from the Royal Cache.

Mummies

Our understanding of the human remains found in the Tomb of the Priests of Amun is seriously compromised given their current state of preservation. From the 153 burials originally found in the tomb, Daressy only published a brief summary of what he had found in 93 mummies,[49] and only a small group of these mummies had been studied from a medical or anthropological perspective.[50]

This wide group of mummies had been unwrapped in two stages. Most of

Fig. 164. The mummy and the "semiotic wrapping" provided by coffin decoration.

8. The divine brotherhood: The tomb of the Priests of Amun

Fig. 165. Examination of a Mummy of the Priests of Ammon (1891). Oil on canvas, by Paul Dominique Philippoteaux. Photo credit: Peter Nahum at The Leicester Gallery, London. Fouquet is depicted at the centre, with Grébaut at his right and Daressy on his left, taking notes. Other Egyptologists witness to the examination: Brugsch, Bazil, Barois and Bouriant.

the mummies were unwrapped between 1891 and 1892, immediately after the arrival of the find (Fig. 165). Daniel M. Fouquet – a French physician who had first examined the mummies found in the Royal Cache – began to unwrap the human remains, under Daressy's supervision, in the premises of the Giza Museum. This process would only be completed in the Egyptian Museum in Cairo, from 1903 onwards, with Elliot Smith directing these examinations, which begun to pay more attention to the study of the medical aspects.

During the unwrapping, Daressy recorded the objects found together with the mummy, such as sandals, rods, and small boxes. The mummies were usually wrapped in a shroud bearing the name and titles of the deceased. Sometimes it was decorated with a large sketch depicting Osiris or even a reference to the High Priest or the Pharaoh under whose orders the mummification had been executed or restored.

A wide variety of reused cloths was utilised to wrap the mummies, such as tunics, clothes, or simply linen sheets. Sometimes these materials show evidence of having been previously used in other burials.

The mummy-braces, either found bent over the mummy itself or on its outer wrappings, are also precious sources for this kind of historical information. Nearly fifty mummies provided this type of historical reference. High Priest Pinedjem II is the most frequently quoted (23 mummies), followed by Menkheperre (11 mummies) and Psusennes (10 mummies). The Tanite kings Siamon and Psusennes II were both mentioned only once.[51]

Nearly 46 burials contained a papyrus scroll with funerary compositions, normally alluding to the Amduat. These papyri were usually placed between the legs of the mummy and sometimes on the chest,[52] around the abdomen,[53] or legs.[54] One burial revealed three papyri, an exceptional find.[55] Normally, these papyri display iconographic compositions.

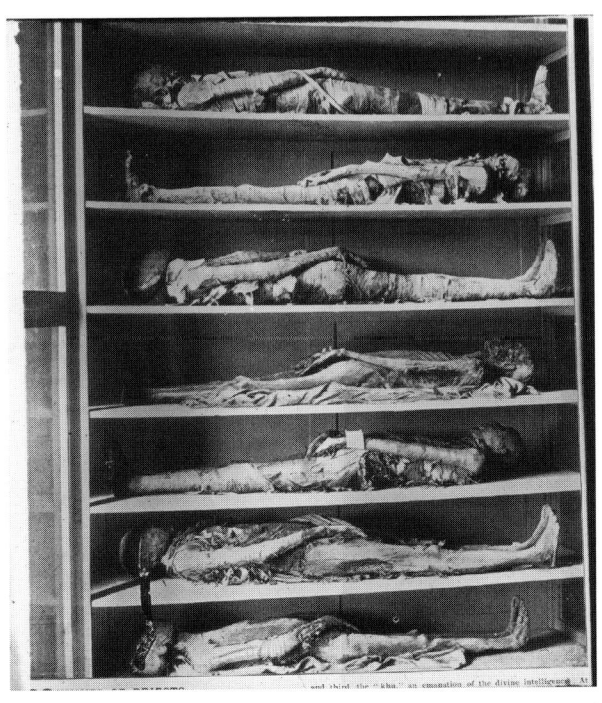

Fig. 166. Showcase with a sample of unwrapped mummies from Bab el-Gasus at the Giza Museum (Room 85/86)

The amulets found in the mummies varied considerably (Fig. 156). In the simplest burials, the mummy was merely equipped with a wax tablet decorated with the *wedjat-eye*[56] and the heart scarab.[57] Other items were included in more luxuriously equipped burials, such as the heart amulet,[58] a falcon-shaped pectoral (usually in gilded bronze or copper),[59] sacred cobras,[60] golden necklaces, some of them with gilded pectorals,[61] bracelets,[62] golden rings,[63] and earrings.[64] Small collections of amulets were sometimes found on the throat.[65]

At least 18 mummies were equipped with wax figurines depicting the four Sons of Horus, or even with *shabtis*.[66]

In addition, a large number of floral garlands were recorded by Daressy[67] and most interestingly bulbs were found under the feet and hands.[68] He also reported the use of mud sprinkled with seeds,[69] possibly resulting from a regeneration ritual comparable to the concept of corn mummies, and wax, as a sealing mainly of the eye-lids.[70]

On the mummies themselves, Daressy supplies little information. We know from his registers that many of them were reduced to the state of a skeleton.[71] According to his records, elderly people were rare in the community buried in Bab el-Gasus. Only one old woman is explicitly referred to in his report,[72] as well as a hunchbacked man.[73]

Among the mummies found in Bab el-Gasus, many of them revealed a premature death, usually before the age of twenty,[74] but it is possible that these estimates might be too low. It is interesting to note the occurrence of a dual burial of a woman and her child (A.83), which is an exceptional occurrence in Egyptian archaeology, where the autonomy of the burials is strictly observed, with the corpses kept in separate coffins.

Unfortunately, the location of these mummies is now lost (Fig. 166). The massive removal of antiquities from the Giza Palace to the Egyptian Museum at Kasr el-Nil played another part in the increasing uncertainty surrounding the current location of the mummies.

The plundering of the tomb

Despite the care involved in increasing the security of the tomb, Daressy noticed intriguing clues suggesting that methodical plunder of the burials took place even before its definitive sealing. While removing the coffin sets from the tomb, Daressy and his team opened the burial assemblages and pulled up separately the outer coffins and the inner coffins. While doing so he remarked that the exterior coffins of the double sets were often found unlocked, whereas the inner coffins remained sealed. Such a pattern resulted from the method used by the Egyptian priests themselves: they had opened up the burial sets and lowered the inner and outer coffins down separately. Perhaps deliberately, when they placed the burial sets in their final location in the tomb the ancient undertakers did not lock them.[75] The fact is that some of the coffin sets reveal intriguing traces of plunder, after their storage in the tomb. As we have seen, the outer coffin of Hori was left undisturbed, but the inner coffins were plundered and their faces and hands were ripped off to remove the gold.

Further evidence of this type of plunder is found in the most splendid coffins buried in the tomb,[76] suggesting that the systematic looting of the burials was taking place in Bab el-Gasus, surely by the personnel that were involved in the management of the site. It is interesting to note that Daressy still found fragments of beards and hands in a box. These objects were left behind probably because the amount of gold involved in the decoration of the faces was superior. It is, therefore, possible that the faces have been first taken out of the tomb and that the remaining objects were kept in a safe deposit waiting to be removed. The beards, in particular, were almost useless in terms of the recycling of gilded foil and for that reason were ripped off the faces to provide better handling of the objects while moving them outside, probably hidden under the clothes.

These are not the only signs of theft. Five pairs of sandals had been found by Daressy between the coffin sets. This type of personal object was normally kept inside the coffins, together with tunics and clothes. These sandals, in particular, seem to have been surreptitiously taken out from the coffin sets where they belonged, but for some reason the thieves were not able to carry them out.

166 *Gilded Flesh*

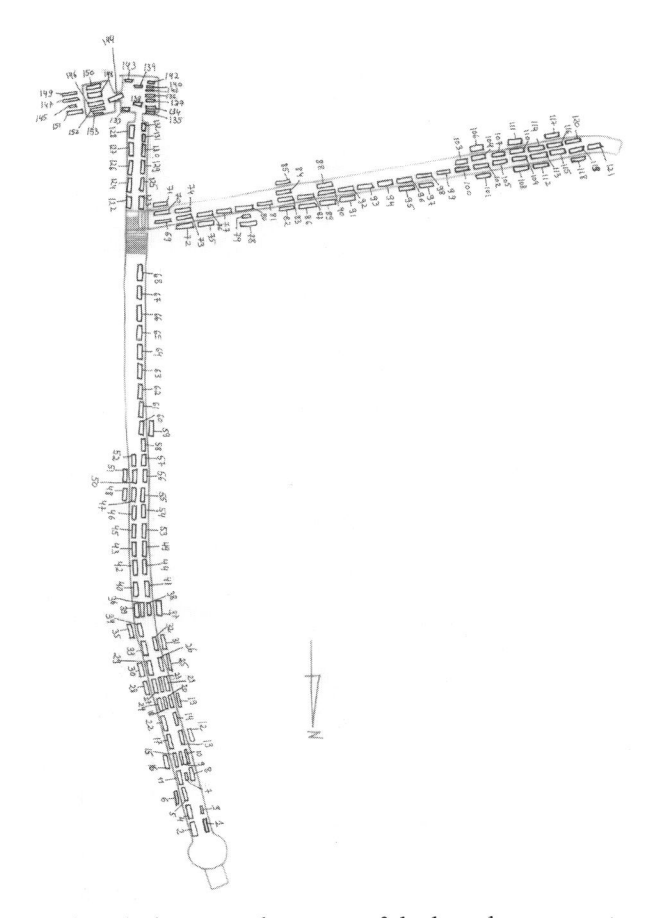

Fig. 167. Plan of the tomb with the original position of the burial sets. Drawing after Niwiński, 21st Dynasty Coffins from Thebes, table 1. The drawing includes the original burial chamber located in the shaft and the reviewed position of the burials, according to the notes published by Daressy (1900: 147-148).

The fact is that, when the tomb was sealed, with its 153 coffin sets buried inside its galleries, it was still well below its storage capacity, which could have easily held at least more 70 coffin sets, if not more (Fig. 167).

All these clues suggest that the sealing of the tomb was unexpected and that it remained open during a relatively short period of time. The closure of the tomb was probably anticipated to prevent the occurrence of further damage to the main burials kept in the burial chambers. However, additional evidence suggests that a "last visit" to the burial chambers took place shortly before the final closure of the tomb. Daressy points out, in his report, that in the stairway moving down to the transversal gallery, a ladder had been improvised by propping a coffin lid against the wall to provide access to the funerary chambers. He found the lid still in position, with the foot-board, hands and face scratched from having served as a stairway.[77] This piece of evidence once again suggests that not only was the sealing of the tomb unexpected, as the personnel involved in the storage of the coffins inside the tomb somehow "mapped" the potential resources provided by the burials and carried out selective plunder.

The definitive proof of this methodical activity was eventually given by the mummies themselves. When, later on, Daressy and his assistants examined the mummies, it became obvious that selective looting had affected the most important mummies before the definitive sealing of the tomb.[78]

Concluding remarks

One of the most intriguing aspects of the coffins uncovered in Bab el-Gasus is the anonymous character of a large part of them, even in the most splendid ones. The anonymous character of these objects suggests that their assignment to a particular individual did not result from an individual acquisition but from the commission of the priesthood of Amun, who would then redistribute them to its own members.

This idea clearly challenges our vision regarding the ownership of funerary artefacts in ancient Egypt. In fact, during the New Kingdom, private coffins are produced under commission and in most of the cases reflect the social status of the owners. This pattern seems to have been observed during the first half of the 21st Dynasty, as most of the coffins from this period show that they were specifically crafted to be used by a certain individual.

However, by the mid-21st Dynasty, possibly after the reopening of the Theban caches, this pattern changed drastically. In the Tomb of the Priests of Amun, the usurped coffins preserve the name of the previous owners, perhaps aiming at enhancing the association of the deceased with a (prestigious?) ancestor. Other coffins reveal in their inscriptions a space left empty so that the name of the future owner could have been inscribed later on, while others do not reveal any interest in mentioning the deceased at all.

The previous remarks have shown that a personal attachment between an individual and the body container is not detected in most of the burial sets found in the tomb. Therefore, coffin decoration during the second half of the 21st Dynasty revolves around the definition of the collective identity of the priests and priestesses of Amun and not the individuals themselves, who did not play any role in the decoration of coffins. Exactly because of that, each one of the priests could relate to the scenes featured on the coffins as if they were sacred chambers where he/she was depicted performing rituals and showing the required esoteric knowledge of his/her rank.[79]

Coffins were used by the priesthood of Amun as positive statements of discrimination of this social group, as a whole. It is reasonable to accept that the Temple of Amun controlled the workshops and managed the funerary artefacts as a "communal" property aiming at redistributing them to their members, probably according to their rank.

During the 21st Dynasty, coffin decoration achieved outstanding levels of complexity and elaboration. The craftsmanship of these objects became a cutting-edge industry which was only paralleled by tomb decoration during the 18th and 19th Dynasties. From the 20th Dynasty onwards, the coffin assumed much of the traditional symbolic role of the tomb, but it definitely ceased to celebrate the individual, privileging the definition of the dominant social group instead.

Hence, coffins became the privileged media to convey the corporative values of the priesthood of Amun. In all, the information collected thus far clearly shows that by the late 21st Dynasty, funerary artefacts were managed as corporative goods, being produced, recycled and redistributed centrally by the Temple of Amun.

The construction of new tombs during the late 21st Dynasty, such as the Tomb of the Priests, reveals a turning moment in the pattern of occupation of the Theban necropolis. With this tomb, a totally different phenomenon emerges: the excavation of a new funerary site designed from the start to be used as a collective burial ground. The decision of building such tombs was probably taken after using the Royal Cache to hold the interments of the High Priest Pinedjem II and his immediate family.[80]

The Tomb of the Priests was excavated at the bottom of a deep shaft, from where the enormous amount of debris hewn out of the rock had to be lifted up to the surface. From a technical standpoint, it represented a tremendous effort, as nothing of this size had been built since at least the reign of Ramesses VI (1143–1136 BC).[81]

The decision to build a collective burial ground presupposes a new awareness of the Theban priesthood as a coherent social group, with a strong sense of collective identity. Such awareness is probably related to other important corporative achievements, such as the construction of communal houses for the priests of Amun in the sacred precinct of Karnak itself. The houses of this priests' quarter were built in mudbrick on the east bank of the sacred lake. They vary in size (58 m^2 for the smallest, 176 m^2 for the biggest), and are well individualised, showing typical features known from terraced houses.[82] It is, therefore, interesting to see that a corporative identity of the priests of Amun was emerging, and not only at the funerary level. Therefore, a collective burial ground such as this one, may not result from defensive purposes alone, but from a new awareness of this social group, with an identity of its own.

In Thebes, the historical antecedent of this type of funerary site is to be found in the Tomb of the Sons of Ramesses II (KV 5),[83] which literally held the brotherhood of the sons of the Pharaoh. It is, therefore, interesting to relate the creation of this new type of burial ground during the theocratic State of Amun with a new ideological definition of the status and identity of the priests of Amun. As a collective burial ground, the Tomb of the Priests of Amun reveals a new understanding of this community as a ritual "brotherhood" of men and women serving under the theocratic rule of Amun, i.e., the "king of gods".[84] This may have implied that a new awareness was rising amongst the priesthood of Amun regarding its identity as a privileged social group.

The most distinctive aspect of the funerary material culture from this period is the prevalence given to iconography. Visual arts literally fill in papyri and coffins giving full visibility to the underworld, a phenomenon typically associated with the "yellow" coffins. With them, Egyptian visual culture shifted from the visibility of the earthly life to the netherworld. From the symbolic standpoint, funerary visual culture of this period is focused on the nightly journey of the sun, while previously it was confined to the daily circuit of the sun.

The yellow coffins thus described the netherworld as a realm of light, where the sun god unites with Osiris, providing the deceased with the nest of light of his/her heavenly mother, and allowing the "gilded flesh" of the deceased to shine over in the midst of deep darkness. In a way, "yellow" coffins created a revolutionary vision of the netherworld by adopting the visual schemes introduced by Akhenaton in his reform and using them to give visibility to the Osirian netherworld. By doing so, they fully solarised Osirian imaginary.

In this highly speculative context, the traditional role played by the Ka and its cult faded away to such an extent that it is only detected in short, one could say secondary, inscriptions. The pursuit of light and rebirth plays by far a bolder role in the funerary equipment of this brotherhood of men and women serving the supreme god Amun-Re, the king of gods.

Notes

1 Reeves and Wilkinson 1996, 205.
2 Reeves and Wilkinson 1996, 205.
3 Taylor 2001, 181.
4 Sousa 2018b, 537–538.
5 Daressy 1900, 142.
6 Daressy 1900, 142.
7 Daressy, 1900, 146; Sousa 2018c.
8 Daressy 1900, 142.
9 Daressy 1900, 143.
10 Daressy 1907, 12.
11 Daressy 1907, 3.
12 Daressy 1907, 3.
13 Grimal 2017.
14 Daressy 1900, 143.
15 Daressy 1900, 144.
16 Orsenigo 2010, 132.
17 Lipinska 1993–1994, 48–60.
18 Lipinska 1993–1994, 48–60.
19 Lot I (France), Lot II (Austria), Lot III (Turkey), Lot IV (United Kingdom), Lot V (Italy), Lot VI (Russia), Lot VII (Germany), Lot VIII (Portugal), Lot IX (Switzerland), Lot X (USA), Lot XI (Netherlands), Lot XII (Greece), Lot XIII (Spain), Lot XIV (Sweden-Norway), Lot XV (Belgium), Lot XVI (Denmark), Lot XVII (Vatican).
20 Bettum 2014, 167–186.
21 Tarasenko 2017.

22 Küffer 2007.
23 Daressy 1900, 146; Sousa 2017c, 21–22.
24 Daressy 1907, 142.
25 Niwiński 1984, 74.
26 The location of these niches is carefully indicated by Daressy in the plans published in 1900, 146.
27 Niwiński 1988, 118.
28 Broekman 2018, 17.
29 His fists grasp *tjet* and *djed*-signs.
30 Niwiński 1988, Pl. XIII.
31 Sousa 2018c.
32 Daressy 1907, 36–37.
33 Lipinska 1993–1994, 48–60.
34 Sousa 2018b.
35 Sousa 2018b.
36 A.60 (Sousa 2018b) A.136 (Sousa 2017a).
37 See burial assemblage A.20, in Sousa 2018b.
38 See A.15 in Sousa 2018b, 532.
39 See A.20 in Sousa 2018b, 532–533.
40 Sousa 2018a.
41 Grajetzki 2013.
42 Sousa 2018a.
43 Coffin A.56, outer coffin from A.60 and inner coffin from A.15.
44 Naville 1896, Pl. XXVI.
45 Weiss 2017, 222–230.
46 Taylor 2016a, 49.
47 Sousa 2018a.
48 Smith 1906, 155–160; Van Walsem 1997, 117.
49 Daressy 1907, 22–38.
50 Daressy 1902, 152–154; Daressy 1902b, 155–157; Daressy 1903, 150–155; Smith 1903, 156–160; Smith 1906, 155–182.
51 Daressy 1907.
52 A.81, A.98, A.127.
53 A.113, A.127, A.150. Daressy 1907.
54 A.152. Daressy 1907.
55 A.127. Daressy 1907.
56 *Wedjat*-plaques were found in nearly 45 mummies. Daressy 1907.
57 Heart scarabs were found in nearly 43 mummies. Daressy 1907.
58 Heart amulets were found in at least nine mummies. Daressy 1907.
59 This type of pectoral was found in 19 mummies. Daressy 1907.
60 Three occurrences were reported, normally on the forehead (A.85, A.98, A.127 e A.151). Daressy 1907.
61 Two occurrences were reported (A.50, A.139), one with golden beads (A.50) and the other composed of small amulets (A.139). Daressy 1907.
62 Three occurrences were reported (A.50, A.133, A.139). Daressy 1907.
63 A.50, A.83. Daressy 1907.
64 A.50. Daressy 1907.
65 A.65, A.84, A.125. Daressy 1907.
66 In A.32. Smith 1906, 155-160.

67 A.66, A.72, A.77, A.116, A.127, A.134, A.148, A.151. Daressy 1907.
68 A.82, A.120, A.151, A.127. Daressy 1907.
69 A.129. Daressy 1907.
70 A.133. Daressy 1907.
71 A.6, A.25. Daressy 1907.
72 A.133. Daressy 1907.
73 A.35. Daressy 1907.
74 A.20, A.50, A.127. Daressy 1907.
75 Daressy 1896, 73
76 Daressy 1900, 143.
77 Daressy 1900, 142.
78 A.130, A.132, and A.143.
79 Gasse 1996, Pl. XXVIII; Araújo Duarte 2014, 89; Liptay 2014, 75–76; Taylor 2010, 132–140.
80 Graefe 2003; Niwiński 1984a, 80; Dodson and Ikram 2008, 273.
81 Compare with the structure of the royal tombs in Reeves and Wilkinson 1996, 165.
82 Millet and Masson 2011, 7.
83 Weeks 1999, 240–241.
84 Sousa 2014, 107.

Chapter 9

Conclusion

Coffin and funerary space

Coffins provided protection, transport and ritual mediation with the mummy during the funerary rites. Besides reaching these goals, coffins were crafted with the funerary setting in mind, where eventually they would be integrated. As the key-piece of the burial set, the coffin was not prepared in isolation, but as part of a wider assemblage that included the tomb, the funerary equipment and of course the mummy itself.

Egyptian elite tombs are strictly codified spaces with a semantic of their own. Objects and representations interact in such a way as to allow a flexible combination of the available resources. For example, the concern for food supply remained an important aspect of material funerary culture until the Ramesside Period. However, the way this concern was materialised greatly differed. During the Early Dynastic Period, graves were provided with a wealth of food supplies but, during the Old Kingdom, representations featuring the process of their production was favoured instead. When decorated tombs ceased to be produced in the Second Intermediate Period, earthly goods returned again to the grave. Later on, during the 18th Dynasty, tomb decoration involved more theological aspects and again earthly goods were included in the burial chamber as most of them were not featured in the tomb paintings. Finally, by the end of the Ramesside Period, the production of food is entirely projected in the mythical Fields of Iaru and entrusted to *shabtis*. Consequently, agricultural scenes and food offerings decreased significantly in these burials.

As in any Nilotic dwelling, the arrangement of the burial ground in a certain necropolis is deeply affected by the social organisation of that particular community. In its roots, the tomb illustrates a social phenomenon rather than an individual will, although at times, we may witness to interesting "personal interpretations" of the funerary space.

In this holistic view, the decoration of the coffin interacts with the tomb, connecting the deceased with the underworld, and the world of the living. Deeply rooted in the primordial need of providing a shelter for the deceased,[1] coffins truly recreate a magical dwelling where images and texts play a protective role. Cosmic integration and protection are the two main purposes that coffin decoration is summoned to fulfil. We will now briefly review how these needs were transposed to the design of coffins and how they interacted with the remaining features of the tomb.

The rebirth hut

Since Predynastic times, the preservation of the body required the development of specialised techniques and skills extended to other forms of craftsmanship, from pottery to masonry, which were necessary to equip the tombs.

In fact, most of the objects found in Predynastic graves were produced specifically for funerary contexts. Pottery vessels are particularly important, indicating a wish to secure an eternal supply of food.[2] Other funerary items include cosmetic palettes and flint tools, perhaps alluding to the rites of passage that would be expected to be performed in the afterlife.

The body was placed in a contracted position, cosmically aligned with the Nile's flood and the sunset, so that the deceased could be begotten by the great mother goddess and live again.

Visual culture clearly plays an important role in the world of the tomb, with most of the objects, including the body of the deceased, used as media to convey a wide set of images alluding to the life on the shores of the Nile. In this way, the same repertoire of symbols is found on tattoos, cloths, pottery and even on mural paintings.

The grave itself was arranged as a household. The dead were buried in oval holes, but over time the tendency grew to cut rectangular graves. This parallels the development from round huts to rectangular houses in the settlement sites.[3] This rectangular shape would eventually be imprinted in the first wooden coffins produced in the transition to the Early Dynastic Period, which interestingly enough, were designed as small huts.

The tomb was completed with a hill of gravel that protected the grave from scavengers and signed its location for the living.

The chthonic shelter

During the Old Kingdom access to the royal necropolis was provided by the king to his most loyal subjects who aspired to serve him forever in their houses of eternity, the mastaba-tombs.

Private tombs were designed as twofold structures, with a "public" area accessible to the living, and a hidden one, where the mummy was buried. The main focus of the superstructure was the false door. Facing the west, this was the magical gate where the

Ka of the deceased could meet the living, and take his funerary offerings, consisting of bread, beer, meat, cloth, alabaster vessels, ointments and, in short, "everything good and neat".

The upper rooms of the mastaba were magically prepared to provide an eternal supply of these goods to the deceased's Ka, thus aiming to assure the sustenance of his vital force. For this reason, an extensive repertoire of scenes was elaborated to decorate the walls. First, they depicted the deceased taking the funerary meal, but soon they included detailed depictions of the goods mentioned in the inscriptions. However, the most important development occurred when the work involved in the production of funerary goods was also included in the repertoire of scenes depicted in the tomb. During the 5th Dynasty, the visual programme depicted on these magnificent reliefs encompassed most of the areas of Nilotic economic life, showing a variety of workers, from carpenters, to farmers and shepherds.[4] A haunting atmosphere is exuded from these scenes, where the behaviour of these characters is so lively featured that these galleries still echo with their voices and speeches.[5] This emphasis on the process rather than on the goods themselves betrays the influence of solar theology, which triggered a true search for the visibility of life itself.

Contrasting with this realm of light, sometimes highlighted by opening a solar courtyard designed after the plan of the royal complexes, the burial chamber was conceived as a secretive realm of darkness and invisibility. The underground burial chamber was entered by a shaft or, less often, a sloping passage roughly carved on the bedrock of the plateau. The unfinished nature of the undecorated burial chamber is often paralleled by the sarcophagus itself, normally a large piece roughly hewn out of a single block shaped as an archaic hut provided with a rounded ceiling.[6]

This absence of decoration was conceived as a semiotic barrier that created a protective opacity around the body of the deceased.[7] The sarcophagus was thus conceived as a chthonic shelter, providing the deceased with an opaque involucre of stone. In this context, wooden coffins were occasionally used. As with the sarcophagus, the coffin is plain and uninscribed.

Evisceration was already carried out and undecorated jars are used to keep the viscera. The body is wrapped in linen but the shape of it, including limbs and head, was preserved as to resemble the statue of the Ka. The mummy was usually placed full length, lying on its left side, facing the sunrise with the head turned to the north. This scheme was borrowed from royal burials, where the north was associated with the Imperishable Stars.

This was the realm of complete darkness where the regeneration of the deceased took place. In this secretive atmosphere, only a few items were disposed, as the visual development in the chapel allowed the reduction of burial goods stored in the underground rooms of the tomb. The images and words literally replaced the funerary goods.[8] When they occur, models of tools and vessels are the most important class of objects found in these galleries.

Positioned between the mysterious opaqueness of the burial chamber and the visual splendours of the chapel, the *serdab* provided shelter for the statue of the Ka. A small hole opened on the walls of this secret chamber allowed the Ka to "see" the offerings provided by the living.[9] In the Tomb of Ti, a second *serdab* was embedded in the walls of the courtyard reflecting the increasing desire of the deceased to see the sunlight.

In all, the sumptuous tombs built during the Old Kingdom are designed with at least three different purposes. With their wealth of decoration, the visible chambers of the superstructure work as an extension of the false door and provide support for the funerary cult. The unfinished burial chamber holds the sarcophagus and the mummy hiding it within its primordial darkness. Positioned on the threshold of the world of the living and the netherworld, the *serdab* keeps the statue of the Ka, allowing the deceased to see the light.

The model of the universe

The drive for gazing at light and life would eventually be imprinted on the design of the coffins themselves. During the 6th Dynasty, an apparently modest development took place. A pair of eyes begun to be depicted on the east side of the coffin, introducing, for the first time, a visible dimension into the burial chamber, breaking the neat divisions formerly established between the three dimensions of the tomb. This eye-panel, alluding to the eyes of the Ka, added to the coffin the magical purpose of the *serdab*, creating a deeper identification between the mummy and the statue of the Ka. From then on, the opaqueness of the body container was broken and a magical link was firmly established between the body and the tomb. With this association, the motifs once associated with the *serdab* and the offering chambers of the mastaba were used in the decoration of the coffin.

The eye-panel thus introduced in the coffin the symbolism of passage, allowing other motifs to be included in coffin decoration, especially the false door design, which began to be depicted inside the coffin, directly behind the eye-panel.[10]

Coffins then began to be used as media to depict the funerary imaginary associated with the cult of the Ka. Coffin decoration was particularly important inside the trough, where lists of offerings are featured together with instruments used in the ritual of the Opening of the Mouth, the most important ceremony carried out to reanimate the deceased's Ka.

These semiotic developments took place in private tombs after royal burials had introduced the written word in the burial chambers of the pyramid complexes. The so-called "Pyramid Texts" shattered the primordial silence of royal tombs and introduced the speeches of gods, summoned to provide the dead king with a new status and identity, that of Osiris, the resurrected king of the netherworld. The Osirification of the burial practices consisted in the creation of representations, both textual and iconographic, for the hidden sectors of the tomb. In private tombs, the development of the Osirian beliefs introduced a new semiotic concern: words and images now provided identification with Osiris.

Coffin decoration was greatly enhanced under this process, with the sides and the lid inscribed with texts alluding to the Heliopolitan gods protecting the corpse of Osiris, notably Geb, the god of earth, Nut, the heavenly goddess, Shu and Tefnut, the primordial couple, and the Sons of Horus.

The lid, associated with the sky, is often inscribed with an address to the sky goddess Nut taken from the Pyramid Texts.[11] On the interior walls, lengthy recitations derived from the Pyramid Texts are inscribed, together with object friezes featuring funerary goods.

The shape of the coffin itself was designed after the Per-nu shrine of Lower Egypt, an elaboration of the archaic hut, which was now seen as the tomb of Osiris.

Osirian semiotics had transformed rectangular coffins not only into a sacred place, but as a miniature version of the cosmos itself, with each of its components associated with the sky, the netherworld, the tomb and the world of the living. This "cosmos", offered the deceased a protective environment where he could literally find his way to regeneration.

The flesh of Osiris

During the Middle Kingdom the Osirification of funerary practices progressed even further, originating new artefacts, conceived specifically for the burial context. Aiming at providing magical aid for the deceased's identification with Osiris, these artefacts moved the emphasis from coffin decoration to the mummy itself.

By the end of the 12th Dynasty, a typical "court type" burial involved a well-defined set of funerary objects arranged in a nested assemblage.

The outer layer consisted of a "sarcophagus" (sometimes crafted in wood when access to stone was not possible), decorated with the eye-panel and inscribed with texts alluding to the key positions of the Heliopolitan gods escorting the corpse of Osiris. Often, the interior was left undecorated.

The second layer consisted of a rectangular coffin with a yet simpler decoration, where the eye-panel stands out as the most prominent feature.

Inside this coffin, the mummy would be positioned resting on its left side so that the head could face the eye-panels featured on the coffins, and see the sunrise. Together with the mummy, a collection of staves, weapons, and sticks was often laid next to it as symbols of status and dignity.

A collection of Osirian objects would be found in direct contact with the mummy, either in its wrappings or directly attached to it. Amidst these objects, the most important one was the mummy mask, which provided the deceased with his divine manifestation as an Osirian god. In some burials, the mummy mask was extended to cover the mummy entirely, originating a new form of body container, the anthropoid coffin.

It is important to emphasise that in these early burials, what we call "anthropoid coffins" would not have been seen as a distinct part of the mummy itself, and might have been regarded as an involucre instead, some kind of an outer wrapping that would be indissociably attached to the body of the deceased. Most are made of very thin wood and often only the metal parts had been preserved.[12]

The paraphernalia of funerary objects is normally hidden under the mummy wrappings, often including royal sceptres, ritual aprons, jewels, and a new category of magical objects, the amulets, which gave hieroglyphs a new use, summoning the ideas they represented to protect the mummy. It is interesting to note that some of the earliest examples of amulets are shaped in the form of *shen*-rings, or *sa*-signs, both revolving around concepts of protection.

The burial chamber is transformed into a sacred place associated with the mysterious resurrection of Osiris. The jars for the viscera are now reinterpreted in the light of the Osirian myth and are positioned under the protection of the Sons of Horus. This Osirification of the funerary jars was achieved by rendering a "mummy mask" on their lids. The Canopic jars were thus seen as "coffins", with the entrails inside equivalent to a mummy.[13]

These burials would be completed with ritual tools, such as a box with seven vessels for the sacred oils, and a long box containing royal insignia and weapons. Pottery consisting of small vessels and plates would briefly and symbolically allude to the cult of the Ka.[14]

The primordial egg (Rishi type)

During the New Kingdom the use of feathered coffins (*rishi*) was restricted to the pharaoh and his queens. In the archaeological record, however, this model appears in Thebes, during the 17th Dynasty, where they were used by the Theban ruling elite and its entourage. These coffins represent a break with the Osirian funerary tradition developed in private burials under the 12th Dynasty. Nevertheless, they were not necessarily a new creation and it is possible that they may have been designed for royal burials when, during the 12th Dynasty, private individuals were allowed to use Osirian regalia.

As Gianluca Miniati points out, Theban *rishi* coffins introduced a whole different set of funerary patterns.[15] First of all, they are no longer used as the innermost container of a coffin set, but as an independent object. In fact, the two halves of the object refer to different aspects of the afterlife.

The case is painted in dark monochromatic paint alluding to the earth and the underworld. It recalls the opaqueness and impenetrability of the undecorated rectangular coffins of old, adopting the square, flattened layout of the rectangular cases.

The lid, on the other hand, refers to the heavenly realm, adopts the anthropomorphic shape but gives it an apparently new reading, showing the deceased as a Ba-bird, with the back of the bird depicted over the human head and the long wings fully stretched as in flying mode. Additionally, on the edge of the footboard, a hill is depicted.

Often, the tomb consisted of a simple grave, therefore, without a formal structure that could have supported pictorial decoration. Hence, objects from daily life entered again in the grave, as it once happened in the Early Dynastic Period and, curiously enough, the Osirian paraphernalia elaborated during the 12th Dynasty ceased to be used.

From the symbolic perspective, *rishi* coffins introduced a different set of ideas regarding the afterlife. During the Middle Kingdom, anthropoid coffins were used as an extension of the body, showing the deceased as a resurrected Osirian god, locked in a static dimension of eternity, which in Egyptian is called *djet*, the realm of everlasting existence. *Rishi* coffins are no longer crafted as an extension of the mummy and they rather work as a "shell", showing a dynamic process, a transformation that occurred in its interior. From the mystical union of Osiris and Re results the rebirth of Osiris/sun god.[16] This rebirth could only occur in the cyclic dimension of time, called *neheh*, where one could return to the beginning of time and be reborn again. Here, solar regeneration and rebirth take place through the annihilation of time.[17]

A coffin of the *rishi* type was thus crafted as an "egg" where the avian manifestation of the deceased was begotten under the protective wings of his divine mother, the vulture goddess featured on the lid, outstretching her wings over him. As the solar aspect of the deceased, the Ba would go forth by day and unite with the sun god in his cosmic circuit, while the mummy rested in the grave, provided with the objects required for the maintenance of the deceased's Ka.

The coffin of Gold ("Black" coffins)

Under Hatshepsut/Thuthmosis III the Theban necropolis witnessed to the growth of exquisitely decorated tombs where an important shift in the funerary representations is documented. The superstructure of the tomb normally displays a T-shaped plan. It is painted in bright colours, with a vibrant and joyful atmosphere, as it was used to accommodate the deceased's family during the Beautiful Feast of the Valley. The scenes of these banquets are shown on the walls of the transversal room.

In these tombs, the longitudinal gallery provided a transitional device to approach the west. Their walls were decorated with new scenes featuring funerary rituals such as the mortuary cortege and the Opening of the Mouth ceremony. Eventually, cult scenes were introduced in this setting, showing the deceased performing offering rituals before the gods of the necropolis. Formerly a royal prerogative, cult scenes subtly equated the status of the deceased with that of a god, transforming each chapel into a private "temple" for the great festival that celebrated the cosmic renewal of Amun-Re.

As the provision of the tomb occupied a relatively small portion in the decorative programme of the chapel, the burial chamber was filled with objects from daily life.

Despite all the novelties introduced in the superstructure, it is in the burial chamber where the most important changes occur.

Here we find the first funerary compositions written on papyri, forming the "Book of going forth by day", currently known as the "Book of the Dead". The accompanying vignettes are the first attempts to illustrate the afterlife but they are particularly relevant because they witness to the extension of the Egyptian visual repertoire of the netherworld, a territory which, with a few exceptions had remained largely beyond the reach of visual representation. The funerary papyri thus literally unfolded the landscape of the Duat over and around the mummy. In fact, the sacred space of the burial chamber started to be arranged and organised after the layout of the vignettes of the Book of the Dead.

The burial chamber, for example, was protected with a special set of amulets: *djed*-pillar, jackal, torch, *shabti*-figure. These images provided identification with the Osirian chamber depicted in Chapter 151.[18]

Certain objects were inscribed with texts from the Book of the Dead, such as the *shabti* figurines, which were often placed in model coffins or model sarcophagi. Under Amenhotep III small shrine-shaped boxes, in which a *shabti* figurine was placed, are attested for the first time.

A new type of coffin is designed in order to accommodate the imagery of the Book of the Dead, forming the so-called "black" type. From the symbolic standpoint, these anthropoid coffins associated two different sets of images. The anthropoid shape of the coffin shows the deceased as an Osirian god, but the images and texts disposed on the sides allude to the mythical burial chamber of Osiris described in Chapter 151 of the Book of the Dead. From this association results the dynamic view of Osiris awakening from the sleep of death under the combined action of the gods that protect his body. Additionally, the effigies of Thoth allude to Chapter 161 of the Book of the Dead, which refers to the triumph of the sun god Re over his enemy Apophis, and to his ascent to the heavens.

Besides resurrection, the nested coffins suggest a progression from the state of complete darkness to full radiance, with the innermost object entirely covered with gilded foil. Thus, the "black" type recreates a process rather than a result in time, leading to a solar rebirth.

Aside from iconography and texts, brightness was a fundamental feature of these objects and it seems to have played a key role during funerary rituals. The coat of black pitch was added to the outer coffins during the funerary rituals themselves, seemingly with the purpose of adding brightness to the objects.[19] This illumination ritual was at the core of the funerary ritual, which of course would not make sense without the mummy itself and it is here where this cosmogonic image was fully achieved. The heart scarab, carved in stone and inscribed with Chapter 30 B of the Book of the Dead, showed the heart of the deceased literally transformed into Khepri, the god of sunrise, rising from the dead corpse of Osiris and irradiating light, recreating the world anew. Heart scarabs, which provided identification with the sun god and rebirth, appeared sporadically in the 13th Dynasty but only became common from the reign of Hatshepsut onwards.[20]

In sum, the gilded decoration of the nested coffins recreated the Chamber of Gold on the depths of the Duat, there where the heart of Osiris awakened in the form of the rising sun.

Arranged for the festival ("Proto-yellow" type)

During the reign of Akhenaten, the Osirian beliefs regarding the afterlife were seriously challenged and the burial practices had been reviewed in the light of the new religious system imposed by the king. The afterlife was now fully seen as the continuing involvement of the deceased in the divine festival of Aten, performed at the Great Temple in Akhetaten, the new capital city. The tombs of the high officials are decorated with scenes alluding to the "daily life" in Amarna, showing the afterlife as a blissful existence in the sacred city of the Aten, where light and life are continuously celebrated.

For the first time, the corpse is shown in Egyptian art: tomb decoration in Amarna clearly depicts the deceased lying on a funerary bier, with the arms alongside the body, wearing festive wig and garments. These scenes, which are normally interpreted as the depiction of the corpse, may actually represent the type of coffin in use for the Amarnian elite, the so-called "festive dress" type. Entirely shaped after the living image of the deceased, this new type of coffin was designed as a private sculpture that could stand in the Temple of Aten. So far coffins of this type remain unattested in the archaeological record, but we have shown elsewhere evidence suggesting that such models did exist by the end of the Amarna Period.[21]

After the Amarna Period, the traditional Osirian archetype was back in favour. However, despite being short-lived, the Amarnian model did not entirely fall into disuse. On the contrary, attempts to integrate the "festive dress" type into the Osirian scheme of decoration played a decisive role in the subsequent evolution of coffin decoration.

These attempts to combine both models in one single coffin, resulting in hybrid objects with the lid following the layout of the "festive dress" type and the sides designed after the "black" type.

These developments are first seen in Saqqara, where most of the court of Tutankhamun, which previously lived in Amarna, was eventually buried. Here we find the first anthropoid sarcophagi showing a hybrid model. In these objects the lid depicts the deceased as living, clad in festive garments. The layout of the sides is designed after the "black" type, featuring the usual figures of the four Sons of Horus and Thoth.

Juxtaposing the layout of the "festive dress" type with that of the "black" type was just the first step towards the full integration of both models. In Thebes, this synthesis between the two models would progress even more when the deceased himself was integrated into the iconographic repertoire of his own coffin, which seems to be a novelty of this period. Anthropoid coffins from Amarna show offering scenes instead of the Sons of Horus, suggesting once again, that the inspiration for these motifs originated in Akhetaten.[22]

The concepts introduced with the "festive dress" type therefore, opened coffin decoration to the exploration of the iconographic resources previously used in tomb decoration only. This was the key to the tremendous success achieved by the emerging model. The lids of the coffins were now decorated with miniature scenes featuring the deceased in (ritual) interaction with the gods of the netherworld, but the case still keeps the layout of the "black" type, forming what can be labelled as the "proto-yellow" coffin.[23]

These coffins were much appreciated as they clearly empowered the deceased and enhanced his/her godlike status. With this new type of coffin, a big change occurred in burial customs. Under Ramesses II, most of the objects from daily life disappear from tombs, and so do the painted scenes from daily life.[24] The chapels of the tombs are now exclusively decorated with vignettes from the Book of the Dead, or with adoration scenes.

Most of the objects placed in the tomb are specially produced for burial and the imagery of the Book of the Dead reshapes them even further. The canopic jars are decorated with the iconography of the Sons of Horus.[25] The number of *shabtis* increase, often placed in a special box, with room for 2 or 3 *shabtis*.

The typical burial equipment includes a papyrus with the Book of the Dead, several types of amulets, the most important of them related to the heart, which are shaped like heart-amulets, heart scarabs, or both.[26] *Wedjat*-plaques are positioned over the left side of the abdomen, "healing" the wound open to remove the viscera.

The body of light ("Yellow" type)

By the end of the Ramesside Period, the definition of the so-called "yellow" type established the full synthesis between the "festive dress" type and the "black" type. In this scheme of decoration, the deceased is integrated into the decoration of both the lid and the case and a new object was created, the mummy-cover.

Contemporary *shabtis*, mummiform[27] or carved after the "festive dress" type,[28] show further evidence that might be helpful to understand the symbolism of the "yellow" coffin. They often bear the inscription *sehedj Osiris N.* ("To make shine the Osiris N".) sometimes using the sun disk as determinative (N 8 in Gardiner's list) pointing out to the solarisation of the Osirian afterlife and depicting the deceased as a solarised god. Illumination and radiance were thus sought as the ultimate expression of a glorious afterlife and the gleaming coating provided to the coffins and *shabtis* expressed this pursuit of light. The extensive pictorial programme featured on coffins sets up a "realm of light" where the deceased lived as if in perpetual celebration with the gods of the underworld. This "realm of light" is arranged as a building providing the deceased with his/her own monument of eternity. The inside of the coffin is decorated with motifs originally found in royal anthropoid sarcophagi.[29] Between the interior and the exterior of the coffins, there is an intense "flow" of decoration. On later coffins, this flow is materialised by the increasing weight of liminal elements in the decoration of the objects. Moreover, the nested assemblages establish visual spheres around the mummy, creating what Eva Liptay calls a "transparency" effect, which is consistent with the vision of the coffin set as a "realm of light".[30]

The outstanding pictorial programme of these coffins provides a counterbalance for the highly impersonal character of the tombs. During the 21st Dynasty, the Theban elite is buried in undecorated tombs. The coffin thus performs the role of the tomb itself, providing the decoration needed for the burial chamber.

"Yellow" coffins provide a safe nest where the mummy unites both with its heavenly mother and solar *ba*, allowing the "gilded flesh" of the deceased to shine over it, unfolding colours, images and texts, around the deceased and giving full visibility to the netherworld and its topography. From the magical standpoint the varnish literally "make divine" the gilded flesh of the deceased, a concern deeply embedded in the magical search for solarisation of the funerary equipment. The result is the coffin literally showing the deceased as a deity irradiating sunlight.

This "solar quest" is rendered in images both in coffins and in papyri. The most distinctive aspect of the funerary material culture from this period is the prevalence given to iconography. Visual culture pervades all sorts of media, from coffins to papyri, stelae or amulets, unfolding the landscape of the netherworld in the same way that reliefs illustrated the earthly life in the mastabas of the Old Kingdom. The main difference between the visual culture displayed on mastabas and "yellow" coffins lies on the aspect of the solar circuit that is depicted. In the mastabas, visual culture illustrates cosmic order when the sun god illuminates the Nile banks, while "yellow" coffins show the netherworld during the nightly journey of the sun on his way to unite with Osiris.

The prevalence of *shabtis* during the 21st Dynasty reflects the same phenomenon. Each burial may include up to 70 statuettes or more. The role of these figurines is directly related to the Fields of Iaru, where the deceased is fed and regenerated. The number of these figurines increases exactly when scenes related to the world of the living, namely those illustrating the provision of the tomb, disappear from the world of the tomb. The representations of the afterlife are exclusively focused on the nightly journey of the sun, so much so that even the provision of the deceased is entirely entrusted to the *shabtis*, the deceased's servants in the netherworld.

This focus led to another innovation introduced in the late Ramesside Period in the funerary material culture, the wooden Osiris figurine, a hollowed-out statue that holds a papyrus with chapters of the Book of the Dead. In a way, *shabtis* relate to this effigy as servants relate to their master. In this context, the traditional role played by the Ka and its cult faded away to such an extent that it is only detected in short, one could say secondary, inscriptions. The pursuit of light and its regeneration plays by far a bolder role in the funerary equipment of this brotherhood of men and women serving the supreme god Amun-Re, the king of gods.

Coffins, workshops, and commissioners

Even before buried in the tomb, coffins play a variety of roles. First of all they generate a socio-economic network where goods and raw materials are traded, sometimes from very distant locations.

Secondly, elite tombs generate an important socio-economic cluster that gathers craftsmen with different types of expertise, such as masons, painters, sculptors, and carpenters, as well as experts versed on textual and iconographic tradition. The close interaction between these professionals is often the cement that gives consistency to the different objects integrating a funerary foundation. Coffins are a good example of this phenomenon. The earliest examples of body containers are crafted in wood, by carpenters, but during the Old Kingdom, the container of choice of high elite burials becomes the sarcophagus, carved by stonemasons, which in turn will adapt the sarcophagus in order to accommodate a wooden coffin within. Later, during the Middle Kingdom, both categories of object share aspects of their decoration, showing that craftsmen with different expertise worked in close association, possibly at the building site itself.

The close interaction between professional experts is probably the most important factor for the creation of anthropoid coffins. Producing an extended version of funerary mask in cartonnage (linen covered with gesso) required the cooperation of a carpenter who mounted the wooden frame and this may have led carpenters to develop the techniques required for the creation of an anthropoid case in wood.

This cooperation also helps to explain the phenomenon of "osmosis" between different media. An interesting example is provided by anthropoid coffins in the late 12th Dynasty. The burial of Senebtisi includes an anthropoid coffin decorated with the royal *nemes*-headdress. The mummy, on the other hand, was equipped with an Osirian set of jewels and regalia in order to define the status of the deceased as a king of the netherworld. In other burials, however, this expensive set of jewels was depicted on the anthropoid coffin instead, thus saving the need to include them in the mummy wrappings.

This example suggests that, when preparing a given elite burial, experts would access how it could be prepared in order to be as complete as possible. When the acquisition of important funerary objects was not possible, the repertoire of coffin decoration was extended in order to accommodate the "missing" objects in the mummy.

As highly prized material goods, coffins required the combined work of several types of artisans, such as carpenters, sculptors, painters, jewellers, goldsmiths, or lector-priests. Their collaboration certainly originated a specific set of tools and techniques to achieve the required result. For example, when black pitch started to be used in the funerary ritual to cover the coffin, the work of goldsmiths became important to enhance decoration. So much so that hieroglyphs and images became moulded in plaster, in raised relief, and covered by gilded foil. Later on, in "proto-yellow" coffins, such as the coffin of Sennedjem, this technique was maintained, not because it was needed but simply because craftsmen were used to it.

This observation leads us to a different set of questions regarding the transmission of practices. Funerary workshops tend to build upon their previous experiences, replicating techniques, knowledge, and outputs. This modus operandi explains why coffin decoration evolves in such an "organic" way, in many ways similar to a phylogenetic pattern. As in the evolution of species, the genealogical link between an older form of life and a more recent one is given by the existence of reminiscent features of the first in the later.

Of course, there is a huge difference between a genetic process of transmission and that used in a workshop. However, we should keep in mind that in antiquity transmission of knowledge and professional skills did follow a genetic line, from father to son, and this certainly shaped the way techniques and outputs tended to be replicated one generation after another.

Of course, disruptive events do take place, such as the creation of the Theban *rishi* coffins during the 17th Dynasty, as it has been pointed out by Gianluca Miniaci.[31] Such disruption is motivated by the discontinuity of social and political structures that seriously compromises the regular activity of workshops. In those moments, the continuity of transmission is broken, and a new "genealogical" line is created with the development of local workshops. These moments of rupture are fruitful in terms of innovations, both technical and symbolical.

However, when political and socio-economic conditions are stable, workshops tend to observe a stable model. Innovations, when they occur, are typically introduced *from above*, *i.e.* by someone who is responsible by the critical assessment of the role performed by coffins in a particular tomb, at a certain moment.

The creation of the "black" type under Hatshepsut/Thuthmosis III provides a typical example of an innovative set of features introduced in coffin decoration, which resulted from changes in the significance of the object and in the ritual role it performed. Once established, this scheme of decoration remained stable and even the most luxurious objects did not differ much in terms of iconography. The quality of execution could differ, as well as the quality of the materials involved, but the scheme of decoration was the same. This stability allowed workshops to carry out most of the work without close supervision, as long as a model was provided.

Ritualistic needs would greatly interfere with the work of craftsmen. The "black" coffins remained "incomplete" when they left the workshop. Seemingly, the black coat of resin was applied during the funerary rituals,[32] and so the decoration had to be highlighted in plaster covered with gilded foil, so to resist the application of black pitch.

A less costly version of the "black" type involved cheaper materials, such as the use of yellow paint instead of gold. These imitations originated yellow painted coffins of the "black" type, which are not to be confused with the objects later on known as "yellow" coffins (in fact most of the "yellow" coffins have been painted white). Other versions are painted with a "black" background overlaid with yellow paint. Unlike luxurious coffins, these imitations had to leave the workshop complete and could not undergo the "coating" ritual.

In this process, the commissioner did not seem to play any relevant role. A stable code defined with accuracy the key-features associated with the different categories of objects. However, this does not mean that the commissioner was entirely passive. Paraphrasing John Taylor, until the 19th Dynasty, "the tomb was the most conspicuous signifier of rank",[33] and so many of the key decisions regarding the decoration of the tomb were surely mediated by the tomb owner.

Another example of how innovations were introduced *from above* is provided by the "festive dress" type. Once again, coffin layout is reshaped at the light of theological concepts serving ideological purposes under the reform put forward by Akhenaten. The creation of anthropoid coffins featuring the deceased as living introduces a deep break with the former tradition, which relied on the Osirification of the funerary setting. Such a break required not only the redefinition of the ideal afterlife but also the setup of new workshops in a new capital city. Despite all these ruptures with the recent past, it is interesting to detect in this reformative impetus the reuse of ideas that had long been discarded from the funerary culture, such as the moulding of the mummy as a statue of the Ka, during the late Old Kingdom. In fact, this was not the only aspect to have been recovered from the Memphite tradition. Old Kingdom visual culture, which revolved around the visibility of life, is preferred to the Osirian imagery and tombs became again entirely decorated with scenes from "daily life". The "Festive dress" type is thus conceived as an update of the solar visual culture, providing the deceased with a statue of his Ka, with the implicit statement that he was no longer featured as an Osirian god as previously occurred.

After the Amarnian reform, an interesting phenomenon occurred from the point of view of material funerary pragmatics. With the "proto-yellow" type, attempts were carried out to achieve a synthesis between the two previous models. Unlike the former types of coffins, which were conceived and planned before they were implemented, this new type of coffin results from an experimental process, which spans two or three generations, as we may see in the Tomb of Sennedjem. This process becomes even more interesting as innovations seem to be mastered by the craftsmen themselves, who assess the results of their own work and foresee the possible developments. The burial equipment of Sennedjem shows how important the personal engagement of the craftsmen in the creation of their own coffins was. It is likely that these results may have been adopted by official workshops which worked under commission for private individuals.

"Proto-yellow" coffins provide an interesting case regarding the impact of innovations introduced *from below*, *i.e.* from the artisans themselves. The development of iconography in these coffins was only possible because transparent yellowish varnish was introduced. Unlike black pitch which hides the pictorial decoration, the varnish was compatible with polychrome decoration as it stabilised the pigments. This varnish consists of pistacia resin, a substance also used as incense in temple ritual, which conferred a godlike radiance to the deceased,[34] and transformed the white paint used as background into a yellowish glow. This technical innovation betrays a deep engagement of coffin decorators in techniques associated with painting materials, which was only possible in a community of artisans. Using a transparent coating material allowed the coffin to be used literally as a canvas and, from this moment onwards, the input of techniques introduced by painters is clear. "Yellow" coffins are covered with linen and a thin layer of plaster so to provide a suitable support for the pictorial work. These technical innovations are put forward by the craftsmen themselves, possibly stimulated by the authorities who supervised their work.

Once established, the scheme ruling the layout of the "yellow" type was already the most complex ever seen in coffin decoration. However, during the 21st Dynasty, this scheme did not cease to be continuously expanded reaching levels of complexity of astonishing proportions. The craftsmanship of these objects truly became a cutting-edge industry, presenting an entirely different character from the phenomenon previously observed in coffin decoration.

In the first place, the tremendous growth of complexity required a totally different organisation of labour. The number of key-features ruling each sector of a coffin was already so high that a careful plan of the coffin as a whole was required. Despite that, innovative inputs had been continuously added, either by adding new key-features or by changing the layout of the scenes. So much so that each "yellow" coffin presents a layout of its own. Such developments would certainly require a larger team of craftsmen and all these factors combined would risk turning coffin decoration into a chaotic enterprise. However, such a risk seems to have been successfully avoided by establishing clear principles ruling the composition of each panel or section and by implementing an effective system to supervise them. This allowed to make progress in reaching increasingly higher levels of complexity.

The evolving nature of coffin decoration therefore, seems to have played a crucial role in the definition of the "yellow" type. Unlike the previous models of coffins, the "yellow" type does not have a static scheme. This does not mean that innovations are introduced aleatory. The seriation of the objects according to the complexity of their compositions clearly reveals that new arrangements were always built upon the former developments creating evolutional sequences that can be helpful when dating these compositions.

During the 21st Dynasty, innovations are thus introduced methodically, by simply manipulating the complex set of key-features that ruled each section. Under these circumstances, given the amount of work, the teams involved in coffin decoration should have been significantly wider than before. Moreover, the supervision should have been much more demanding and it should be expected that these workshops would be installed in the premises of a temple, most probably Medinet Habu, where most of the villagers from Deir el-Medina had moved in.

As we have seen the three stages of development detected in coffin decoration during the 21st Dynasty present subtle differences in terms of symbolism. Curiously enough, these differences are consistent with a varying degree of work involved in the craftsmanship of the coffin.

Traditionally, the most time-consuming part of the anthropoid coffin was the headboard. This is exactly what we expect when we think that anthropoid coffins were created as extensions of the funerary mask. With the "festive dress" type, the workforce required to craft the headboard became even more expanded.

Only with the "yellow" type, we witness to a change in the global economy of the coffin. In the basic scheme, the most important section of the lid was the lower section, the largest and the most profusely decorated. In the classical scheme, the central panel became the most intricate composition of the coffin. In the complex scheme the upper section gained a bolder role with the increasing importance given to the floral collar, and the lower section is much reduced or even excluded.

Therefore, changes in the layout of the coffin had an important impact in the economy of decoration and a greater investment of the workforce was carried out in the areas that in a certain moment would be perceived as more important by the community that was supposed to use them.

Necessarily, coffins played an important role in Theban society during the Libyan theocracy, as they were used by the priesthood of Amun as positive statements for the discrimination of this social group, as a whole. It is reasonable to accept that the Temple of Amun controlled the workshops and managed the funerary artefacts as a "communal" property aiming at redistributing them to their members, probably according to their rank. The craftsmanship of such complex objects was viable from an economic standpoint only because they were prepared for the corporation of Amun as a group, and not for an individual person.

Hence, coffins became the privileged media to convey the corporative values of the priesthood of Amun. In times of economic scarcity, funerary goods became an important way to assure abidance and conformity of the Theban elite to the "Libyan" theocratic regime.

Notes

1 Van Walsem 2014.
2 Grajetzki 2013, 4.
3 Grajetzki 2013, 4.
4 Van Walsem, 2008.
5 For these speeches, Van Walsem 2008 (Mastaba of Ti).

6. Van Walsem 2014.
7. Nyord 2014.
8. Grajetzki 2013, 14.
9. Grajetzki 2013, 14.
10. Taylor 1989, 16.
11. Williams 2018.
12. Grajetzki 2013, 27–54.
13. Grajetzki 2013, 27–54.
14. Grajetzki 2013, 55–56.
15. Miniaci 2018.
16. Miniaci 2010.
17. Assmann 2001, 109.
18. Grajetzki 2013, 68.
19. Sousa 2018a, 31–32.
20. Grajeztki 2013.
21. Sousa 2018a.
22. Stevens 2018.
23. Sousa 2018a.
24. Grajetzki 2013, 95.
25. Grajetzki 2013, 66.
26. Sousa 2011.
27. *Shabti* of Khabekhnet, from TT 1. See Hornung, Bryan 2002, 143.
28. *Shabti* of Sunur. See Taylor, 2001, 123.
29. Taylor 2017.
30. Liptay 2017, 269.
31. Miniaci 2018.
32. Ikram and Dodson 1998, 211.
33. Taylor 2018, 349.
34. Taylor 2016a, 57.

Bibliography

Altenmüller, H. (2001) A vida quotidiana na Eternidade – Mastabas e túmulos rupestres dos funcionários. In *Egipto: O mundo dos Faraós*, R. Schulz and M. Seidel (eds), 79–93. Colónia: Köneman.

Andreu, G. ed. (2002) *Les Artistes de Pharaon: Deir el-Medineh et la Vallée des Rois*. Paris-Turnhout: Brepols, Réunion des Musées Nationaux.

Andrews, C. (1994) *Amulets of Ancient Egypt*. London: British Museum Press.

Arnold, D. (1999) Les relations entre la statuaire et l'architecture. In *L'Art Égyptien au temps des pyramides*, C. Ziegler (ed.), 64–71. Paris: Réunion des Musées Nationaux.

Arnold, D. (2005) Royal cult complexes of the Old and Middle Kingdoms. In *Temples of Ancient Egypt*, B. Shafer (ed.), 31–85. Cairo: American University in Cairo Press.

Arnold, D. (2008) *Middle Kingdom Tomb Architecture at Lisht*. New York: Metropolitan Museum of Art Egyptian Expedition.

Assmann, J. (2001) *The Search for God in Ancient Egypt*. Ithaca-London: Cornell University Press.

Assmann, J. (2003) *Mort et au-delà dans l'Égypte ancienne*. Monaco: Éditions du Rocher.

Aston, D. (2009) *Burial assemblages of Dynasty 21-25: Chronology, typology, developments*. Vienna: Verlag der Österreichischen Akademie der Wissenschaften.

Bayard, E. (1891) Les découvertes de Louqsor. *L'Illustration* 49, 304–5.

Bettum, A. (2014) Lot XIV from Bab el-Gasus (Sweden and Norway): The modern history of the collection and a reconstruction of the ensembles. In *Body, Cosmos and Eternity: New research trends in the iconography and symbolism of ancient Egyptian coffins*, R. Sousa, (ed.), 167–86. Oxford: Archaeopress.

Bianucci, R., Habicht, M.E., Buckley, S., Fletcher, J., Seiler, R., Öhrström, L.M., Vassilika, E., Böni, T. and Rühli, F.J. (2015) Shedding new light on the 18th dynasty mummies of the royal architect Kha and his spouse Merit. *PLOS-One* 10(7).

Bolshakov, A. (1997) *Man and his Double in Egyptian Ideology of the Old Kingdom*. Wiesbaden: Harrassowitz.

Bourriau, J. (1997) Beyond Avaris: The Second Intermediate Period in Egypt outside the Eastern Delta. In *The Hyksos: New Historical and Archaeological Perspectives*, E.D. Oren (ed.), 159–82. Philadelphia: University of Pennsylvania.

Broekman, B. (2000) On the chronology and genealogy of the second, third and fourth prophets of Amun in Thebes during the Twenty-First Dynasty in Egypt. *Göttinger Miszellen* 174, 25–36.

Broekman, G. (2018) The 21st Dynasty: The theocracy of Amun and the position of the Theban priestly families. In *The Coffins of the Priests of Amun: Egyptian Coffins from the Collection of the National Museum of Antiquities in Leiden*, L. Weiss (ed.), 13–20. Papers on Archaeology from the Leiden Museum of Antiquities (PALMA) 17. Leiden: Sidestone Press.

Bruyère, B. (1952) *Tombes Thébaines de Deir el-Medineh à décoration monochrome*. Le Caire: Imprimerie de l'Institut français d'archéologie orientale.

Bruyère, B. (1959) *La Tombe No 1 de Sen-Nedjem à Deir el-Medineh*. Cairo: Institut Français d'Archaeologie Oriental.

Bryan, B. (2000) The 18th Dynasty before the Amarna Period (c. 1550–1352 BC). In *The Oxford History of Ancient Egypt*, I. Shaw (ed.), 218–71. Oxford: Oxford University Press.

Cherpion, N. (1999) La conception de l'Homme à l'Ancien Empire, d'après les bas-reliefs figurant les notables. In *L'Art Égyptien au temps des pyramides*, C. Ziegler (ed.), 83–95. Paris: Réunion des Musées Nationaux.

Clayton, P. (1994) *Chronicle of the Pharaohs: The Reign-by-Reign Record of the Rulers and Dynasties of Ancient Egypt*. London: Thames & Hudson.

Cooney, K. (2007) *The Cost of Death: The social and economic value of ancient Egyptian funerary art in the Ramesside Period*. Egyptologische Uitgaven 22. Leiden: Nederlands Instituut voor het Nabije Oosten.

Cooney, K. (2011) Changing burial practices at the end of the Ramesside Period: Evidence of tomb commissions, coffin commissions, coffin decoration, mummification and the Amen Priesthood. *Journal of the American Research Center in Egypt* 47, 3–44.

Cooney, K. (2014a) Ancient Egyptian funerary arts as social documents: Social place, reuse, and working towards a new typology of 21st Dynasty coffins. In *Body, Cosmos & Eternity: New Research Trends in the Symbolism of Coffins in Ancient Egypt*, R. Sousa (ed.), 45–66 Egyptology Series 3. Oxford: Archaeopress.

Cooney, K. (2014b) Private sector tomb robbery and funerary arts reuse according to West Theban documentation. In *Deir el-Medina Studies. Proceedings Helsinki June 24-26, 2009*, J.T. Viitala, T. Vartiainen, and S. Uvanto (eds), 16–28. Occasional Papers 2. Helsinki: Finnish Egyptological Society.

D'Abbadie, J.V. and Jourdain, G. (1939) *Deux Tombes de Deir El Médineh (1) La Chapelle de Khâ (2) La tombe du scribe royal Amenemopet*. Le Caire: Imprimerie de l'Institut français d'archéologie orientale.

Daressy, G. (1896) Contribution à l'étude de la XXIe dynastie égyptienne. *Révue Archéologique* 28(3), 72–90.

Daressy, G. (1900) Les sépultures des prêtres d'Ammon à Deir el-Bahari. *Annales du Service des Antiquités de l'Égypte* 1, 141–8.

Daressy, G. (1902) Procès-verbal d'ouverture de la momie No 29707. *Annales du Service des Antiquités de l'Égypte* 3, 151–4.

Daressy, G. (1902a) *Fouilles de la Vallée des Rois (1898-1899)*. Catalogue Général des Antiquités Égyptiennes du Musée du Caire (Nos. 24001–24990). Le Caire: Institut Français d'Archéologie Orientale.

Daressy, G. (1902b) Inscriptions sur les objets accompagnant la momie de Ta-du-Maut. *Annales du Service des Antiquités de l'Égypte* 3, 155–7.

Daressy, G. (1903) Ouverture des momies provenant de la seconde trouvaille de Deir el-Bahari. Procès-verbaux d'ouverture. *Annales du Service des Antiquités de l'Égypte* 4, 150–5.

Daressy, G. (1907) Les cercueils des Prêtres d'Ammon (Deuxieme Trouvaille de Deir el-Bahari). *Annales du Service des Antiquités de l'Égypte* 8, 3–38.

Daressy, G. (1909) *Cercueils des Cachettes Royales*. Catalogue Général des Antiquités Égyptiennes (Nos. 61001–61044). Le Caire: Institut Français d'Archéologie Orientale.

Daressy, G. and Smith, E.G. (1903) Ouverture des momies provenant de la seconde trouvaille de Deir el-Bahari. *Annales du Service des Antiquités de l'Égypte* 4, 150–60.

de Araújo Duarte, C. (2014) Crossing the landscapes of eternity: Parallels between Amduat and funeral procession scenes on the 21st Dynasty coffins. In *Body, Cosmos, and Eternity: New Research Trends in the Iconography and Symbolism of Ancient Egyptian Coffins*, R. Sousa (ed.), 81–90. Egyptology 3. Oxford: Archaeopress.

Del Vesco, P. (2015) The Old Kingdom: An eternity of stone. In *Museo Egizio*, C. Greco (ed.), 182–93. Turin: Fondazione Museo della Antichità Egizie di Torino.

Delvaux, L. and Therasse, I. (2015) *Sarcophages: Sous les étoiles de Nout*. Brussels: Éditions Racine-Musées royaux d'Art et Histoire.

Dodson, A. (2016) Go west: on the ancient means of approach to the Saqqara Necropolis. In *Mummies, Magic and Medicine in Ancient Egypt: Multidisciplinary Essays for Rosalie David*, C. Price, R. Forshaw, A. Chamberlain and P. Nicholson (eds) 3–18. Manchester: Manchester University Press.

Dodson, A. and Ikram, S. (2008) *The Tomb in Ancient Egypt*. London: Thames & Hudson.

Eremin, K., Goring, E., Manley, W. and Cartwright, C. (2000) A Seventeenth Dynasty Egyptian Queen in Edinburgh. *Kmt – A Modern Journal of Ancient Egypt* 11(3), 32–40.

Farid, H. and Farid, S. (2001) Unfolding Sennedjem's Tomb. *KMT: A Modern Journal of Ancient Egypt*, 1–8.

Ferraris, E. (2015) The tomb of Kha. In *Museo Egizio*, C. Greco (ed.), 244–53 Turin: Fondazione Museo della Antichità Egizie di Torino.

Gasse, A. (1996) *Les sarcophages de la Troisième Périod Intermédiaire du Museo Gregoriano Egizio*. Aegyptiaca Gregoriana 3. Città del Vaticano: Monumenti Musei e Gallerie Pontificie.

Graefe, E. (2003) The Royal Cache and the tomb robberies. In *The Theban Necropolis, Past, Present, Future*, N, Strudwick and J.H. Taylor (eds), 74–84. London: British Museum Press,

Grajetzki, W. (2013) *Burial Customs in Ancient Egypt*. London: Duckworth.

Grajetzki, W. (2018) The burial of the king's daughter Nubhetepti-khered. In *Ancient Egyptian Coffins: Craft, Traditions and Functionality*, J. Taylor and M. Vandenbeusch (eds), 231–46. Leuven: Peeters.

Grimal, N. (2017) *Daressy: un savant, des archives – Trente-six années en Égypte au tournant du XXe siècle*. Paris: Collège de France.

Guichard, H., Pagès-Camagna, S. and Timbart, N. (2017) The coffin of Tanetshedmut of the Musée du Louvre: First study and restoration for the Vatican Coffin Project. In *Proceedings of the First Vatican Conference (Vatican Museums, 19–22 June 2013)*, A. Amenta and H. Guichard (eds), 169–78. Vatican: Edizioni Musei Vaticani.

Hayes, W. (1953) *The Scepter of Egypt: A Background for the Study of the Egyptian Antiquities in the Metropolitan Museum of Art. Part I: From the Earliest Times to the End of the Middle Kingdom.* New York: Metropolitan Museum of Art.

Hayes, W. (1959) *The Scepter of Egypt: A background for the study of the Egyptian Antiquities in the Metropolitan Museum of Art*. Part II: *The Hyksos Period and the New Kingdom (1675–1080 BC)*. New York: Metropolitan Museum of Art.

Holm-Rasmussen, T. (1983) Amons sangerinde. *SFINX* 6, 99–102.

Hornung, E. and Bryan, B. (eds) (2002) *The Quest for Immortality: Treasures of Ancient Egypt*. Washington DC: National Gallery of Art.

Ikram, S. and Dodson, A. (1998) *The Mummy in Ancient Egypt. Equipping the Dead for Eternity*. Cairo: American University in Cairo Press.

Jánosi, P. (1999) Les tombes privés, des 'maisons d´éternité'. In *L´Art Égyptien au temps des pyramides*, C. Ziegler (ed.), 56–63. Paris: Réunion des Musées Nationaux.

Jones, J., Higham, T., Chivall, D., Bianucci, R., Kay, G., Pallen, M., Oldfield, R., Ugliano, F., Buckley, S. (2018) A prehistoric Egyptian mummy: Evidence for an 'embalming recipe' and the evolution of early formative funerary treatments. *Journal of Archaeological Science* 100, 191–200.

Kemp, B. (1996) *El Antiguo Egipto: Anatomia de una civilization*. Barcelona: Crítica.

Küffer, A. and Siegman, R. (2007) *Unter dem Schutz der Himmelsgöttin: Ägyptische Särge, Mumien und Masken in der Schweiz*. Zürich: Chronos.

Lichtheim, M. (1973) *Ancient Egyptian Literature: The Old and Middle Kingdoms* (Vol. 1). Berkeley: University of California Press.

Liptay, É. (2014) Representations of passage in ancient Egyptian iconography. In *Body, Cosmos, and Eternity: New Research Trends in the Iconography and Symbolism of Ancient Egyptian Coffins*, R. Sousa (ed.), 91–109. Egyptology 3, Oxford: Archaeopress.

Liptay, É. (2017) The ancient Egyptian coffin as sacred space: Changes of the sacred space during the Third Intermediate Period. In *Proceedings of the First Vatican Coffin Conference, 19–22 June 2013*, A. Amenta and H. Guichard (eds) 259–70. Vatican: Edizioni Musei Vaticani.

Lipinska, J. (1993–1994) Bab el-Gusus: Cache-tomb of the priests and priestesses of Amen. *KMT. A Modern Journal of Ancient Egypt* 4(4), 48–59.

Loring, E. (2012) They were not yellow: 21st Dynasty Theban coffins from the 'Royal Cache' TT 320, In *Achievements and Problems of Modern Egyptology: Proceedings of the International Conference held* in Moscow on September 29-October 2, 2009, G. Belova and S. Ivanov (eds), 208–13. Moscow: Russian Academy of Sciences.

Mace, A. and Winlock, H. (1916) *The Tomb of Senebtisi at Lisht*. New York: Metropolitan Museum of Art Egyptian Expedition.

Mahmoud, A. (2011) *Catalogue of the Funerary Objects from the Tomb of the Servant in the Place of Truth Sennedjem*. Cairo: IFAO.

Malek, J. (2003) *Egypt: 4000 years of Art*. New York: Phaidon Press.

Manley, W. and Dodson, A. (2010) *Life Everlasting: National Museums Scotland. Collection of Ancient Egyptian coffins*. Edinburgh: National Museums of Scotland.

Manley, W., Eremin, K., Shortland, A. and Wilkinson, C. (2002) The facial reconstruction of an Ancient Egyptian Queen. *Journal of Audiovisual Media in Medicine* 25(4), 155–159.

Marochetti, E.F. (2013) Gebelein. In *UCLA Encyclopedia of Egyptology*, W. Wendrich (ed.), Los Angeles: University of California.

Maspero, G. (2003) *Lettres d'Egypte. Correspondance avec Louise Maspero (1883-1914)*, E. David (ed.), Paris: Seuil.

Meyer-Dietrich, E. (2006) *Senebi und Selbst: Personenkonstituenten zur rituellen Wiedergebut in einen Frauensarg des Mittleren Reiches*. Orbis Biblicus et Orientalis 216. Freiburg: Göttingen.

Millet, M. and Masson, A. (2011) Karnak: Settlements. In *UCLA Encyclopedia of Egyptology*, W. Wendrich (ed.). Los Angeles: University of California.

Miniaci, G. (2010) The iconography of the *rishi* coffins and the legacy of the Late Middle Kingdom. *Journal of the American Research Center in Egypt* 46, 49–61.

Miniaci G. (2011) *Rishi Coffins and the Funerary Culture of Second Intermediate Period Egypt*. London: Golden House Publications in Egyptology 17.

Miniaci, G. (2014) The collapse of faience figurine production at the end of the Middle Kingdom: Reading the history of an epoch between Postmodernism and Grand Narrative. *Journal of Egyptian History* 7, 109–42.

Miniaci, G. (2018) Burial equipment of *rishi* coffins and the osmosis of the 'rebirth machine' at the end of the Middle Kingdom. In *Ancient Egyptian Coffins: Craft, Traditions and Functionality*, J. Taylor and M. Vandenbeush (eds), 247–74. Leuven: Peeters.

Miniaci, G. and Quirke, S. (2009) Reconceiving the tomb in the late Middle Kingdom: the burial of the accountant of the Main Enclosure Neferhotep at Dra Abu el-Naga. *Bulletin de L'Institut Francais d'Archeologie Orientale* 189, 339–384.

Moiso, B (2016) *La storia del Museo Egizio*. Turin: Fondazione Museo della Antichità Egizie di Torino.

Naville, E. (1896) *The Temple of Deir el Bahari (2): The Ebony Shrine, Northern Half of the Middle Platform*. London. Egypt Exploration Fund.

Niwiński, A. (1984) The Bab el-Gusus tomb and the Royal Cache in Deir el-Baḥri. *Journal of Egyptian Archaeology* 70, 73–81.

Niwiński, A. (1988) *21st Dynasty Coffins from Thebes, Chronological and Typological Studies*. Theben 5. Mainz am Rhein: Philipp von Zabern.

Nyord, R. (2009) *Breathing Flesh: Conceptions of the Body in the Ancient Coffin Texts*. Copenhagen: Museum Tusculanum Press-University of Copenhagen.

Nyord, R. (2014) Permeable containers: Body and cosmos in Middle Kingdom coffins. In *Body, Cosmos & Eternity: New Research Trends in the Symbolism of Coffins in Ancient Egypt*, R. Sousa (ed.), 29–44. Egyptology Series 3. Oxford: Archaeopress.

Orsenigo, C. (2010) Turning points in Egyptian archaeology (1850–1950). In *Egypt and the Pharaohs: From the Sand to the Library - Pharaonic Egypt in the Archives and Libraries of the Università degli Studi di Milano*, P. Piacentini (ed.), 117–72. Milan: Università degli Studi di Milano.

Petrie, W.F. (1909) *Qurneh*. London: British School of Archaeology in Egypt 16.

Ranke, H. (1935) *Die Ägyptischen Personennamen*. Glückstadt: J.J. Augustin.

Reeves, N. (2000) *Ancient Egypt: The Great Discoveries: A Year-by-year Chronicle*. London: Thames & Hudson.

Reeves, N. (2013) Amenhotep, overseer of builders of Amun: An Eighteenth-Dynasty burial reassembled. *Metropolitan Museum Journal* 48, 7–36.

Reeves, N. and Wilkinson, R.H. (1996) *The Complete Valley of the Kings*. Cairo: American University Cairo Press.

Roehrig, C. (1988) *Mummies and Magic: An Introduction to Egyptian Funerary Beliefs*. Boston: Museum of Fine Arts.

Russo, B. (2012) *Kha (TT 8) and his Colleagues: The Gifts in his Funerary Equipment and Related Artefacts from Western Thebes*. London: Golden House.

Saleh, M. and Sourouzian, H. (1987) *The Egyptian Museum in Cairo: Official Catalogue*. Mainz am Rhein: Philipp von Zabern.

Shedid, A.G. (1994) *Das Grab des Sennedjem*. Mainz am Rhein: Philipp von Zabern,

Smith, E. (1906) An account of the mummy of a priestess of Amen supposed to be Ta-usert-em-suten-pa, *Annales du Service des Antiquités d'Égypte* 7, 155–60.

Smith, S. (1998) *The Art and Architecture of Ancient Egypt*. New Haven-London: Yale University Press.

Sousa, R. (2011) *The Heart of Wisdom: Studies on the Heart Amulet in Ancient Egypt*. Oxford: British Archaeological Report S2211.

Sousa, R. (2014) 'Spread your wings over me': Iconography, symbolism, and meaning of the central panel on yellow coffins. In *Body, Cosmos, and Eternity: New Research Trends in the Iconography and Symbolism of Ancient Egyptian Coffins*, R. Sousa (ed.), 91–109. Egyptology 3. Oxford: Archaeopress.

Sousa, R. (2017a) *Burial Assemblages from Bab el-Gasus in the Geographical Society of Lisbon*. Monumenta Aegyptiaca XIV. Turnhout: Brepols.

Sousa, R. (2017b) Building catalogues: the concept of "architectonisation" and the description of coffins of the 21st dynasty. In *Proceedings of the First Vatican Conference (Vatican Museums, 19-22 June 2013)*, A. Amenta and H. Guichard (eds) 515–520. Vatican: Edizioni Musei Vaticani.

Sousa, R. (2018a) *Gleaming Coffins: Iconography and Symbolism in Theban coffin decoration (21st Dynasty)*. Coimbra: Coimbra University Press.

Sousa, R. (2018b) The coffins of the Tomb of the Priests from an art historical perspective: Lot V at the Egyptian Museum of Florence. In *The Tomb of the Priests of Amun: Burial Assemblages in the Egyptian Museum of Florence*, R. Sousa (ed.), 515–44. Gate of the Priests Series 1 – Culture & History of the Ancient Near East 97. Leiden, Boston: Brill.

Sousa, R. (2018c) The tomb of the priests of Amun at Thebes: The history of the find. In *The Coffins of the Priests of Amun: Egyptian Coffins from the Collection of the National Museum of Antiquities in Leiden*, L. Weiss (ed.), 21–34. Papers on Archaeology from the Leiden Museum of Antiquities (PALMA) 17. Leiden: Sidestone Press.

Sousa, R. (2018d) Começar de novo: A 'Repetição do Nascimento' e a transformação política do Egipto na viragem para o I milénio. In *Arqueologias de Império*, D. Leão, J. Ramos and N. Rodrigues (eds), 57–74. Lisboa: Universidade de Lisboa.

Sousa, R. and Nørskov, V. (forthcoming) – Tabasety, the temple singer in Aarhus. *Trabajos de Egiptologia* 9.

Steindorff, G. (1913) *Das Grab des Ti*. Leipzig: J.C. Hinrichs.

Stevens, A. (2018) Beyond iconography: The Amarna coffins in social context. In *Ancient Egyptian Coffins: Craft Tradition and Functionality*, J. Taylor and M. Vandenbeusch (eds), 139–60. Leuven-Paris-Bristol: Peeters.

Tarasenko, M. (2017) The Third Intermediate Period coffins in the museums of Ukraine. In *Proceedings of the First Vatican Conference (Vatican Museums, 19-22 June 2013)*, A. Amenta and H. Guichard (eds), 529–40. Vatican: Edizioni Musei Vaticani.

Taylor, J. (1989) *Egyptian Coffins*. Aylesbury: Shire.

Taylor, J. (2000) The Third Intermediate Period (1069–664 BC). In *The Oxford History of Ancient Egypt*, I. Shaw (ed.), 330–69 Oxford: Oxford University Press.

Taylor, J. (2001) *Death and the Afterlife in Ancient Egypt*. Chicago: University of Chicago Press.

Taylor, J. (ed.) (2010) *Journey Through the Afterlife: Ancient Egyptian Book of the Dead*. London: British Museum Press.

Taylor, J. (2016) Coffins from the Middle Kingdom to the Roman period. In *Death on the Nile: Uncovering the Afterlife of Ancient Egypt*, H. Strudwick and J. Dawson (eds), 49–74. Cambridge: Fitzwilliam Museum, D Giles.

Taylor, J. (2017) *Sir John Soane's Greatest Treasure: The Sarcophagus of Seti I*. London: Pimpernel.

Taylor, J. (2018) Evidence for social patterning in Theban coffins of Dynasty 25. In *Ancient Egyptian Coffins: Craft traditions and functionality*, J. Taylor and M. Vandenbeusch (eds), 349–388. Leuven-Paris-Bristol: Peeters.

Taylor, J. Antoine D. and Vandenbeusch, M. (2014) *Ancient Lives, New Discoveries: Eight Mummies, Eight Stories*. London: British Museum Press.

Troalen, L., Guerra, M.-F., Manley, W. and Tate, J. (2009) Technological study of gold jewellery from the 17th and 18th Dynasties in Egypt. *ArcheoSciences: revue d'archéométrie* 33, 112–19.

Ugliano, F. (2015) The Predynastic Period: Life in Egypt before the pharaohs. In *Museo Egizio*, C. Greco (ed.), 38–45. Turin: Fondazione Museo della Antichitá Egizie di Torino.

Vassilika, E. (2010) *The Tomb of Kha: The Architect*. Torino: Fondazione Museo delle Antichita Egizie.

Veldmeijer, A.J. and Bourriau, J. (2009) The carrier nets from a burial at Qurna. *Journal of Egyptian Archaeology* 95(1), 209–22.

Van Walsem, R. (1997) *The Coffin of Djedmonthuiufankh in the National Museum of Antiquities at Leiden. Vol. I: Technical and Iconographic/Iconological aspects*. Egyptologische uitgaven 10. Leiden: Nederlands Instituut Boor Het Nabije Oosten.

Van Walsem, R. (2005) *Iconography of Old Kingdom Elite Tombs: Analysis and Interpretation, Theoretical and Methodological Aspects*. Ex Oriente Lux. Dudley, MA: Peeters.

Van Walsem, R. (2008) *Mastabase: The Leiden Mastaba Project*. Leiden: Peeters-Leiden University.

Van Walsem, R. (2014) From skin wrappings to architecture. The evolution of prehistoric, anthropoid wrappings to historic architectonic coffins/sarcophagi; separate contrasts optimally fused in single Theban 'stola' coffins (±975–920 BC). In *Body, Cosmos, and Eternity. New Research Trends in the Iconography and Symbolism of Ancient Egyptian Coffins*, R. Sousa (ed.), 1–27. Egyptology 3. Oxford: Archaeopress.

Weeks, K. (1999) *The Lost Tomb: The Greatest Discovery at the Valley of the Kings since Tutankhamun*. London: Phoenix.

Weiss, L. (2017) I am Re and Osiris. In *Imaging and Imagining the Memphite Necropolis: Liber Amicorum René Van Walsem*, V. Verschoor, A.J. Stuart and C. Demarée (eds), 215–30. Leuven: Peeters-Neberlands Instituut Voor Het Nabije Oosten.

Wild, H. (1953) *Le Tombeau de Ti. La chapelle* (Part 1). Le Caire: Imprimerie de l'Institut français d'archéologie orientale.

Wild, H. (1966) *Le Tombeau de Ti. La chapelle* (Part 2). Le Caire: Imprimerie de l'Institut français d'archéologie orientale.

Williams, H. (2018) The coffins of the lector priest Sesenebenef: a Middle Kingdom Book of the Dead? In *Ancient Egyptian Coffins: Craft Traditions and Functionality*, J. Taylor and M. Vandenbeusch (eds) 3–16. Leuveen: Peeters.

Yamazaki, S. (2018) Archaeological and iconographic analysis of the use of funerary personal adornments in the Middle Kingdom of Ancient Egypt. *Sociology and Anthropology* 6(4), 433–46.

Yoshimura, S., Baba, M., Yazawa, K., Jaeschke, R. and Uda, M. (2018) Intact Middle Kingdom anthropoid coffin of Sobekhat from Dashur North: Discovery, conservation and X-ray analysis. *Journal of Egyptian Studies* 24, 158–77.